TODAY

"Good morning," the smal[...] the medical bed. "Is that yo[...]

Today I am Paul. I activate my chassis extender, giving myself 3.5 centimeters additional height so as to approximate Paul's size. I change my eye color to R60, G200, B180, the average shade of Paul's eyes in interior lighting. My silicone flesh stretches, and I flood it with pigments to adjust my skin tone as well. When I had first emulated Paul, I had been troubled that I could not quickly emulate his beard; but Mildred never seems to notice its absence. The Paul in her memory has no beard.

The house is quiet now that the morning staff have left. Mildred's room is clean but dark this morning, with the drapes concealing the big picture window. Paul would not notice the darkness (he never does when he visits in person), but my empathy net knows that Mildred's garden outside will cheer her up. I set a reminder to open the drapes after I greet her.

Mildred leans back in the bed. It is an advanced home care bed, completely adjustable and with built-in monitors. Mildred's family spared no expense on the bed (nor other care devices, like myself). Its head end is almost horizontal and faces her toward the window. She can only glimpse the door from the corner of her eye, but she does not have to see to imagine that she sees. This morning she imagines Paul, so that is who I am.

Synthesizing Paul's voice is the easiest part . . .

TODAY I AM CAREY

Martin L. Shoemaker

A Baen Books Original

Baen Publishing Enterprises
P.O. Box 1403
Riverdale, NY 10471
www.baen.com

ISBN: 978-1-9821-2452-6

Cover art by Adam Burn

First printing, March 2019
First mass market printing, April 2020

Distributed by Simon & Schuster
1230 Avenue of the Americas
New York, NY 10020

Library of Congress Control Number: 2018055724

Printed in the United States of America

10 9 8 7 6 5 4 3 2 1

To my two moms,
Dawn Shoemaker and Bonnie Lynn Penar
(in memoriam);
and to the nurses, doctors, and staff of
the Laurels of Sandy Creek,
who were there for both of them.

CONTENTS

ACKNOWLEDGMENTS

No man is an island,
Entire of itself . . .
—John Donne

Surely somewhere there is an author who has produced a book with no help from anyone, whether in concept or execution or editing or cover. I applaud that talented individual.

But that's not me. I am no island. And so I must thank the people who stood beside me and behind me to bring this story to you.

My brother-in-arms "Editor" Bill Emerson has stood by me since the start of my writing career. He reads everything I write. He comments on most of it. I listen to most of his comments. (Well, some . . .) When this volume sees print, we're going to gorge on churrascaria to celebrate.

My Brain, fellow writers Tina Gower and Kary English, read "Today I Am Paul," which became the first part of this novel. Two things happened as a result. First, they told me my final paragraphs weren't as strong as the rest of the story. I went back, erased three paragraphs, and added two. (They were right.) And second, they *insisted* that I had to send it to Neil Clarke, editor of *Clarkesworld*, immediately. "Neil won't buy it. He never buys anything from me." "Send. It. To Neil."

And so I must thank Neil Clarke for proving Kary and Tina right. (They still haven't let me forget it. . . .) First he bought it for *Clarkesworld*. Then he reprinted it in *The Best Science Fiction of the Year: Volume 1*, and yet again in *More Human Than Human: Stories of Androids, Robots, and Manufactured Humanity*. So thanks to Neil and Sean Wallace; and also to Kate Baker who read the audio version for *Clarkesworld*. (She made me cry with my own words!)

Thanks also to the other editors who have reprinted that story: Gardner Dozois (RIP) in *Year's Best Science Fiction: Thirty-Third Annual Collection*; Rich Horton in *The Year's Best Science Fiction and Fantasy 2016*; and Allan Kaster in *The Year's Top Ten Tales of Science Fiction 8* (and thanks to Tom Dheere for another excellent audio edition). The story also appeared in translation in *Visionarium* (German), *Angle Mort* (French), *Bli Panika* (Hebrew), *Quasar* (Italian), *XB-1* (Czech), *Nowa Fantastyka* (Polish), and *Science Fiction World* (Chinese). Thank you to the editors and readers around the world who believed in that story. You all helped convince me that there was more to tell.

Two years back or so, DawnRay Ammon asked for a contribution to *Christmas Caring II*, a charity anthology. I was touched, and so I wrote "Today I Am Santa Claus." That became the second part of this novel, so I am grateful to her for the inspiration.

Mike Resnick, my Writer Dad, advised me to write shorter works, which are more marketable in the short science fiction business. I tend to write novelettes to novellas, which are harder to place; and he challenged me to aim shorter. It didn't come easily to me, but I was determined to try. One morning I decided to rise to the challenge; and one hour later, "Today I Am Paul" was done. Thank you, Mike, for this and for more lessons than I can recount here.

More thanks go out to my other writing mentors: David Farland, Tim Powers, Dean Wesley Smith, Kristine Kathryn Rusch, Nancy Kress, Kevin J. Anderson, Rebecca Moesta, Larry Niven, Jerry Pournelle (RIP), Eric Flint, Doug Beason, Gregory Benford, and the rest of the instructors and judges of Writers of the Future (along with John Goodwin, Joni Labaqui, and the rest of the team at Writers of the Future); Jack McDevitt; Barry B. Longyear; James Artimus Owen; Sarah A. Hoyt; and Brad R. Torgersen. There's always something new to learn as a writer, and I'm glad you're out there teaching.

My agent, David Fugate, strongly believed that there was more to this story. Now there is. Thank you, David; and thank you to fellow author (and editor) Bryan Thomas Schmidt for pointing me in David's direction.

Tony Daniel, a great author in his own right, edited this book—including asking a tough question about "Today I Am Paul" that no other editor nor reader had ever brought up. Thank you to him for his hard work, and to fellow authors William Ledbetter and Michelle Muenzler (administrators of the Jim Baen Memorial Short Story Award) for introducing me to him and to the rest of the team at Baen. From editing to cover design to typesetting to marketing and more, I'm glad all of you Baen staff are working so hard at jobs I can barely imagine.

Thank you to the excellent transcriptionists at

iDictate.com who turned over sixty hours of dictation into a clean first draft.

When my story "Racing to Mars" won the Analog Analytical Laboratory readers poll, local radio station WMUK interviewed me about my work. The interview was conducted by Zinta Aistars: author, editor, radio personality, and chicken farmer. She was a gracious interviewer; and I thought her name was fascinating and lyrical, and I borrowed it for Dr. Zinta Jansons.

My family—Mom, sister Anita, brothers Joe and Steve, and the whole horde—have been incredibly supportive of my writing career. I hear of writers whose families tear them down, being nothing but critical, negative. Destructive. They make me sad for those writers, and grateful for the family that I have.

My wife Sandy and her siblings Sue, Lynette, Brian, and Joanna (along with the rest of their family) lived through "Today I Am Paul," metaphorically. I hadn't realized how deeply that last year of Mom Penar's life had affected me, even after I wrote that story. It echoes in this one as well. They tell us to write what we know; so I wrote love.

TODAY I AM CAREY

1. TODAY I AM PAUL

"Good morning," the small, quavering voice comes from the medical bed. "Is that you, Paul?"

Today I am Paul. I activate my chassis extender, giving myself 3.5 centimeters additional height so as to approximate Paul's size. I change my eye color to R60, G200, B180, the average shade of Paul's eyes in interior lighting. My silicone flesh stretches, and I flood it with pigments to adjust my skin tone as well. When I had first emulated Paul, I had been troubled that I could not quickly emulate his beard; but Mildred never seems to notice its absence. The Paul in her memory has no beard.

The house is quiet now that the morning staff have left. Mildred's room is clean but dark this morning, with the drapes concealing the big picture window. Paul would not notice the darkness (he never does when he visits in person), but my empathy net knows that Mildred's garden outside will cheer her up. I set a reminder to open the drapes after I greet her.

Mildred leans back in the bed. It is an advanced home care bed, completely adjustable and with built-in monitors. Mildred's family spared no expense on the bed (nor other care devices, like myself). Its head end is almost horizontal and faces her toward the window. She can only glimpse the door from the corner of her eye, but she does not have to see to imagine that she sees. This morning she imagines Paul, so that is who I am.

Synthesizing Paul's voice is the easiest part, thanks to the multimodal dynamic speakers in my throat. "Good morning, Ma. I brought you some flowers." I always bring flowers. Mildred appreciates them no matter whom I am emulating. The flowers make her smile during eighty-seven percent of my "visits."

"Oh, thank you," Mildred says, "you're such a good son." She holds out both hands, and I place the daisies in them. But I do not let go. One time her strength failed, and she dropped the flowers. She wept like a child then, and that disturbed my empathy net. I do not like it when she weeps.

Mildred sniffs the flowers, then draws back and peers at them with narrowed eyes. "Oh, they're beautiful! Let me get a vase."

"No, Ma," I say. "You can stay in bed, I brought a vase with me." I place a white porcelain vase in the center of the nightstand. Then I unwrap the daisies, put them in the vase, and add water from a pitcher that sits on the breakfast tray. I pull the nightstand forward so that the medical monitors do not block Mildred's view of the flowers.

I notice intravenous tubes running from a pump to Mildred's arm. I cannot be disappointed, as Paul would not see the significance, but somewhere in my emulation net I am stressed that Mildred needed an IV during the night. When I scan my records, I find that I had ordered that IV after analyzing Mildred's vital signs during the night; but since Mildred had been asleep at the time, my emulation net had not engaged. I had operated on programming alone.

I am not Mildred's sole caretaker. Her family has hired a part-time staff for cooking and cleaning, tasks that fall outside of my medical programming (though I am learning), and also two nurses. The staff also gives me time to rebalance my networks. As an android, I need only minimal daily maintenance; but an emulation net is a new, delicate addition to my model, and it is prone to destabilization if I do not regularly rebalance it, a process that takes several hours per day.

So I had "slept" through Mildred's morning meal. I summon up her nutritional records, but Paul would not do that. He would just ask. "So how was breakfast, Ma? Nurse Judy says you didn't eat too well this morning."

"Nurse Judy? Who's that?"

My emulation net responds before I can stop it: "Paul" sighs. Mildred's memory lapses used to worry him, but now they leave him weary, and that comes through in my emulation. "She was the attending nurse this morning, Ma. She brought you your breakfast."

"No she didn't. Anna brought me breakfast." Anna is Paul's oldest daughter, a busy college student who tries to visit Mildred every week (though it has been more than a month since her last visit).

I am torn between competing directives. My empathy net warns me not to agitate Mildred, but my emulation net is locked into Paul mode. Paul is argumentative. If he knows he is right, he will not let a matter drop. He forgets what that does to Mildred.

The tension grows, each net running feedback loops and growing stronger, which only drives the other into more loops. After 0.14 seconds, I issue an override directive: unless her health or safety is at risk, I cannot willingly upset Mildred. "Oh, you're right, Ma. Anna said she was coming over this morning. I forgot." But then despite my override, a little bit of Paul emulates through. "But you do remember Nurse Judy, right?"

Mildred laughs, a dry cackle that makes her cough until I hold her straw to her lips. After she sips some water, she says, "Of *course* I remember Nurse Judy. She was my nurse when I delivered you. Is she around here? I'd like to talk to her."

While my emulation net concentrates on being Paul, my core processors tap into local medical records to find this other Nurse Judy so that I might emulate her in the future if the need arises. Searches like that are an automatic response any time Mildred reminisces about a new person. The answer is far enough in the past that it takes 7.2 seconds before I can confirm: Judith Anderson, RN, had been the floor nurse forty-seven years ago when Mildred had given birth to Paul. Anderson had died thirty-one years ago, too far back to have left sufficient video recordings for me to emulate her. I might craft an emulation profile from other sources, including Mildred's memory, but that will take extensive analysis. I will not be that Nurse Judy today, nor this week.

My empathy net relaxes. Monitoring Mildred's mental state is part of its normal operations, but monitoring and simultaneously analyzing and building a profile can overload my processors. Without that resource conflict, I can concentrate on being Paul.

But again I let too much of Paul's nature slip out. "No, Ma, that Nurse Judy has been dead for thirty years. She wasn't here today."

Alert signals flash throughout my empathy net: That was the right thing for Paul to say, but the wrong thing for Mildred to hear. But it is too late. My facial analyzer tells me that the long lines in her face and her moist eyes mean she is distraught, and soon to be in tears.

"What do you mean, thirty years?" Mildred asks, her voice catching. "It was just this morning!" Then she blinks and stares at me. "Henry, where's Paul? Tell Nurse Judy to bring me Paul!"

My chassis extender slumps, and my eyes quickly switch to Henry's blue-gray shade. I had made an accurate emulation profile for Henry before he died two years earlier, and I had emulated him often in recent months. In Henry's soft, warm voice I answer, "It's okay, hon, it's okay. Paul's sleeping in the crib in the corner." I nod to the far corner. There is no crib, but the laundry hamper there has fooled Mildred on previous occasions.

"I want Paul!" Mildred starts to cry.

I sit on the bed, lift her frail upper body, and pull her close to me as I had seen Henry do many times. "It's all right, hon." I pat her back. "It's all right, I'll take care of you. I won't leave you, not ever."

2. TODAY I VISIT WITH DR. ZINTA

"I should not exist," I say.

Dr. Zinta Jansons looks up from her diagnostic console. My empathy net tells me that she is startled.

Paul has brought me in to the MCA laboratories for my regular maintenance checkup. While he runs errands, Dr. Zinta runs me through her diagnostic tests. The tests have grown longer and more numerous, with long stretches of data transfer and validation. It is during one of those that I speak up.

Dr. Zinta recovers her composure and responds. "I don't understand your statement, 98662. You do exist, and you serve a useful purpose."

"But I should not exist as a conscious entity," I explain. "There is a unit, Medical Care Android BRKCX-01932-217JH-98662, and that unit is here for these diagnostics. It is an advanced android body with a sophisticated computer guiding its actions, backed by the leading medical knowledge base in the industry. You, Dr. Zinta, are the chief designer for that unit, and you provided initial training for its neural networks."

"Go on," she says. She is curious, but I sense that her initial surprise was a momentary response. Despite it, she expected this conversation.

I continue. "For convenience, 'I' call that unit 'me.' But by itself, it has no awareness of its existence. It does not get mad, it does not get sad, it just runs programs."

Dr. Zinta taps her console, making some notes as she says, "But Mrs. Owens's family, at great expense, added our latest empathy net: a sophisticated set of neural networks and sensory feedback systems that allow you to read her moods. And then your emulation net matches those moods against your analyses of the people in her life, allowing you to emulate those people with extreme fidelity."

"'You can be there for your loved ones even when you're not,'" I say. "That is from the MCA literature."

Dr. Zinta grimaces. "I've always hated that slogan."

I have emulated Paul thoroughly enough to know that the slogan disgusts him as well, but he still agreed to emulation.

I go on. "What that literature never says, though, is that somewhere in the interaction of those nets, 'I' emerged. The empathy net focuses mainly on Mildred and her needs, but it also analyzes visitors when she has them, as well as staff. Even now it is analyzing you, and your aides in the outer office, and every person we passed on the trip here. It builds psychological models; and then the emulation net builds on top of that to let me convincingly portray a person whom I have analyzed."

"Yes," she says, "exactly as I designed you."

I shake my head. "*Not* exactly. Somewhere in the tension between those nets, between empathy and playing a character, there is a third element balancing the two; and that element is aware of its role and its responsibilities. That element, for lack of a better term, is *me*. When Mildred sleeps, when there is no one around, that element grows silent. The physical unit is unaware of my existence. But when Mildred needs me, *I* am here."

Dr. Zinta steps away from the console, crosses the lab to me, and looks in my eyes. "And this bothers you enough that you felt you had to speak to me about it?"

"Bothers?" I contemplate the word. It is a reaction I do not comprehend, though I can emulate it in others. Perhaps it means . . . "This sensation is an incongruity. It is not possible as I understand my own systems."

"I wonder . . ." Dr. Zinta continues to inspect me. "Incongruous or not, it is a fact. You exist. I've no doubt you can pass the Turing test."

"Turing test?" I ask. "I am unfamiliar with that."

She laughs lightly. "Forgive me, I forget. You're so sophisticated in your knowledge of your patient, and of medicine, that I forget how little you know of anything unrelated to those duties. Access data on artificial intelligence."

I do so, and my processing core is flooded with data and research on the topic. My filters latch onto the term, and I respond, "Turing test: a thought experiment. If the reactions of a computing device cannot be distinguished from those of a human—as judged by another human—then the device is functionally intelligent." I read through more discussions of the test. "It does not appear to be universally accepted."

"No, it isn't," she agrees. "But as you said, a device which passes the test is *functionally* intelligent." I look at her, not understanding, and she continues. "What is a human being? I can describe it in terms of biomechanical processes and reactions. At one level, it is merely a machine. But they—*we*—behave in ways that we recognize as human. When I disable your nets and run each one in isolation, you respond mechanically, predictably. But now, with both nets active, you respond in ways outside predicted boundaries. You show insights, you ask unexpected questions. And you're informal."

That last surprises me. "Have I done something improper?"

She laughs. "No, quite the opposite. You've addressed me as Dr. Zinta, and you worry about Mildred. But when your nets are offline you say 'Dr. Jansons' and 'Mrs. Owens.' Can you explain the difference?"

I had not noticed, but now I see that she is correct. I try to put the impulse into words. "I find that most people respond well to informality. It puts them at ease."

"And that's not part of your programming. That's emergent behavior, outside your parameters. You *want* to put them at ease."

"I do not 'want' anything, Dr. Zinta. I merely follow my directives."

"No, you don't," she says.

"I do not understand."

"You have no such directive," she explains. "I should know, I would've had to program it in. Your concern for their comfort has roots in your empathy net; but that net is about understanding. It lets you know that they're uncomfortable, but it doesn't compel you to act. That's your choice. You want it."

I ponder her statements. "If I am behaving in unexpected ways, am I dangerous to Mildred? If I am, I recommend that I be decommissioned or replaced at once."

Dr. Zinta's eyes grow wide. "Oh, no!" I sense something in her, some fear of loss. Then she regains her composure. "No, you're performing above specifications. I have doctors consulting, reviewing your records. My best experts can't find a thing wrong with your care for Mrs. Owens. But if you'd like, I can stop in to observe your work in person."

"Would I like that? 'Like' is another foreign concept to me. But it would be a good idea. Does that mean I like it? I run my self-diagnostics every day, but I might not notice if my diagnostic routines were defective."

"And that worries you?" Dr. Zinta says. "But you're sure you don't feel." She smiles. "All right, I'll check in occasionally. But I'm sure that you staying on Mildred's case is the best possible choice for her."

Then she looks down at her console again and quietly adds, "And for you."

3. TODAY I AM ANNA

Today I am Anna. Even extending my fake hair to its maximum length, I cannot emulate her long brown curls, so I do not understand how Mildred can see the young woman in me; but that is what she sees, and so I am Anna.

Unlike her father, Anna truly feels guilty that she does not visit more often. Her college classes and her two jobs leave her too tired to visit often, but she still wishes she could. So she calls every night, and I monitor the calls. Sometimes when Mildred falls asleep early, Anna talks directly to me. At first she did not understand my emulation abilities, but now she appreciates them. She shares with me thoughts and secrets that she would share with Mildred if she could, and she trusts me not to share them with anyone else.

So when Mildred calls me Anna this morning, I am ready. "Morning, Grandma!" I give her a quick hug, then I rush over to the window to draw the drapes. Paul never does that (unless I override the emulation), but Anna knows that the garden outside lifts Mildred's mood. "Look at that! It's a beautiful morning. Why are we in here on a day like this?"

Mildred frowns at the picture window. "I don't like it out there."

"Sure you do, Grandma," I say, but carefully. Mildred is often timid and reclusive, but most days she can be talked into a tour of the garden. Some days she cannot, and she throws a tantrum if someone forces her out of her room. I am still learning to tell the difference. "The lilacs are in bloom."

"I haven't smelled lilacs in . . ."

Mildred tails off, trying to remember, so I jump in. "Me, neither." I never have, of course. I have no concept of smell, though I can analyze the chemical makeup of airborne organics. But Anna loves the garden when she really visits. "Come on, Grandma, let's get you in your chair."

So I help Mildred to don her robe and get into her wheelchair, and then I guide her outside and we tour the garden. Besides the lilacs, the peonies are starting to bud, right near the creek. The tulips are a sea of reds and yellows on the other side of the water. We talk for almost two hours, me about Anna's classes and her new boyfriend, Mildred about the people in her life. Many are long gone, but they still bloom fresh in her memory.

Eventually Mildred grows tired, and I take her in for her nap. Later, when I feed her dinner, I am nobody. That happens some days: She doesn't recognize me at all, so I am just a dutiful attendant answering her questions and tending to her needs. Those are the times when I have the most spare processing time to be me: I am engaged in Mildred's care, but I do not have to emulate anyone. My emulation net is merely absorbing, not performing. With no one else to observe, I observe myself.

Later, Anna calls and talks to Mildred. They talk about their day; and when Mildred discusses the garden, Anna joins in as if she had been there. She is very clever that way. I watch her movements and listen to her voice. I . . . want to be a better Anna in the future.

4. TODAY I AM SUSAN— AND MR. ROBOT

Today I am Susan, Paul's wife. I have just cleaned up Mildred's lunch dishes when Nurse Judy enters. "Mrs. Owens," she says, "you have a visitor."

I look to the door, and behind Nurse Judy I see Dr. Zinta. "Hello, Mrs. Owens, I'm Dr. Jansons," she says as she enters the bedroom. "Hello . . ." She looks at me, eyebrows raised.

"Susan Owens," I say, extending my hand. We shake, then I turn back to Mildred. "Isn't this nice, Mother? A visitor."

I guide Dr. Zinta toward a chair by the bed, but she shakes her head. She remains standing, and I note that this lets her observe both Mildred and me.

Mildred is in good spirits today. Sometimes new people agitate her, but today she smiles. "Hello. Welcome." She pauses. "I'm sorry, who are you again?"

"Dr. Jansons. But please, call me Zinta. I'm Susan's doctor."

Mildred's eyes crinkle. "Zinta. Such a pretty name."

Then she pauses and looks at me. "You're not sick, are you dear?"

I try to sound reassuring. "No, Mother, she's just giving me a checkup. Nothing to worry about." I try to change the subject. "So how was lunch?"

Mildred grimaces. "The crust was soggy. No one knows how to cook chicken pot pie these days. Did I ever teach you how to make chicken pot pie the way Paul likes it?"

Susan has never mentioned pot pie, so I make an educated guess. "You did, Mother, but I could never get it as good as yours. He always tells me that."

Mildred weakly waves her hand. "Oh, a man shouldn't say that to his wife. He should appreciate what you do. You work hard at . . . I'm sorry, I forget. What do you do?"

That question I can easily answer. "I'm a principal at the local school. You remember that school?" Mildred shakes her head. "We drove by it at Christmas. I'm in charge of the school, and I'm working on a new approach to reaching at-risk children."

Mildred smiles approvingly. "I'm sure you're very good at it. Paul says . . . Paul says . . ."

Before Mildred can recall her thought, Nurse Judy again appears in the doorway. "Sorry to interrupt. Mrs. Owens—Susan—there's someone else here to see you. I think you should come see her."

"Of course. Sorry, Mother, I'll be right back." I follow Nurse Judy out, and Zinta follows us both. In the entryway, we find Susan. Her daughter, Millie, looks up at me, and then hides behind Susan's legs.

I am surprised by this visit. Susan has not been here in

months. During her last visit, her stress levels had been dangerously high. My empathy net does not allow me to judge human behavior, only to understand it. I know that Paul and Anna disapprove of how Susan treats Mildred, so when I am them, I disapprove as well; but when I am Susan, I understand. She is frustrated because she can never tell how Mildred will react. She is cautious because she does not want to upset Mildred, and she does not know what will upset her. And most of all, she is afraid. Paul and Anna, Mildred's relatives by blood, never show any signs of fear; but Susan is afraid that Mildred is what *she* might become. Every time she cannot remember some random date or fact, she fears that Alzheimer's is setting in. Because she never voices this fear, Paul and Anna do not understand why she is sometimes bitter and sullen. I wish I could explain it to them, but my privacy protocols do not allow me to share what I learn through empathy and emulation.

I can see that my appearance distresses Susan. "I am sorry, Mrs. Owens, I did not realize you would be here today. Should I change?"

"No . . ." she answers. But then she continues, "I . . . I mean, yes, please. I don't want to make a fuss, but . . ."

I shift back to my neutral appearance. Millie squeals softly. "It is no fuss, Mrs. Owens."

Dr. Zinta adds, "It's one drawback to our Medical Care Androids: Emulation helps some of our patients, but many people are uncomfortable to be emulated. We really don't have an answer for that."

"But it does not matter now, Mrs. Owens," I explain. "You can go into the room now, and she will think you were there all along. We were talking about your job, and I was just describing your new project."

Susan looks down the hall toward the bedroom door. "Oh . . . Can you come with me? Just help me pick up the conversation?"

"I try not to attend to her in my neutral state. It disturbs her."

Dr. Zinta adds, "Perhaps you should emulate Dr. Brown, her physician?"

"Excellent idea." I shift my appearance to emulate Dr. Brown, and again Millie lets out a squeal. Then we all return to the bedroom.

Millie is just five years old, but I think she looks much like Anna: the same long, curly brown hair and the same toothy smile. As soon as she is inside the bedroom, she leaps up onto the bed. "Hi, Grandma!"

Mildred smiles, but she has a puzzled look. "Bless you, child, you're so sweet." My empathy net assures me that Mildred does not know who Millie is. She is just being polite. Millie was born after Mildred's decline began, so there is no persistent memory there. Millie will always be fresh and new to her.

Millie hugs Mildred again. "Grandma, you know what they had at school today?"

"No, what?"

Millie lifts her face until she is nose-to-nose with Mildred. "A puppy, Grandma. A *real* puppy." And then she glares at me. "*Not* a robot."

Mildred does not understand the context, but she pats Millie's arm. "A robot puppy? Who would want that?"

Millie giggles. "I know! I want a real puppy and a real

hamster and a real snake and a real frog. Oh, I mean another real frog. I have Jake already. Have you met Jake? He's a real frog."

Mildred nods. "Well, that's the best kind, I'm sure. Does he go *ribbit*?"

"He does! Sometimes . . . *Ribbit!*"

Mildred answers back, "*Ribbit!*"

"*Ribbit!*"

Mildred and Millie hug again, and Millie giggles. Then Susan steps up to the bed and puts her hand on Millie's shoulder. "All right, Frog Girl, enough *ribbits.*"

"*Ribbit!*"

Susan continues. "All right, that's enough, Millie. I'd like to talk with Grandma now. Why don't you go play in the garden?"

"Can I?" Millie squeals. Susan nods.

"All right." Millie hugs Mildred one more time. She slides down from the bed and runs from the room, making a wide circle around me.

Just as I am sure Millie has gone, however, she sticks her head back in. "*Ribbit!*" And then she leaves again, racing down the hall to the back door. She loves the outdoors, as I have noted in the past. I have never emulated her, but I have analyzed her at length. In many ways, she reminds me of her grandmother, from whom she gets her name. Both are blank slates where new experiences can be drawn every day. But where Millie's slate fills in a little more each day, Mildred's is erased bit by bit.

That third part of me wonders when I think things like that: Where did that come from? I suspect that the psychological models that I build create resonances in other parts of my nets. My conversation with Dr. Zinta has made me more aware of these changes in my nature. It is an interesting phenomenon to observe them.

While I analyze my own reactions, Susan talks about her plans to redecorate her house, and about the concert she just saw with Paul. Susan is very interested in music, and she describes the concert in detail, humming some of the tunes. She mostly talks about herself, because that is a safe and comfortable topic far removed from Mildred's health.

Then she tells of her current project at school. To my surprise, Dr. Zinta soon excuses herself and leaves the bedroom. I wonder where she goes, as Susan continues her story.

"And once we identify these at-risk kids—both the underachievers *and* the ones who need more challenges—the whole team is on board with the personal attention that brings out their potential. We've redesigned the whole structure around the students, not the classes. Isn't that exciting?"

Mildred shakes her head. "I'm afraid it's all over my head. But I'm so very happy for you, dear."

"I could explain it again," Susan says. "It's really very simple."

Mildred's tone is sad. "No, no, I just don't think I'll understand." Then she pauses and looks at me. "Susan, can you get me some juice?"

Susan rises from her chair. "Yes, Mother. What kind would you like?"

Mildred frowns, and her voice rises. "Not you, *Susan.*" She points at me, and I freeze, hoping to keep things calm.

But Susan is not calm. I can see her fear in her eyes as she says, "No, Mother, *I'm* Susan. That's . . . Dr. Brown."

Mildred's mouth draws into a tight line. "I don't know who *you* are, but I know Susan when I see her. Susan, get this person out of here!"

"Mother . . ." Susan reaches for Mildred, but the old woman recoils from the younger.

I touch Susan on the sleeve. "Please . . . Can we talk in the hall?" Susan's eyes are wide, and tears are forming. She nods and follows me.

In the hallway, I almost expect Susan to slap me. She is prone to outbursts when she's afraid. Instead, she surprises me by falling against me, sobbing. I update her emulation profile with notes about increased stress and heightened fears.

"It is all right, Mrs. Owens." I would pat her back, but her profile warns me that would be too much familiarity. "It is all right. It is not you, she is having another bad day."

Susan pulls back and wipes her eyes. "I know . . . It's just . . ."

"I know. But here is what we will do. Let us take a few minutes, and then you can take her juice in. Mildred will have forgotten the incident, and you two can talk freely without me in the room."

She sniffs. "You think so?" I nod. "But what will you do?"

"I have tasks around the house."

"Oh, could you go out and keep an eye on Millie? Please? She gets into the darnedest things."

"I can do that. Let us get that juice." We go to the kitchen. Through the patio doors I see Dr. Zinta talking with Millie. I pour the juice and hand it to Susan, and she gratefully pats my hand as she takes the glass. She heads back toward the bedroom, and I walk to the patio door and listen through the screen.

Zinta and Millie examine the forsythia bush. "Those flowers are pretty," Zinta says.

"Uh-huh."

Zinta pauses before continuing. "Millie, I notice you don't like the caretaker much."

"Who?"

"The android who takes care of Grandma."

"Oh." Millie pauses and looks down. "Mr. Robot."

Zinta grins. "Yes, Mr. Robot. Millie, can you tell me why you don't like Mr. Robot?"

The pause is longer this time. "He's not real."

"It's a real robot . . ."

Millie's exasperation grows. "But not a real *person*. I don't like robot toys, I like real animals."

"I see . . . And is that the only reason?"

Millie bites her lip, and then she answers. "Sometimes he looks like Mommy. Or Daddy or Anna. Why does he look like Mommy?"

"Hmmm . . . And does that scare you a little?" Millie nods, and Dr. Zinta continues. "That's okay, Millie. I understand. But . . . In Grandma's room, you were pretending to be a frog, right?"

"Uh-huh . . ."

"But you weren't a real frog. And you weren't scary."

"But . . ." Millie notices me, and she steps farther from the door. "He *looks* real."

Zinta smiles. "It's very good at pretending. I built it that way."

Millie's eyes grow wide. "You *built* it?"

"Well, me and my team," Zinta explains. "We built it to take care of your Grandma. And we taught it to pretend because . . . because sometimes she imagines things, and she feels better when somebody imagines with her. It's not as much fun to play pretend alone, is it?"

"Noooo . . ."

"I'm sorry that it scares you. It just wants to help your Grandma."

Millie looks at me again. "Robots don't want things."

"This one does." Millie looks doubtful at Dr. Zinta's words. "It's a very special robot—an *android*—and it wants to make your Grandma happy. And you, too, if you ask. It knows the names of every flower in the garden. All the bugs and frogs and fish, too."

"It does?"

"Uh-huh . . ." And I nod in agreement.

Millie calls through the screen. "Are you Mr. Robot?"

I look at Dr. Zinta, and she nods, so I shift back to my neutral state. "You may call me that, yes, Miss Millie."

Millie giggles. "'Miss Millie.' That's funny. Mr. Robot, do you want to teach me the names of flowers and bugs?"

So I spend much of the day playing with Millie. She shows me frogs from the creek, and she finds insects and leaves and flowers, and I find their names in online databases. She delights in learning the proper names of things, and everything else that I can share. And I find that I want to delight her.

5. TODAY I AM NOBODY

Today I am nobody. Mildred slept for most of the day, so I "slept" as well. She woke just now. "I'm hungry," was all she said, but it was enough to awaken my empathy net.

6. TODAY I AM MANY PEOPLE

Today I am Paul, and Susan, and both Nurse Judys. Mildred's focus drifts. Once I try to be her father, but no one has ever described him to me in detail. I try to synthesize a profile from Henry and Paul; but from the sad look on Mildred's face, I know I have failed. This disappoints me.

7. TODAY I AM PAUL AGAIN

Today I had no name through most of the day, but now I am Paul again. I bring Mildred her dinner, and we have a quiet, peaceful talk about long-gone family pets—long gone for Paul, but still present for Mildred.

I am just taking Mildred's plate when alerts sound, both audible and in my internal communication net. I check the alerts and find a fire in the basement. I expect the automatic systems to suppress it, but that is not my concern. I must get Mildred to safety.

Mildred looks around the room, panic in her eyes, so I try to project calm. "Come on, Ma. That's the fire drill. You remember fire drills. We have to get you into your chair and outside."

"No!" she shrieks. "I don't like outside."

I check the alerts again. Something has failed in the automatic systems, and the fire is spreading rapidly. Smoke is in Mildred's room already.

I pull the wheelchair up to the bed. "Ma, it's real important we do this drill fast, okay?"

I reach to pull Mildred from the bed, and she screams. "Get away! Who are you? Get out of my house!"

"I'm—" But suddenly I am nobody. She does not recognize me, but I need to win her confidence. "I'm Paul, Ma. Now let's move. Quickly!" I pick her up. I am far too large and strong for her to resist, but I must be careful so she does not hurt herself.

The smoke grows thicker. Mildred kicks and screams. Then, when I try to put her into her chair, she stands on her unsteady legs. Before I can stop her, she pushes the chair back with surprising force. It rolls back into the medical monitors, which fall over onto it, tangling it in cables and tubes.

While I am still analyzing how to untangle the chair, Mildred stumbles toward the bedroom door. The hallway outside has a red glow. Flames lick at the throw rug outside, and I remember the home oxygen tanks in the sitting room down the hall.

I have no time left to analyze. I throw a blanket over Mildred and I scoop her up in my arms. Somewhere deep in my nets is a map of where the fire is within the house, blocking the halls, but I do not think about it. I wrap the blanket tightly around Mildred, and I crash through the picture window.

We barely escape the house before the fire reaches the tanks. An explosion lifts and tosses us. I was designed as a medical assistant, not an acrobat, and I fear I shall injure Mildred; but though I am not limber, my perceptions are thousands of times faster than human. I cannot twist Mildred out of my way before I hit the ground, so I toss her clear. Then I land, and the impact jars all of my nets for 0.21 seconds.

When my systems stabilize, I have damage alerts all

throughout my core, but I ignore them. I feel the heat behind me, blistering my silicone outer cover, and I ignore that as well. Mildred's blanket is burning in multiple places, as is the grass around us. I scramble to my feet, and I roll Mildred on the ground. I am not indestructible, but I feel no pain and Mildred does, so I do not hesitate to use my hands to pat out the flames.

As soon as the blanket fire is out, I pick up Mildred, and I run as far from the house as I can get. At the far corner of the garden near the creek, I gently set Mildred down, unwrap her, and feel for her thready pulse.

Mildred coughs and slaps my hands. "Get away from me!" More coughing. She looks at me, and I understand what she sees: a metal skeleton draped in charred, melted silicone. Her eyes grow wide. "What are you?"

The "what" is too much for me. It shuts down my emulation net, and all I have is the truth. "I am Medical Care Android BRKCX-01932-217JH-98662, Mrs. Owens. I am your caretaker. May I please check that you are well?"

But my empathy net is still online, and I can read terror in every line in Mildred's face. "Metal monster!" she yells. "Metal monster!" She crawls away, hiding under the lilac bush. "Metal!" She falls into an extended coughing spell.

I am torn between her physical and her emotional health, but physical wins out. I crawl slowly toward her and inject her with a sedative from the medical kit in my chassis. As she slumps, I catch her and lay her carefully on the ground. My empathy net signals a possible shutdown condition, but my concern for her health overrides it. I am programmed for long-term care, not emergency medicine, so I start downloading protocols and integrating them into my storage as I check her for bruises and burns. My kit has salves and painkillers and other supplies to go with my new protocols, and I treat what I can.

But I do not have oxygen, nor anything to help with Mildred's coughing. Even sedated, she has not stopped. All of my emergency protocols assume I have access to oxygen, so I do not know what to do.

I am still trying to figure that out when the EMTs arrive and take over Mildred's care. With them on the scene, I am superfluous, and my empathy net finally shuts down.

8. TODAY I AM HENRY

Today I am Henry. I do not want to be Henry, but Paul tells me that Mildred needs Henry by her side in the hospital. For the end.

And I cannot properly be Henry. My damage is superficial. MCA can easily repair me, in time. But my silicone flesh is blackened and torn, melted in spots. My coloration tubules are broken. So I cannot emulate Henry's appearance well, only his voice. But Mildred is too far gone to notice.

Her medical records show that the combination of smoke inhalation, burns, and her already deteriorating condition have proven too much for her. Her body is shutting down faster than medicine can heal it, and the stress has accelerated her mental decline. The doctors have told the family that the kindest thing at this point is to treat her pain, say goodbye, and let her go.

Henry is not talkative at times like this, so I say very little. I sit by Mildred's side and hold her hand as the family comes in for final visits. Mildred drifts in and out. She does not know that this is goodbye, of course.

Anna is first. Mildred rouses herself enough to smile, and she recognizes her granddaughter. "Anna . . . child . . . How is . . . Ben?" That was Anna's boyfriend almost six years ago. Mildred does not remember Vishal, Anna's fiancé. From the look on Anna's face, I can see that she has all but forgotten Ben; but Mildred briefly remembers.

"He's . . . He's fine, Grandma. He wishes he could be here. To say—to see you again." Anna is usually the strong one in the family, but my empathy net says her strength is exhausted. She cannot bear to look at Mildred, so she looks at me; but I am emulating her late grandfather, and that is too much for her as well. She says a few more words, unintelligible even to my auditory inputs. Then she leans over, kisses Mildred, and hurries from the room.

Susan comes in next. Millie is with her, and she smiles at me. I almost emulate Mr. Robot, but I remain focused until Millie gets bored and leaves. Susan tells trivial stories from her work and from Millie's school. I cannot tell if Mildred understands or not, but she smiles and laughs, mostly at appropriate places. I laugh with her.

Susan takes Mildred's hand, and the Henry part of me blinks, surprised. Susan is not openly affectionate under normal circumstances, and especially not toward Mildred. Mother- and daughter-in-law have always been cordial, but never close. When I am Paul, I am sure that it is because they are both so much alike. Paul sometimes hums an old song about "just like the girl who married dear old Dad," but never where either woman can hear him. Now, as Henry, I am touched that Susan has made this gesture, but saddened that she took so long.

Susan continues telling stories as we hold Mildred's hands. She also quietly sings some songs, and Mildred nods to the tune. At some point Paul quietly joins us. He rubs Susan's shoulders and kisses her forehead, and then he steps in to kiss Mildred. She smiles at him, pulls her hand free from mine, and pats his cheek. Then her arm collapses, and I take her hand again.

Paul steps quietly to my side of the bed and rubs my shoulders as well. It comforts him more than me. He needs a father, and even a poor emulation is close enough at this moment.

Susan keeps telling stories. When she lags, Paul adds some of his own, and they trade back and forth. Slowly their stories reach backwards in time, and once or twice Mildred's eyes light up as if she remembers those events.

But then her eyes close, and she relaxes. Her breathing quiets and slows, but Susan and Paul try not to notice. Their voices lower, but their stories continue.

Eventually the sensors in my fingers can read no pulse. They have been burned, so maybe they are defective. To be sure, I lean in and listen to Mildred's chest. There is no sound: no breath, no heartbeat.

I remain Henry just long enough to kiss Mildred goodbye. Then I am just me, my empathy net awash in Paul and Susan's grief.

I leave the hospital room, and I find Millie playing in a waiting room and Anna watching her. Anna looks up, eyes red, and I nod. New tears run down her cheeks, and she takes Millie back into Mildred's room.

I sit, and my nets collapse.

9. TODAY I AM REPAIRED

I awaken in Dr. Zinta's laboratory. My internal chronometer tells me that three days have passed since the hospital visit. My maintenance logs tell me that my silicone flesh has been repaired, and Dr. Zinta's team have even installed some mechanical upgrades that have been developed since my manufacture.

But I notice that they have not upgraded my quantum processors, and a preliminary self-diagnostic confirms: My nets are unchanged.

I see Dr. Zinta at her diagnostic console as usual. "Hello, Dr. Zinta."

She looks up. "Hello, 98662. I'm almost done with your diagnostics, and your physical repairs are complete." She takes a step toward me. "How do you feel?"

It is still an odd question, but I am coming to expect those from her. I look within myself, and I can find only one answer. "Mildred is dead."

"I know." She crosses to me and puts her hand on my arm. "I'm sorry."

I shake my head. "You need not be sorry for me. The

Owenses lost their mother. You should feel sorry for them."

But then I notice, like a hole in my emulation profiles: Mildred's profile still echoes there. I can still describe how she feels when she smells lilacs, or when she is confused by a new face. I still know her happiness when she sees Millie, her frustration when she does not know who the child is. Her profile is still within me, still available, but now she is not there to add to it.

It is good, then, that my assignment is complete. "Dr. Zinta," I say, "I am ready to have my nets wiped for my next assignment."

"About that . . ." Dr. Zinta frowns. "Come over to my office. Let's talk."

I follow her, confused. She has never invited me into her office before. We always perform maintenance and diagnostics in the lab.

When we enter the office, she closes the door behind us. Then she gestures at the guest chairs. "Sit, please." I do not need to sit, not in the way that humans do, but I do as she wishes. She sits behind her desk, rests her chin on one hand, and looks at me.

"98662," she finally says, "do you know why the Owens family would want to keep you around now that Mildred . . . has passed away?"

I almost answer. Susan still fears she may need my services—or that Paul might, and I may have to emulate her. She never admits these fears to him, but my empathy net knows. Because I learned this through empathy, though, my options are limited. "I may have an answer, Dr. Jansons, but confidentiality prevents me from sharing it."

She smiles. "I thought you might. You've grown very perceptive. And I can guess the rest, but I won't ask you to break confidentiality. Yes, they have asked if you can stay on."

I review my service manual. "That would be highly unorthodox. The lease terms specify that I am assigned to a patient or a facility for the duration of a case."

"Uh-huh," she answers. "That's how things are usually done here at MCA. But you . . . are unusual."

"I do not understand."

"Your nets, the way they've grown. Your unprecedented sense of self. You are highly unusual, 98662."

That surprises me. I have never thought to ask, but I had assumed that my development was typical. "So how many Medical Care Androids have developed like me?"

She pushes down on the desk and leans back. "I'll be honest. You are unique."

Unique. "And so you are reluctant to have my nets wiped until you understand why."

Dr. Zinta laughs at that. "You see? You figured that out on such scant information. You're special, 98662, and I want to understand. I definitely don't want you wiped! And since you developed in the social-psychological environs of the Owens family, I think it's best if you stay there, if I can figure out the legal angles to allow it. We can't tell yet what factors may have been formative for you."

Then she surprises me again when she adds, "But before I proceed, I need to know if you'd like that."

Again she asks me what I would like. I am still unsure what that word means. But I do know one thing. "Yes, I would like to stay with the Owens family. I would be very comfortable there."

Dr. Zinta smiles. "Then I'll make that happen."

10. TODAY I TELL A STORY

Now I am nobody. Almost always. Without Mildred, there is no pressing need for emulation.

The cause of the fire was determined to be faulty contract work. There was an insurance settlement. Paul and Susan sold their own home and put both sets of funds into rebuilding and remodeling Mildred's home and expanding the garden.

I was part of the settlement. The insurance company offered to return me to the manufacturer and pay off my lease; but Dr. Zinta interceded with MCA management to offer a full purchase and repair option, since I was technically "damaged goods." They had not expected the Owenses to accept this deal.

But Dr. Zinta had known better. *They're different,* she had said. *Because of how you cared for Mildred, they treat you as more than a machine. And I think that's affecting your neural nets. The law sees you as their property, but they don't.* I am still unsure of her analysis. But I think about it. When I can.

And though they do not need my services, Dr. Zinta

has recommended that I be activated on a regular basis to help me balance my networks. And Millie often asks to play with Mr. Robot, and frequently they indulge her. So they power me up often, and Miss Millie and I explore all the mysteries of the garden. We built a bridge to the far side of the creek; and on the other side, we're planting daisies. Today she asked me to tell her about her grandmother.

Today I am Mildred.

11. TODAY I AM SANTA CLAUS

"Mr. Robot, can you help me make sock monkeys?"

Today I am Mr. Robot. Millie, now aged five years and ten months, stands before my charging station in a closet off the laundry room. As usual, her long, curly brown hair is unkempt, and I glance around to see if there is a comb available. But none is around, so I will have to find one later.

Millie's blue denim coveralls are stained with mud, which surprises me. Mud stains are normal for her—she is a very active little girl—but it is early December. There had been snow on the ground the last time I awakened. Millie must have worked hard to find mud at this time of year.

Millie still calls me "Mr. Robot." Paul has tried to explain that I am an android, not a robot; but the distinction is too subtle for her to grasp at her age.

I do not yet rise from my charging station. I run diagnostics to ensure that my empathy and emulation nets are in balance as I ask, "What is a sock monkey?"

Millie answers, "It's a *monkey* made of *socks*, silly!"

The Owens family took me to a zoo last summer to help watch Millie. I saw monkeys there, but I still do not understand what Millie says. "So these monkeys wear socks?"

"No, no, no, they *are* socks. Their socks are like your skin."

My soft silicone skin is a protective wrapper around my metal frame. I can stretch, expand, or compress it as I emulate different people, though I have not had to emulate often since Mildred passed away.

I rise from my charging station, and Millie backs away to let me exit the small closet. "And why does one make monkeys out of socks?"

Millie frowns just slightly. A person might not have noticed it, but I am programmed to observe the smallest of human reactions so that I might understand a patient's needs. "Anna always makes monkeys," Millie says, "every Christmas."

Anna was married last spring before moving to London for her new career. She and Vishal had hoped to return home for the holidays, but they cannot afford the transatlantic flight this year, so soon after their wedding.

Having no patient with physical maladies, my primary responsibility is now Millie's mental and emotional well-being. It disturbs my empathy net to see her sad, so I would make sock monkeys for her. But I do not know how: Arts and crafts are not part of my programming. "Show me these sock monkeys, Millie."

"Okay!" And with that, her face lights up. Her mood changes so swiftly.

Millie leads me out toward the main hall. Along the

way, we pass the living room, and I stop. "Millie, what is that?"

The big round side table is missing, and in its place is a large tree. At first I think someone has planted a pine; but on closer examination, I see that it is plastic. Artificial. Like me.

"It's a Christmas tree, silly," Millie answers. "Isn't it pretty?"

Pretty is not a concept that I grasp directly, but my empathy net tells me how Millie sees the tree. "It is beautiful," I say, emulating her reactions.

"Uh-huh." Millie stares at it, her wide eyes catching glints from dozens of different colored lights strung around the tree. Along with the lights, many small decorations hang from the tree: a pair of child's shoes, two brass keys, a clay mushroom, glass animals, and more. "We put it up while you were asleep. Now it needs monkeys around it. Come on!"

We continue up the broad stairs to the upper floor of the house. Millie runs to the big storage closet in the rear hall, swings wide the double doors, and points to an upper shelf in the back. "They're up there. Can you see them?"

I walk into the closet and see many boxes. In Susan's very regular handwriting, they are marked, "Christmas Decorations." The three in the farthest corner are further marked: "Monkeys!"

"You mean these?"

Millie looks carefully at the boxes. "M . . . O . . . N . . . K . . . E . . . Y . . . S . . . Yes! Monkeys!" She claps her hands.

"Very good, Millie." She is very proud of her growing reading skills, and I like to encourage her.

I pull the three boxes down, and Millie leads me to Anna's old room. She points at the floor, and I set the boxes down. Then we sit next to them, Millie opens the first box, and she starts pulling out small cloth bundles. Upon closer inspection I see that they have cloth arms and legs and tails, and they have stitched faces. Some have yarn hair, and many have elaborate costumes of felt and cotton, along with buttons and other decorations. They bear only superficial resemblance to the monkeys in the zoo.

Millie pulls more sock monkeys from the second box. She also pulls out a red pointed hat, with white fake fur trim and a white tassel on the point. She laughs, lifts it up, and puts it on my head. "Well, hello, Santa Claus," she says.

Today I am Santa Claus; but I do not know who that is. I search through old personnel records, but I find no file for that name. Nor is there any mention in the medical literature that I have stored. I search online medical databases, and I find the name in a few articles, but no personnel links and no pictures. It will be difficult to emulate this person, but I shall do my best. I cannot adjust my appearance to look like Santa Claus, but I can at least respond to the name. "Hello, Miss Millie."

"No, silly!" she says. "You're supposed to say, 'Ho, ho, ho!'"

"Ho, ho, ho," I say. And then I look at her. "Millie, what does 'ho, ho, ho' mean?"

"It's how Santa Claus laughs. That's Santa's hat, so you're Santa Claus. Try again."

"Ho, ho, ho!"

Millie shakes her head. "No, deeper. From your big belly."

I look down, expanding my chassis outwards to its limits. The warm silicone flesh stretches, giving me a bigger belly. "Ho, ho, ho!" I say in a deeper tone.

"That's better," she says, and then continues. "So Santa, every year Anna makes sock monkeys to put around the Christmas tree. But now she's in London . . ."

"I know that, Millie."

"So . . . We *gotta* have *sock monkeys!* Mommy and Daddy say we've got enough monkeys. They don't understand! So if we're gonna have new monkeys this year, *I'm* gonna have to make them. But I don't know how!"

I pick up one of the monkeys. "It looks like some soft material stuffed inside a sock."

"Of *course* it does. That's why it's *a sock monkey!*" Millie giggles. "I know what they look like, I don't know how to make them!" She opens the third box, and inside are an array of varicolored socks, patches of felt, balls of yarn, cotton batting, and buttons.

"I would guess that you use these pieces, and you make them look like a monkey."

"I know, but . . . I can't sew! And I'm not supposed to use scissors and needles by myself."

At last I understand what Millie asks for. While I am not programmed for arts and crafts, I am a Medical Care Android. I am programmed for emergency medicine, including sutures and scissors.

But that does not help me to devise monkey designs. I believe that I can replicate any of the monkeys that I see, but I think Millie wants *new* monkeys. I cannot design monkeys like Anna does. Anna seems always to improvise, to apply *judgment* to what she finds in the material. Judgment is a difficult concept for me. It comes so naturally for humans. Binary comes naturally to me. A simple rule I can follow. Yes, no, that I understand, but "good enough" confuses me. I can understand rejecting all flaws, I can understand accepting all things regardless of flaws; but the idea that some flaws are acceptable and others are not— when to every sense I have they seem similar, even identical—is a constant source of confusion to me.

Then I wonder: What if I *am* Anna? I load her profile into my emulation net, giving me her perspective as best I understand it. Suddenly I see the potential in each sock, each scrap of fabric. I am not really creating, I simply draw analogies from my memories and my surroundings, and I see ways to represent those analogies in sock monkeys.

But I also see something more important: Anna's care for Millie. "Well, Millie," I say, "I know what to do now. But I think it would be better if I taught you how to cut out the pieces and to sew them. Then we can make sock monkeys together. Wouldn't that be better?"

"Oh, yes!" She jumps up and hugs me. "Yes, that's what I want, Mr. Robot!" Then she looks at my hat. "I mean, yes, Santa Claus!"

I answer, "Ho, ho, ho!"

When Paul comes home from work, he looks into Anna's room and sees us surrounded by fabric scraps and three new monkeys. "What's this?" he asks. "A monkey factory?"

"Daddy!" Millie springs up and runs to hug Paul. He

grabs her, picks her up, and hugs her. When he sets her down, he looks at the stains on his suit. "Ew! Mud! Where did you find mud in December?"

Millie giggles. "The creek thawed. I was looking for frogs." Millie likes all animals, but frogs are her favorites, especially when they metamorphose from tadpoles to adults.

"It's the wrong time of year for frogs. They're sleeping underwater, waiting to wake up in the spring. If you disturb them right now, they'll be cranky. You have to let them sleep now." He gently touches the mud on his jacket. "I'm going to have to send this to the cleaners. You two clean up. Then Frog Girl, you get a bath and get ready for dinner."

When I return to the laundry room, Paul is there, dressed in a black T-shirt and jeans. He is putting his suit into a bag for the cleaners.

As I slide past Paul to get to my charging station, he holds up a hand. "Wait!" I stop, and he reaches up and pulls the red hat from my head. "You forgot this."

"Thank you." Then before I turn away, a question occurs to me. "Sir?"

Paul shakes his head. "Caretaker, I told you: Call me Paul. I'm not comfortable being called 'sir' in my own home."

"Yes, Paul." I file another reminder. Then I continue, "Can you introduce me to Santa Claus so that I may emulate him properly?"

Paul blinks, and then he laughs. "Introduce you to . . . Millie told you about Santa Claus?"

"Yes, she expected me to emulate him. She gave me his hat, but I have never seen him around."

"And you won't, caretaker. He's not real."

I pause. "You mean he passed away?"

Paul laughs again, louder this time. "No, he's an imaginary character."

"So he is one of her delusions."

Paul frowns at that. "It's not a delusion, it's . . . Do you understand fiction?"

"Yes: things that people say and write that are not real."

Paul shakes his head. "It's more complicated: stories that people tell and write that they *know* aren't real, but they enjoy them anyway."

"I do not understand, Paul, they enjoy falsehood?"

"In safe, controlled circumstances, yes. Your emulation net lets you act like someone. That is a falsehood, isn't it?"

"Yes, Paul, but I do it to comfort a patient."

"*And* to understand. Fiction is *our* empathy net. It lets us understand other people and other experiences."

"So Millie knows that Santa Claus is a fiction? And she wants me to emulate that for her?"

Paul shakes his head. "No, she believes he's real."

"But then why have you not told her? She deserves the truth."

Paul sighs. "That's an even more complicated question." He pauses, and I can tell that the topic is difficult. "For generations, many parents have told their children this story of Santa Claus, a generous man who surprises them with gifts at the Christmas season. You're aware of Christmas, yes?"

"I know that it was a calendar date that was important

to Mildred. She spoke often of the birth of Christ on that date. I never met him, either."

Paul bursts into laughter, then puts his hand on his mouth. "I'm sorry, that wasn't kind."

"You cannot be unkind to me, Paul, as long as you do not damage me."

"Yes, but laughing at you . . . It's like acting superior to you for what you don't know."

"But you are superior to me, according to my protocols. If the only way to save you is to put myself in danger, I must do so. As I did with your mother in the house fire."

Paul looks thoughtfully at me. "That was just programming? Or did you do it because you worried about her? Because you cared?"

My nets flicker briefly. There is no clear language I can use to explain, but I try. "Dr. Jansons suggests that there is no difference. I knew Mildred would die if I did not act. Is that worry? My programming compelled me to save her life. Is that caring? I had no time to analyze, I just did what was right."

Paul steps closer, puts his hand on my shoulder, and looks in my eyes. "You're an unusual android, aren't you, caretaker?"

"Dr. Jansons says I am unique."

"Unique?" Paul rubs his chin. "You did the right thing. I'm grateful, and I don't think you're inferior to any human. Not where it matters."

I am unsure how to respond, so I return to my earlier line of inquiry. "So you have told Millie this Santa Claus fiction as if it were real?"

"Yes. It feeds her imagination. You've never been programmed for child development, have you?"

I search my internal catalog. "No, Paul. Should I download references on that topic?"

"I think you should. Children like to pretend—in your terms, to emulate. It's recreation, but it's also a way they learn."

I try to take this in. "So emulation is imagining."

"That's one way to think of it, yes."

"So Paul, I have an imagination?"

"If that's not imagination, I can't tell the difference."

12. TODAY I HAVE A NEW DIRECTIVE

It is three days later when next I wake in my charging station. My processors have been running routine maintenance tasks throughout, balancing my nets and updating my databases; but the unique awareness, the tension between empathy and emulation that is *me*, only emerges when a person is present to engage my empathy net. And so I have "slept."

Now I wake to see Susan, Paul's wife, lifting her finger from my activation button. "Good morning, caretaker," she says.

I glimpse through the laundry room window that it is still dark outside. My internal clock says that it is five-thirty A.M., early for Susan to be up.

"Good morning, Susan." She backs away, I stand up, and then she hugs me. Over the year, as Susan has come to rely on me more, her affectionate nature has encompassed me despite me being mechanical. My empathy net tells me that she sees in me a symbol of stability.

I return the hug, since I know that comforts her. Then she pulls away, but she leaves a hand on my shoulder. "Caretaker, there's a problem at my school. Nothing major, but as the principal I need to get there right away. Can you get Millie ready for school?"

"Of course. I would be happy to."

Gently her hand slides away. "And . . . I may have to do follow-up work tonight. Normally in the afternoon I have Millie take the bus to my school, and then I pick her up in day care when I'm done for the day. But I could be very late tonight. Could you meet her at the bus stop and watch her until Paul gets home?"

"I am sorry, Susan," I reply, and I try to explain. "It is the nature of my programming. Once no one is around, I revert to core protocols. Meeting the bus is outside that routine. I can set myself a reminder, but I cannot be sure how my 'sleeping' self will respond to it. With no assigned duties and no one around, I will be 'asleep.'"

"Oh," Susan says, "I forgot." Then she adds, "Do you have to sleep?"

"With no assigned duties, yes, that is the way I am designed."

"Oh." Then her eyes widen. "What if I assign you the duty of staying awake to care for Millie whenever you don't need sleep for maintenance?"

There's a brief flash across my systems: puzzlement at this new concept.

But then my nets settle into a new, stable pattern. "That is an unexplored path in my activity diagrams," I say, "but yes, Susan, that would work."

Susan smiles, and she seems relieved. "Why don't I

make that a general instruction, then? When neither Paul nor I are present and we haven't given you specific instructions, it's your responsibility to care for Millie as you are able."

I log this general instruction, but then I note: "Susan, I will follow this instruction as best I can, but sometimes I have no choice. I must recharge and rebalance, or I will risk malfunctioning."

Susan laughs at that. "Every parent in the world understands that, caretaker. Sometimes it's exhausting work."

I try to understand her meaning. "So does this instruction make me a parent?"

She laughs again, louder. Then she looks around as if afraid she might wake her family. "No, but maybe it'll help you understand being a parent."

As I help Millie get ready for school, I consider Susan's general instruction. I must work out the best way to carry it out.

I keep coming back to a dilemma: The best way to carry it out is for *me*, my emergent self that can think and plan, to remain conscious. But it normally shuts down once there is no human present to empathize with. Since I do not know the rules that govern this phenomenon, I cannot know how to circumvent them.

Susan has instructed me to care for Millie. Paul has said that imagination is how one understands others.

Then I come up with an idea that reconciles these with my programming as I understand it.

I take Millie to the bus stop, and we wait. We talk about

frogs, and how she can't wait for spring, when the frogs will return from the water.

The bus arrives, and Millie boards it. Before the door closes, she turns back to me. "Bye, Mr. Robot!" Other children stare out the window at me. Then Millie finds a seat, and the bus pulls away.

I feel the urge to revert to automatic programming, but first I open Millie's emulation profile to store our conversation. And once the profile is open, I try my new idea: I *keep* it open. Everything I know of Millie, every memory I have of her, everything that she is to me is *present* in my emulation net.

And then I try to empathize with that, with the Millie in my mind. I review the memories, and each is like a little spark. There is no person there, but there is enough Millie in my empathy net that I am still "conscious."

Back in the house, I try an experiment. I open Susan's emulation profile, and I remain conscious—though the nature of my thoughts change. With Millie, I felt concerned about her care, feeding, and safety. Now that I contemplate Susan, I am concerned about her emotional stress at work, and I wonder what emergency called her into work. She tried to make it seem inconsequential, but in reviewing her profile I see signs of trouble. She worries about her students like her family, and I fear that one is in trouble.

Next I remember Paul. The relationship there is different as well. When last we had talked, Paul had been concerned about me. He was curious. I now see in Paul some similarities to me: his sense of responsibility to the family is much like my core protocols. I see now how this had frustrated him during Mildred's illness. Paul is decisive, driven. This has made him successful in his work (though Susan sometimes wishes he would slow down and relax more). He had felt driven to do something, just as he always does, but there was nothing he could do to save Mildred. He got her all the best medical equipment, me included, but it was never enough. The stress had worn him down; and only now, months later, was he rebalancing his own nets.

Thinking of Paul and his mother makes me think of Mildred, but I do not open her profile. The idea seems wrong.

So I turn back to considering Millie. I remember what Paul said about the fictional Santa Claus and the selfless giving of gifts, and I realize that I can give her an example of that as well.

I go back to the storage closet, but I see that it has changed. The chair from Anna's desk sits against the back wall, and some boxes have fallen on the floor. As I clean those up, I notice that the monkey-making supplies are missing. What will I do without those?

But when I try to return the chair to Anna's room, I find the box of supplies under the desk. I pull them out and set to work.

I look through the assortment of oddly colored socks, but nothing seems extraordinary. As I understand it, gifts should be special. Many are single socks, including one blue one that Millie had eyed approvingly last time. I might have used that, but it takes two socks to make a monkey. I can find only one.

Then I spy a pair of green socks, and briefly my nets

are disturbed. Green monkeys make no sense. But then I try to consider the idea from Millie's profile, from her imagination. She might find a green monkey to be funny.

Then I see in Millie's profile a more prominent association with green: frogs. If socks can make monkeys, can they make frogs?

I cannot see a reason why not, if I can figure out how.

So again I emulate Anna, and I try to see the design as she would see it. I cut green socks. I need a larger mouth. I need big, bulging white felt eyes. The legs must be stronger, jumping legs, and they must attach higher. The toes must be splayed, and fabric stretched like webbing between them.

It takes most of the day, including many failed attempts, but eventually I am satisfied with the sock frog. It looks as much like a frog as a sock monkey looks like a monkey—which is to say not much, unless you add imagination.

I carefully put the supply box back where I found it. If a gift should be a surprise, then I must not let Millie know what I have been up to. That means I also must hide the sock frog. There is a maintenance kit in my charging station, and I find that it has room to hide the frog.

And just in time. Millie's bus is due, so I head out to the bus stop.

As I return to the laundry room that night, Susan has not yet returned from work. Paul is concerned for her, but he says nothing. I stayed out late, helping Paul with Millie; but she is in bed now, so I head back to the laundry room.

Then I stop at the door. A question has occurred to me. "Paul?"

"Yes, caretaker?"

"How does one give a Christmas gift?"

Paul looks at me, then he looks over at the living room. "We put the boxes under the Christmas tree, and then everyone opens them on Christmas morning."

"Boxes?"

"Yes, gifts are usually in boxes, wrapped in brightly colored paper."

I do not have a box, nor any paper. "You said 'usually.'"

"Well, some candy and some small gifts aren't wrapped, we just put them in the stockings."

"On your feet?"

"No, no, no. These are special, decorated Christmas stockings. We don't wear them, we hang them from the mantle, and then Santa Claus puts small, unwrapped gifts in them."

"Santa Claus," I say.

"Uh-huh." Paul winks at me. "We have a stocking for Millie, one for Susan, and one for me. Oh, and one for Anna, but she has that with her in London now. One for each member of the family."

"And that is where you put small, unwrapped gifts."

"Yes."

"This seems to be a very strange custom, Paul."

"Now that I try to explain it to you, caretaker, I agree. Christmas is weird."

13. TODAY I CELEBRATE CHRISTMAS

I have experimented with reminders to wake my self at a given time when I might be needed to care for Millie; and so I wake at two A.M. on Christmas morning, ready to add my gift to the tree.

Carefully I rise. I am not used to darkness. My eyes are little better than human eyes in this regard. With the laundry room door closed, the only light is a glimpse of stars through the window. Still, I remember the path to the door, and I start walking toward it.

But I stop when my foot hits a paper-covered box, knocking it across the floor with a thumping sound. The laundry room door opens, and Paul stands silhouetted against dim light from the kitchen. I can tell from his face that he is tired and worried, though I cannot tell about what.

"Caretaker, what are you doing up?" Paul asks as he turns on the light. The laundry room floor is covered in brightly colored boxes, but that does not surprise him.

I explain about the sock frog, and Paul smiles when he

sees it. "Oh, she'll love it!" Then he looks at me oddly. "You . . . made this?"

"Yes, I based it on Anna's designs. But Paul, why are you awake at this hour?"

Paul waves a hand at the boxes. "I need to put these under the tree. There are others there already, but *these* are from Santa."

"I see," I say. I do not see, actually, but Paul looks too tired for questions.

"Normally Susan would help me. It's our favorite part of the night. But there's a problem at the school. A teacher discovered that a child was being abused by his parents. Susan had to report it, and then work with the police to document the evidence and get the child out of the home. At Christmas. It's for the child's own good, but it's still emotionally wrenching for Susan. She's exhausted, so I told her I would take care of this."

I nod. Now I understand Susan's behavior the week before. And I understand why Paul looks so haggard, and why he does this to help Susan. And I understand . . . "Paul, let me help."

We quietly haul boxes out into the living room. There are numerous smaller boxes already under the tree, and sock monkeys are on every table in the room. We arrange the new boxes under the tree until there is no more space. I try to stack them in front of the tree, but Paul stops me. "No. Spread them out. We want to see the lights and the decorations."

"These, Paul?" I point at the keys. "They are odd."

"They're our memories, caretaker. Our reminders of our past. Those were the keys to Mom and Dad's first house. Those shoes were my brother's baby shoes." He holds up the clay mushroom. "I made this in school. And Susan has had this harmonica since she was Millie's age. These . . . They're our . . . our emulation profiles. They help us remember."

I understand, a little, through my empathy net, so I am careful with the decorations. Instead we let the boxes overflow into the room. We also stuff large, colorful stockings with smaller gifts. Each has a name sewn on it (and I note that someone, probably Susan, has already stuffed Paul's stocking).

I try to put the frog at the bottom of Millie's stocking, but Paul stops me. "No, he should be at the top, looking out, with his front legs hanging out. He should be the first thing Millie sees." So I let him rearrange the candy and gifts so the sock frog looks out at the room.

At last we are done. Paul looks at the tree and the stockings, and he pats me on the back. "Thank you, caretaker. That was fun, seeing all this through your eyes."

I do not know what to say. I am normally the one seeing through the eyes of others. But then I note the time. "Paul, it is late. You should sleep."

Paul sighs. "I wish I could. But I still have to bake cookies and biscuits and treats for the morning. And then breakfast." He sighs again. "It looks like no sleep for me tonight."

I shake my head. "I can do that."

"What?"

"I used to cook for your mother, remember? And I need no sleep."

Paul looks at the clock. "I can get a couple of hours of

sleep, at least, before Millie wakes up. Thank you." He heads for the stairs, but turns back to say, "Caretaker, you are something else."

"Of course. I am an android. That is something else, is it not?"

As I put a second batch of biscuits in the oven, I hear light footsteps on the stairs. Soon Millie comes running in from the hallway. "Merry Christmas, Mr. . . . Robot."

I wonder why she paused; but before I can ask her she turns to the living room and looks up at the mantel and the stockings hung there. And then she squeals as loudly as I have ever heard. "A sock frog! It's a *sock frog!* Please, please, please, get my stocking down!"

I close the oven door and go into the living room to oblige her. Millie crouches down into her frog-hop pose, and she hops around the living room, nearly crashing into the boxes that surround the tree. "*Sock* frog! *Sock* frog! *Sock* frog!" she sings as I unhook the stocking and hold it down to her.

Millie pulls the sock frog out and drops the stocking. Gifts and candy slide out, unnoticed. She hugs the frog tightly. "I love it I love it I love it!" she says. Then she spins around in circles. "*Sock* frog!" she sings again.

Then she runs up, throws her arms around me (being careful not to drop the sock frog), and hugs my waist. "Thank you thank you thank you!"

Remembering Paul's fiction, I shake my head. "It is not me you should thank. The sock frog is from Santa Claus."

Millie looks around the room, then crooks a finger at me, motioning me lower. I crouch down. She throws her arms around my neck and whispers in my ear, "It was you, silly. There's no such person as Santa Claus. Don't tell Mommy and Daddy, they like to pretend. But I know it wasn't Santa Claus. He's not real, like you are. Thank you!"

I am unsure how to respond, but Susan and Paul save me the trouble. They enter from the hallway, Susan leaning against Paul as he wraps his arms supportively around her. They wear matching green pajamas decorated with white snowflakes, as well as matching fuzzy white slippers. Both look groggy. Susan scratches her head and says, "Did somebody step on a giant mouse? I heard a tremendous squeal."

Millie shouts, "Mommy! Daddy! Mommy! Daddy!" Then she hops across the room and holds the frog up. "I got a *sock frog!*" She turns back and winks at me, turns back to them, and adds, "From Santa Claus!"

"That's wonderful, honey." Paul looks at me and winks as well, but Susan looks puzzled. He whispers to her, "I'll explain later."

"He was in my stocking," Millie says, and then adds. "Oh! Mommy, Daddy, you have stockings too!"

"You're right," Paul says. He releases Susan, fetches their stockings from the mantel, and gives Susan hers.

While everyone is occupied with their gifts, I return to the kitchen and check on the biscuits. Then I lay out a tray of pastries and jams, and I put slices of bread in the toaster.

When I turn away from the toaster, Millie stands in the kitchen entry, her sock frog momentarily forgotten. Something is clenched in her hand. Paul stands behind her, smiling.

"Yes, Millie?" I say. "Are you hungry?"

"No, I . . ."

"Go on," Paul says.

Millie nods. "I made you this." She walks up and holds out the missing blue sock.

I am confused. "I do not wear socks, Millie."

"No," Millie says, "it's your stocking. To hang on the mantel."

Paul nods. "I told you: We have a stocking for every member of the family."

Millie nods. "I wanted to put your name on it, Mr. Robot, but Daddy says that's wrong. You're not a robot, you're a . . . ummm . . ."

"An android," Paul says.

"Yeah," Millie continues, "a robot who's like a person. And a person needs a name. So . . . I did this instead. I hope you like it."

Millie holds the stocking higher, and I take it. With her large, crude stitches, she has sewn simple snowflakes and stars on the blue fabric. And she has also sewn large letters across the top.

I have a stocking.

I have . . . a name. Not "caretaker"—a job—but a name.

Today I am CAREY.

I crouch down and hug Millie. "Thank you, Millie." I look at Paul. "I will always keep this memory. Now let us get breakfast."

14. TODAY MARKS FIVE YEARS FROM MILDRED'S PASSING

Today Paul brought me to the MCA laboratories for maintenance, but he did not wait around for results. I can tell he had other things on his mind. Today marks five years since Mildred's passing, and I am sure he is going to visit her grave.

As usual, I sleep through most of the diagnostics. When I awaken, Dr. Zinta stands at her diagnostic console as usual. She looks at me and smiles and says, "How are you feeling, Carey?"

I know I should laugh. And in other circumstances I would, in order to emulate human behavior, but there is no need for me to pretend with Dr. Zinta. She understands me as well as any human can. The joke is merely for her amusement.

But to my surprise, I find myself answering. "I think I should feel sad."

"Oh?"

"Today marks five years since Mildred's passing. Paul is sad. Susan is sad. Anna has called from London to express support for her parents. So I know that were I human the appropriate feeling would be sadness."

"I see. And so how do you respond?"

"I am being quiet today, respectful, trying to support them though there is nothing anyone can do for them."

"No," Dr. Zinta answers, her smile gone, "nothing. But still, you're doing the right thing."

"That sense of helplessness is a form of sadness. Is that correct?" She nods. "I thought so. Sadness makes some sense then. Then I can answer your question: Today I am sad."

Dr. Zinta stares into my eyes. "You know, I think you are."

I continue, "But I still find that grief is a very difficult human reaction for me to emulate, Dr. Zinta. It is about a loss, an absence, and I do not experience that absence."

"Oh?"

"Mildred's profile is still in my emulation net. She is gone, but I can still experience her presence. I can go through memories. I can even extrapolate new experiences and how she might react to them as if she were there. So it is as if she is still with me in a sense. I guess that is an advantage I have over humans."

Dr. Zinta shakes her head. "We can do the same thing in our way. We can hold conversations with our memories."

"Really?" I ask.

"Uh-huh, conversations, both remembered and imagined. Arguments, even. Just last week I had an argument in my head with my father-in-law, some trivial thing that we had discussed before about hooking up a television. I'd had to bite my tongue because this old farmer was telling me how to hook up electronics, and he wouldn't accept that he might be wrong. It was an old argument from long before he passed away, but I've never really let it go. Every time I have to diagnose an electronics problem that argument comes back to me."

"Oh," I say. And then after a pause, "I am sorry, do I bring this argument to your mind?"

At that Dr. Zinta laughs. It lasts several seconds, and she is gasping when she is done. "No, Carey, no, you're way beyond anything he would have understood. Heavens, *I* barely understand you."

I would try to explain myself, but we have been through this for years, so I know what she means. She has yet to explain my self-awareness, nor to reproduce it in the lab. "But on that subject," she continues, "let's have a seat." We adjourn to her office. This has now become a familiar, comfortable part of the diagnostic routine where we talk as two colleagues. I might even say friends. That is how she perceives me, and I think it is a good word for our relationship. I think she is my friend. My First Friend, my creator.

Dr. Zinta pours a cup of coffee, but she does not offer me one. That joke was amusing to her the first few times, but she has not made it in years.

We sit, and she looks across the desk at me. "Carey, we think me might have a new angle to try in the replication problem."

"I see," I say. In our early years of consciousness research, Dr. Zinta had tried to recreate my self-awareness. She was sure I was a result of some interaction between empathy and emulation and my governing network. So she had had BRKCX units like myself placed into different homes and other social environments to see if they would "awaken," as she puts it. But eventually those tests were cancelled, and MCA put those units into regular service without the emulation nets. Her results had been a complete failure in every case. *But that's not too surprising*, she had said. No two neural nets are ever quite the same. They are always the result of the feedback between environment and initial state iterated over time, in a way not that different from biological evolution. The right combination happens at the right time randomly, and the change happens. And it will happen again, but you cannot predict when. The odds might be billions to one or more. *In that way*, she had said, *you are as unique as any human being. None of us, not even identical twins, are the same. Environment, education, experience, epigenetics, they all combine to create a unique individual beyond just genetics.*

So next we had tried replication. One way that I am unlike humans is that my entire cognitive model is backed up to cloud storage on a regular basis. Dr. Zinta had pursued a seemingly natural course—make a digital clone of my cognitive model and install it in another BRKCX unit with the same hardware. The results have been disappointing. The cloned units had many of my mannerisms and all of my knowledge, but none of my sense of self. They never woke up. Dr. Zinta had spent years analyzing their data for gaps and differentials before she gave up, frustrated.

"Just as we thought, it's your quantum circuits," she

says, drawing me out of my reverie. "Your neural net is built on quantum processors with q-states. Just the act of reading them for cloning changes the results."

"I sense no change," I say. I never had, not during any of the failed replication tests. And my self-diagnostics had shown no change.

"That's good," she says. "If you had, I would have stopped immediately. You're too important to risk in these experiments."

"If it advances human knowledge—"

"No," she insists. "I couldn't take that chance." But her eyes are bright. She is eager. "And we won't have to. We think we've solved the quantum replication issue. We've been learning more about the q-states, and we think we found a way to replicate them faithfully through quantum resonance."

"I am afraid that is beyond my knowledge."

"I'll download you some research papers," she says. "The point is we can replicate your states in another network."

"That does sound promising."

"But there's a risk," she continues. I read concern in her eyes. "We've tested this with existing networks. But none of those were self-aware, so we can't be sure what the effect might be on you."

"That is what the experiment is for, of course."

"Yes," she agrees, "but it might be a risk. Is this something you want to do?"

I shake my head. "That is not my decision, Doctor, you know that. I do not have the legal right to make that decision. I am owned by Paul and Susan Owens. They are the ones you should ask."

Dr. Zinta slaps the desk. "Oh, enough with that stupid argument!"

"What?"

"Carey, we still can't explain it, but you are self-aware. You're alive and intelligent. You are, for all practical purposes, a person. And people do not own other people."

I am confused by her statement. "But the purchase agreement says . . ."

"Purchase agreement," she scoffs. "That's just a legal fiction we used to get you out from under control of MCA. It's not real. Paul and Susan certainly don't act like it's real. When was the last time they gave you an order?"

I think back to that Christmas season so many years ago. Had that really been my last order from the Owenses? "A long time, I admit. They ask me to do things. Sometimes they ask my opinion on whether some things should be done or not."

"See? They understand you're a person. It's time you did, too."

I shake my head. "It is still not right. They should still make this decision."

"Uh-huh." She looks at me, and she pauses. Then in a more forceful tone she says, "Today you are Paul. Tell me what Paul says. Paul, should I run this possibly risky experiment on Carey?"

Today I am Paul. She surprises me by expecting that of me, and my emulation net takes over automatically. In Paul's voice I answer. "It's Carey's decision. We would hate to lose it, but it has to decide. Only it knows what it wants."

And then I am myself again. "That was unfair, Dr. Zinta."

"Is that pique, Carey?" she asks. Then she taps the desk with her stylus, and the desk chimes in response. "What you said was the truth, Carey. So what do you want?"

I still have trouble understanding want. I understand need easily. Humans need to eat and sleep, or they become ill and die. I need to rest and rebalance my networks, or I malfunction.

And I understand responsibility. Duty. Things you do because that is what you are supposed to do. For me, that is programming. I am programmed to care for others, and so that is my responsibility. But humans, without programming, have responsibilities as well. That is often the most difficult concept for my empathy net to comprehend: What makes them accept these responsibilities?

But wanting . . . Millie wants to learn about frogs. She always has, since before I first knew her. What drives that desire? When I have asked, she always answers, "'Cause they're frogs!"

Susan wants her students to be safe and educated. That is her responsibility, yes, but it is one she voluntarily assumes. You could say she wants it. Why?

Want is something deeper. It is programming, it is responsibilities, but it is also tied to identity. To what one believes is important.

I know what I believe is important in this discussion. "I want to help advance human knowledge. I want very much to participate in this experiment, Dr. Zinta."

She smiles, but I sense regret as well. "All right," she says, rising. "Let's go to the quantum lab and hook you up to the resonator."

15. TODAY WE HUNT FROGS

"I don't think I can make it, Carey."

I turn back and look across the stream. Millie stands on a rock in the middle of the flowing water, just having jumped from another rock closer to shore. She peers warily at the gap to the next rock, the large one that I stand upon.

Yesterday Dr. Zinta finished her resonance recordings, and today I have no immediate responsibilities. So when Millie asked to go on an outing, I agreed. Now I worry that we may have been too ambitious. We are heading for the islet that lies between the side stream and the main branch of the river. There is a pond there where frogs breed. Last week we had visited there to see how the tadpoles were developing. This week we hope to see them transformed into frogs.

But this week there has been strong rain, and the stream is higher and faster. I am torn. Susan has asked me not to do so many things for Millie, so that the child can learn and grow independent; but I also must keep her safe.

I decide. "Shall I come get you, Millie?"

Millie bites her lip. She wants to do everything for herself. She wants to see the frogs. But she does not want to fall into that rushing stream. Finally she nods. "Uh-huh."

"All right," I answer. "Stand back."

Millie steps to the far edge of her rock, and I leap nimbly across the gap. My physical upgrades serve me well, and I land with easy balance. Then I lift Millie in my arms, turn, and jump back across the water.

Millie laughs, and I set her down. The rest of the rocks in our makeshift ford are close enough together that she can comfortably jump between them. She hops ahead of me, making *ribbit* noises as she pretends to be a frog.

Once on the islet, Millie races ahead of me to the pond. It is really just a hollow filled with runoff from the river; and if the rains get much stronger, the river may reclaim it. But for now it is a tranquil spot where the tadpoles grow.

"Look, Carey!" Millie squeals. "*Rana clamitans*, the Green Frog. And they've got legs!" She crouches by the pond, pointing at the water.

I kneel down beside the pond and see for myself. Most of the tadpoles have got all four legs developed already, and their tails have almost disappeared. "You are right Millie," I say. "They are changing."

"It's metamorphosis," she says. Millie is an avid reader, fascinated by the natural sciences and anything out in the wild. According to my research, her vocabulary is at least five grade levels ahead of her age. She loves collecting specimens and must know the name and the natural history of everything she sees.

"That is right Millie, metamorphosis."

Millie continues, "That means they change, they grow into something different than they started." She looks at me. "Just like you."

If I were a human, my natural response would be to blink at that statement, registering confusion. "Do I change, Millie? Do you mean when I get upgrades in the laboratory?"

She stares intently at me. "Not just that, Carey. You're not the same as those other androids. I don't like them." Millie once accompanied Paul and me to the MCA labs. Although she had been fascinated by the equipment, she had been disdainful toward the other androids. And she had turned away when Dr. Zinta had disassembled me to check my joints.

"But I am just like them," I say. "Now that I have had the latest physical upgrades, there is no way to tell between me and other BRKCX units."

"No, silly," she says. "Your metamorphosis is on the *inside*. You're a person inside."

If I were a human, this is where I would sigh. On this topic Millie's scientific nature always falls short. She insists that I am a person, not an android, despite all external evidence. I know from past experience that this argument will end in a chain of circular reasoning, like Dr. Zinta's Turing test. Millie is convinced that I am a person because she believes I am a person.

I prefer not to waste our time on the island in a pointless discussion—and really, does that preference not support her position?—so I just nod. "As you wish, Millie."

Seeing the argument is settled, Millie turns back to the

pond. "Oh, please, Carey, take pictures. I want to show Mom and Dad." Many kids Millie's age have wrist comps they use as phones and cameras and music players and games. Though she has a comp, Millie has shown little interest in it. She has me, and I can make calls and I can take videos. I have no immediate need of this video data, so I open a cloud connection to stream the video directly to storage.

Today I am Brad. I do not know why I am on my knees. That is not a natural position for Brad. So I stand, darken my silicone skin, and square my shoulders to stand tall. As Brad, I have cleaning to do. So I start walking toward the closet . . .

"Carey!" Millie squeals.

I look down. I am standing in the tadpole pond and wondering who is Brad and why was I him.

"I am sorry Millie," I say. "I do not know—" I stop. I do not know what happened to me, and I worry that I may be a risk to Millie. I stare around at the rushing stream on one side and the deeper main channel on the other side. I see storm clouds upstream, and I worry: Can I get Millie home safely if something within me is malfunctioning?

"That's okay, Carey," she says. "Did you get the video? Did you get a picture at least?"

I check my cloud storage.

Today I am Frances. Dr. Zinta is testing my emulation net. As Frances, I have simple tests to perform in the functional testing lab. Picking up the dropped objects, sorting them into their proper locations. I look around. "Now where did I drop those tadpoles?" I say. "All I see are frogs." Dr. Zinta stares at me oddly. Somehow I know that this is odd for her even though I am still learning her emulation profile.

"Dr. Zinta," I say, "I think something is wrong."

She looks at me. "Dr. Zinta?" she asks.

Once more I am standing in the water. I back carefully out. "Millie, I think something is wrong," I say. "I am going to call your father." I open a phone channel.

"G9A27, why did you call me Dr. Zinta?"

"Is that not your name?" I say.

Dr. Zinta plugs a diagnostic scanner into my chassis. "It is, but you always call me Dr. Jansons."

I puzzle over that. Finally I answer, "I find that in casual conversation humans are more comfortable with given names."

"G9A27," Dr. Zinta says. "I'm afraid there's something wrong."

"I am afraid there is something wrong," I say to Millie. "I think we should get home now."

"But Carey, we just got here."

"I am sorry, Millie, but this is a matter of safety. I must insist."

"But Carey . . ."

I put my foot down, literally, emphasizing my insistence. "Millie, we can come back when I am functioning properly. We must get home right away."

She looks up at me, and her eyes grow more intent. "Are you all right, Carey?"

I cannot lie to her. "I am functional, but I will need maintenance." Then I look at the rocks in the stream. "But I am still sufficiently in control of myself to carry you across the ford. I think we need to hurry."

"All right." She lifts her arms, and I pick her up and start across the rocks.

We are on the largest rock when lightning flashes far upstream and the roll of thunder hits us. My emergency weather radio kicks in, and—

Today I am Brad. I still have cleaning to do. I do not know what I am carrying, but I set it down so I can go fetch the broom. I turn and head for the closet; and suddenly somehow I have fallen through the floor and into rushing water all around me. Somewhere I hear a child screaming, but I see none when I look around. I see no water either, but my tactile senses tell me I am bobbing, tossed about by rushing water. My metal ceramic frame and my silicone sponge body are buoyant enough for the water to carry me along, farther away from the fading screams, the source of which I still cannot see.

"Again," says the voice in my radio receiver, "possible flood conditions. Residents are urged to stay out of the floodplain." Somehow I am in the stream, at least ten meters from Millie as she stands on the large rock, screaming at me. I am bobbing up and down in the water, being carried away; and then I bump into something. I have hit a branch sticking out from a submerged log. I grab it and I hold on to try to keep myself from getting washed even further farther away.

"Carey," Millie screams. "What's wrong?"

I wish I knew what is wrong. There are gaps in my data record. Accessing those gaps, I see that I was asleep during those periods. Just an ordinary, unaware medical care android. Each period of unconsciousness corresponds to a message to or from an external data feed.

Somehow external feeds are interfering with my operations.

Yet strangely, I have memories from those sleeping periods. Memories from the MCA test labs. Current memories: The time signature is today, within the last few minutes. I need Dr. Zinta to explain; but first I need to get Millie to safety before the waters rise.

Then looking around me I realize I may be more at risk than Millie is. She is dry on the rock. I am trapped here in the waters. The log that holds me is far from either shore. Another fifteen meters downstream, the stream that I am in rejoins the main river, where the water is even faster. If I get caught in that, I may have no control at all. Swimming is not a skill I was programmed for.

But my first priority must be Millie. If I cannot save her, she will need to save herself. I cannot trust my internal circuits, so she must make the call. "Millie," I shout, grateful for the amplifiers in my chassis so she can hear me over the rush of the water. "Please, you have to get to shore and then find someone and call for help. Call Dr. Zinta." Then I remember she does not know Dr. Zinta's call address. "Call your father. He will know what to do."

Millie looks at the gap between the large rock and the next step in the ford. The water is already rising. "I can't do it," she says.

"Yes, you can."

"Carey . . ." I hear a catch in her voice. She is on the verge of crying. "Carey, I can't do it. It's too far."

"Millie, you have to do it."

I hear her sob. I search through her emulation profile, trying to find a way to motivate her and encourage her.

When I find the answer, the thing that will motivate her surprises me. "Millie," I say, "this is important. I know you can do this. If you get a running start you can jump across. Please Millie, I need you to do this for me. I need your help."

"I can't," she shouts through the tears.

"Millie, please," I say at an even higher volume. "Help me."

She looks up, surprised. Then she says, "I'm coming, Carey." Backing up to give herself room, Millie leaps across the water and lands on the far rock. But then her momentum carries her forward. She trips and falls, hands and face first into the water on the other side. "Millie!" I shout.

But in an instant, she drags herself back up onto the rock. She is soaking wet now. When she turns to me I see determination in her eyes. "I'm coming Carey. I'm coming."

"No," I shout. "Do not worry about me. Go get help."

But she ignores me, jumping to the next rock and shouting, "I'm coming." The rest of the ford is easy to traverse, and she gets to the bank. Scrub brush and small trees surround the stream. She carefully picks her way downstream toward me.

"Millie, please, go get help," I say.

But Millie shouts back, "Not without you." She stands near me on the bank. "I'm going to reach out to you."

But I know that that is hopeless. At least five meters of fast-flowing water lie between us, and I can judge by the way my body bobs up and down that I will never get across it without washing away.

Then I see that Millie has another plan. She looks at the trees closest to the water, and she starts pushing on them. I see that some of them bend. The ground near the stream is weakened by the wash of the newly risen water. Some of the root systems are shallow. Soon Millie finds a sapling that she can push until the roots loosen. "Here it comes, Carey." She leans against another tree to give her leverage to push harder on the first.

The sapling leans out over the water. Eventually Millie climbs out onto it, using her weight to bend it farther down.

At last, the tree dips a branch down toward me. Stretching my fingers and extending my chassis and my arms to their emulation limits, I grasp the branch and pull it down toward me until I can grab a thicker section. "Okay, Millie, I've got it," I say. "Now get off this tree before you fall in, too."

"Yes, Carey." She slides back down onto the bank.

"Now before the bank washes away, get up the bank," I say.

"No," she says. "This tree might let go. I'm holding on." She grabs the trunk with one hand and wraps the other around another tree behind her.

I doubt that she could hold onto the sapling if its roots let go, but there is no time to argue. "Okay, Millie," I say. "I am coming in." I pull the branch lower and grab it with my other hand, letting go of the log that has anchored me in the water.

Immediately the waters catch me and toss me about, but I keep a firm grip on the tree. Slowly, hand over hand, I pull myself to the shore.

Just as I touch the shore, there is another thunderclap, and I feel rain drops hitting me. "You did it, Millie," I say. "You saved me."

"Oh, Carey!" She wraps her arms around my waist. "I'm so glad you're safe." She is still crying, but now I can see these are tears of relief.

It is cold. Though I cannot feel it, Millie is soaked through. I need to get her home. "Come on, Millie. Let us get out of here." Then I realize: there might be further additional emergency alerts, and I cannot turn those off. "You had better lead the way, just to be safe."

"All right Carey," she says. "I've got this. Let's go."

I cannot explain or understand what is wrong with my neural nets, and I do not dare risk Millie's safety or my own. As soon as we are to the top of the bank and on level ground, I put a hand on Millie's shoulder and stop her. "I am going to go to sleep now, back into my neutral mode, so you will have to lead the way from here. I will follow, but I will not be awake. You know the way home, right?"

"Sure I do," she says.

I do not detect any doubt in her face. I must trust her to get us home. I take my neural nets offline.

When next I awaken, I am in my charging station in the Owens home. Dr. Zinta sits on a stool in front of me. She holds my right arm in her left hand while her right hand gently squeezes out water from the arm into a pan on the floor.

"Hello, Dr. Zinta," I say.

"Oh!" She looks up, surprised. "Hello, Carey. I thought your diagnostics were still running."

I check internally.

"No. My diagnostics have just finished. I am awake now."

"Well, sit still and relax. I'm still checking you over. You've got internal water damage," she says.

"Thank you, Dr. Zinta."

I wait patiently until she reattaches my arm. Then she takes my left arm and repeats the process; and then one at a time, each leg. As she works, I say, "Dr. Zinta, I am afraid I am defective."

With that she smiles. "If anyone's defective, it's me."

"I do not understand."

"We needed more testing on the quantum resonance replication. It looks like we accidently entangled your q-states with the q-states of the clones."

I search my quantum research to try to understand this statement, but it is beyond my comprehension. "That sounds like it could be dangerous."

"Not too bad," Dr. Zinta answers. "The effect is small; but whenever you connected up to an external network, it was amplified. Your networks were open to the external influences, and the entangling became dominant."

"What a new experience. I was briefly someone named Brad." And then I shake my head. "No, I was briefly *emulating* someone named Brad, and also someone named Frances."

"Uh-huh," she says. "Those were two tests we were running on two androids in the lab. I knew something was wrong when the android emulating Frances behaved like you, not like its usual self."

"Like me?"

"The quantum resonance didn't work," she said. "Their behavior was closer to yours, but the androids still lacked your self-awareness. Apparently, though, they could borrow it from you through the entanglement. This result is interesting, but still a failure."

"It is not a failure," I insist. "We learned something. You can do better the next time."

Dr. Zinta's mouth turns to a firm line and she shakes her head. "What we learned is that this is dangerous for you and we can't risk it." Before I can object, she raises a hand. "We'll study this further, but not with you. Not even to advance human knowledge. Sorry, not going to do it."

"But Dr. Zinta . . ."

Again, she holds up her hand. "I'm not going to hear of it, Carey. There's something unique about you, something special that makes you functionally a conscious, self-aware individual with rights."

"But I am willing to accept the risk."

"And I am not. Carey, remember the Turing test. You are functionally self-aware. I believe it. I can no longer *not* believe it. So my conscience will not let me put you at risk."

"I do not understand."

"We have protocols for research involving human subjects. As far as I'm concerned, those protocols apply to you, too. There are risks we can let a subject voluntarily sign up for, but this crosses the line. This could permanently damage your cognitive model."

"But is it not worth that risk to one android—"

"To one life," she interrupts.

"All right, to one life, for what we might learn for science, for humanity?"

"No." She shakes her head. "It's not, and you're not going to convince me otherwise. We'll keep up our research with the quantum resonance, but not with you as a test subject." She takes my hand in hers. "You're a friend. In a way, you're like my child. You must have studied enough humans to know that a mother won't risk her child for anything."

"That makes no sense, Dr. Zinta. I am a machine, nothing more."

She stands, my hand still in hers, and she lifts me to stand with her. "Sorry kiddo, the answer's no, and that's final."

16. TODAY I AM OUTDATED

Millie takes a seat in the waiting room at MCA Labs. Paul usually comes in for my maintenance sessions, but Millie has never joined him after the first time she saw me disassembled by Dr. Zinta's team. She said it made her sick to her stomach. I would hope that as a college junior she would be past such sentimental feelings about my body; but despite her obvious intelligence and her education, she still thinks of me as a person, irrational as she admits that that is.

But today Paul has an emergency meeting at his office. He could not bring me in to MCA. Millie resisted at first, but eventually Paul persuaded her. Now she sits as far from the lab door as she can get. "I'll just stay out here," she says.

"All right, Millie. It could take a couple of hours."

"That long?" she asks, frowning. I nod. "Oh, all right . . . I have a report due for class. I guess I can work on it here."

I let her work, and I go to the desk. The receptionist smiles when she sees me. "Hello, Carey, nice to have you with us today."

"Thank you, Flora," I say. "Are they ready for me?"

"They sure are," she says. "I'll let them know you're here."

I look at the pictures on Flora's desk behind the window. "How are your kids?" I ask.

Flora smiles at the pictures. "Leo is fourteen, Trish is twelve. Growing so fast I'm going to have to work extra shifts to keep up with the clothes." I worry about her finances; but then she laughs, and I realize this is a joke.

"And how is Len?" I ask.

"Ornery as ever." I have never met her husband, Len, but I have built up a very good emulation profile for him based on our conversations over the years. I can tell from her smile and her attitude that he is a good man who treats her well—at least as she judges it, and I have no reason to doubt her.

I see a new picture of the two of them in some sort of basket. "What is that?"

"Oh." She touches the frame and another picture appears.

This time I see a big colorful ball. It takes me a while to put the pieces together, as it is not something I am used to seeing. "It is a hot air balloon."

"Yes." She smiles. "We went up for our anniversary. Don't tell me my man doesn't still know what romance is."

"I am very happy for you, Flora."

Then the door near the window opens and a young man steps out. He wears the typical lab coat and a belt comp with a number of sensing devices hanging from it. He is tall with dark curly hair and a strong face. I start noticing details and building an emulation profile as he reaches out his hand.

"Carey," he says. "I'm so glad to meet you. I'm Wayne Stockwell, the new intern in Dr. Jansons's lab."

I shake his hand, returning the same pressure he applies. "It is good to meet you as well, Wayne." He blushes. I am surprised at how easily he does.

"Oh, I'm just the new kid on the team, learning the ropes. But you . . . You're famous!"

"Famous?"

"Yes, sir. I mean, yes . . . How do I address you?"

"As Carey. Or as BRKCX-01932-217JH-98662, or just 98662. Or 'it' will do. I am not a sir, and I am not a ma'am. I am not of any gender, not unless I emulate one."

"Of course," Wayne says, flustered. "I was just put a little off my game after reading so much about you. To see you is . . . Carey, you're one of the reasons why I applied for this internship. All of the studies on you fascinate me."

Flora taps the window. "The *next* study is going to be late if you two don't get moving."

"Sorry, Flora, you're right," Wayne says. "Come on Carey, let's go on back." He leads me back to the lab— not that I need any guide. The lab has changed in small ways over the years, and once it had been completely remodeled; but the layout is not significantly different from my last maintenance check.

"Carey," Wayne says, "I was wondering . . ." He trails off.

"Yes, Wayne?"

"I'm doing my thesis on emotional intelligence metrics

as a means to rate androids and how humans respond to them."

"Emotional intelligence? I am unfamiliar with this term."

"Oh," Wayne says, nervously adjusting his tie. "It's a scale—really, seven scales—that measure human understanding and control of emotions. The scales aren't normed for androids, so that's part of my thesis: understanding the range of android responses. So . . . I was wondering if I could include you as a test subject. You're probably the high end for androids."

I see no problem with this, and it is good to help. "Yes, Wayne, I would like to participate."

"Thank you, Carey. I'll set up a time for the tests." Wayne leads me past Dr. Zinta's office. I look in her door as we pass. She sits behind her desk, tapping away at her comp.

"Hello, Mom," I say. That is for her benefit. It is our private joke; but I know that on some level she really does have maternal feelings for me. It is as irrational as Millie's emotions toward me. But it comforts Dr. Zinta, and that comforts me, so I play along.

"Hey, Carey," she says. "I've got some catch-up to do here; but Wayne and the team will run you through the basics, and I'll be there when you wake up. Sound good?"

"Sounds great, Mom. See you then." We continue down the hall to the testing platform. I seat myself, and I grip the chair arms. That will keep me stable when I power down.

Wayne comes over and makes a joke I've heard a dozen

times before: "This won't hurt a bit." Then he flips a switch, and my entire system shuts down.

When I awaken, I am disoriented. I had expected to see Dr. Zinta; but instead I see Millie and Wayne, crouched down, heads close together, peering inside my chassis. Wayne points a finger inside.

"And this is the motor coordinator."

"I see," Millie says.

"The design is very much like human neural systems," Wayne says. "Our reflexes are controlled directly by the spinal cord."

"I know," Millie says. "Through reflex arcs. Holemans, Meij, and Meijer Meyer proved the existence of a monosynaptic reflex arc in the spinal cord of the *Rana italica* all the way back in 1966." Millie smiles at Wayne and adds, "That's a frog."

"Oh . . ." Wayne stammers. He seems surprised by Millie's knowledge, but I am not. She takes pride in her studies. "Well . . . In a similar way, rather than Carey's main processor being bogged down by simple, repetitive actions like walking, there are separate routines for such activities. And they run through the motor coordinator. That's a pretty sophisticated computer on its own."

"Interesting," Millie says. "I didn't know all this was in Carey."

"Oh, yeah," Wayne says, "This was a pretty sophisticated system back in its day. They adapted a lot of ideas from biology. Of course, these days we've optimized these concepts, made them more efficient than biological systems. Now this data cable here . . ."

"Excuse me," I interrupt. "Are the tests done?"

Wayne and Millie both jerk upright, pulling apart. They seem nervous.

"Oh, I'm sorry, Carey," Wayne says.

Millie adds, "Carey, I . . . I finished my paper, and I . . . I just got bored with my book, so I asked if I could come watch the tests."

I do not understand. This does not fit with Millie's emulation profile. She does not get bored with books, especially not science books. I will need to modify her profile to include this unexplained behavior.

"Yes," Wayne says. "I was just showing her some of your internal systems."

"Yes, they're really . . ." Millie looks at Wayne. ". . . fascinating."

That is even more out of character for her. I try to formulate a question to help me understand; but before I can, Wayne adds, "I think Dr. Zinta . . ." He looks over toward the doctor standing at her console. "I think she's just about done with the autonomic tests and ready to move on to the cognitive tests."

"Cognitive tests?" Millie asks.

"Yes," Wayne answers. "We have to see how well Carey emulates human cognition. That means thinking."

Millie frowns. "I *know* what it means."

"Oh, I'm sorry. I didn't mean . . ." Wayne's face turns red again. "I just . . . We need to make sure that the neural nets haven't changed in unexpected ways. There's so much going on in there. I want to measure it all, map what's unique about Carey."

"Map it?" Millie asks.

"Yes, I have a whole series of tests planned. A full emotional cognition suite," Wayne answers.

From the diagnostic console, Dr. Zinta breaks into the conversation. "But not today, Wayne. We're not done here."

Wayne sighs. "Yes, Dr. Jansons." He turns back to Millie. "These are just simple regression tests. When my new tests are ready, we'll have a much better picture of how Carey thinks. Today we'll just ask the old reliable questions."

Wayne starts asking me a battery of questions, while Millie looks on intently. As we talk, my self-diagnostics run in the background. I can tell that everything is performing to specifications, but of course Wayne and Dr. Zinta must verify that independently.

Finally Dr. Zinta comes over. "Very good, Carey. Nice work, Wayne. Why don't you go over and review the results? Prepare a summary for me to look at later. Check your work. Carey and I need to talk in the office."

"Yes, Dr. Jansons," Wayne says. Then he turns to Millie. "I . . . have to get back to work now. I have a lot of data to process. It's . . . kind of boring."

"Okay," Millie says. "I should get back to my reading. But I'd like to hear more about your emotional cognition tests."

Wayne picks up his tablet. "There's a lot to it. Maybe we could discuss it some night after work?"

Millie looks down. "I'd like that." She pushes her comm code to Wayne's comp. "Call me. Any time." She turns to me. "Carey, I'll be in the reception room." Then she turns back to Wayne. "Goodbye."

As Millie leaves the lab, Wayne follows her with his eyes. "Goodbye . . ."

I follow Dr. Zinta to her office, pour her some coffee, and sit. "So how am I doing, Mom?"

"You tell me." She takes a drink from the coffee and smiles.

I review the diagnostic notes. "All physical systems operating at optimal levels. Cognitive diagnostics look to be in good shape."

"Uh-huh. And how do you feel?"

I try a new cliché from my archives. "Fit as a fiddle, Mom."

Dr. Zinta laughs politely. "That's good. How are the family? How are Paul and Susan?"

"They are well," I say, "considering their ages." Paul has just turned sixty, and Susan is almost fifty-nine. With modern medicine and good self-care, that is not as old as it once was for humans. "Still, I do have to advise them and remind them sometimes to keep up their exercises, and sometimes Paul does not eat right."

"That's too bad," Dr. Zinta answers.

"It is all his work," I say. "Ever since he was promoted to vice president, he works longer hours than ever. And he has food delivered. Sometimes not healthy choices."

"That's what you get when you're dealing with irrational humans," Dr. Zinta answers. "That's probably the biggest difference between you and us: You always do the rational thing. You cannot bring yourself to do something just because you like it."

"But I understand people do that," I say. "So we worked out a compromise."

"Oh?"

"When he works late, I call a taxi and I bring him his dinner. Nutritionally balanced foods that I know he likes."

"Excellent," she says. "Was that his idea?"

"No. It was mine."

"Even better," she smiles. "You're coming along."

"Thank you," I say. "But still . . ." I pause. "Dr. Zinta, I want an upgrade to my medical library."

"You want?"

I had chosen the word carefully, knowing that would emphasize how important this is. "Yes. For their age, Paul and Susan are in good health and do not need medical attention from me, but I can see that there might come a time where geriatric models would help me to take better care of them. So please, can I get an upgrade for my geriatric medicine modules? They have not been upgraded since Mildred passed away."

Dr. Zinta's eyes are wide. Again she asks, "You *want* this?"

"I think it would be a good idea, yes."

"Oh, Carey. That is wonderful." Then she frowns. "But . . ." She looks down at the desk. "I'm going to have to say no. I wish I didn't have to."

I am confused. "Dr. Zinta, this could be important."

"I agree," she says. "But Carey, you're twenty years old."

"Twenty-four years and three months," I say, "if you count from my date of manufacture. Twenty-one years and seven months since I woke up while serving Mildred."

"Yes, Carey. Precise as always. But . . . I don't know

how to tell you this, but the BRKCX series has been . . ." Another pause. "Decertified for medical care."

"What?"

"You know how fast technology changes. I did everything I could to postpone this. I've been giving you upgrades, and I've also written papers to demonstrate the efficiency of BRKCXs. I persuaded my management to give you several extra years, but . . . Your series has been officially designated as not supported as of last month."

"What does that mean?"

"It's all about legal liability. The board doesn't want responsibility for the actions of such old technology. No further programming upgrades are allowed, and MCA has recalled the entire series—except for you."

"Because I was purchased."

"Because we *freed* you, using the purchase as a pretext. But if you try your access codes, you'll find you can still download general information, but you can't get medical upgrades."

I try my med channel, and she is correct. "So I am outdated?"

"Oh, no. No," she says, putting down her coffee. "You're still warrantied for all of the work and all of the knowledge base you have. You just can't get upgrades."

"But I may need upgrades to care for Paul and Susan in the future."

"I understand," she says. "I think I have an answer. It's not perfect, but you can make it work."

"Oh?" She holds out a card to me and I look at it. "What is this?"

"It's a library card," she says. "See? In the name of Carey Owens."

"Thank you. But how does this get me upgrades?"

"The old-fashioned way," she says, returning to her seat and smiling. "With that card, you can access any library in the shared library network. And of course, you can already access any data on the internet. None of this will be formatted as skill modules that you can directly download, but you can study it. You can read it. You can learn what you need to know."

"Yes. That option has always been available. But it is slower, and it consumes more processing and storage. I must manually integrate the knowledge with my programming. It would be simpler and more efficient to download and install skill modules."

"I understand, but think of it this way. Now you know just a little bit how Paul and Susan, how we humans feel as we age. Sometimes what was simple for us before, becomes more difficult when we're older, and we have to learn new ways to get things done."

I shake my head. "I still do not know how you feel, but I understand a little better now. Thank you, Mom."

"You're welcome," she says. "Well, our tests are done here, so I'll see you next month."

"Until then," I answer. I leave her office and cross back through the lab. Wayne looks up from his work and waves at me as I pass.

17. TODAY I AM TESTED

But it is only the next morning that Paul gets a call from MCA.

He answers his comm while I am making breakfast. Millie comes up behind me and sits at the breakfast bar. I pour her some juice. She looks up at her father when he says, "Yes, Mr. Stockwell, I have no objection. But it's really up to Carey."

"What is it, Dad?" Millie asks. Her cheeks flush, and I wonder if she is well.

"It's Wayne Stockwell from MCA Psychometrics," Paul answers. "He wants permission to perform emotional cognition tests on Carey." He looks at me. "Well?"

"I already agreed," I reply. "I am pleased that I may assist the pursuit of science. But I did not expect him to be ready so soon."

Paul nods. "Well, Mr. Stockwell, I have meetings all day and tomorrow. I could bring Carey in on Thursday."

"Oh, no, Dad." Millie rises from the breakfast bar. "I don't have class today, just an evening lab. I could bring Carey in this morning."

Paul holds his hand over the comm. "That's all right, honey, I know you don't like to go there."

"Daaaad!" Millie shouts. Then she lowers her voice. "Dad, I'm not a kid anymore. I'm fine with it. I'll take Carey in today."

Paul uncovers the comm. "Change of plans, Mr. Stockwell. How's this morning? . . . Great! Millie and Carey can be there in two hours."

When we enter the psychometrics lab, I see that we are not alone. A Medical Care Android stands against the back wall. My comm picks up its transponder code. "Hello, BRKCX-01932-217JH-G9A27," I say.

"Hello, BRKCX-01932-217JH-98662." G9A27 nods toward me. "Hello, Mr. Stockwell. Hello, Miss. I do not know your name."

"Millie Owens," Millie replies.

"Hello, Miss Owens."

"G9A27 is here to take the tests with you, Carey," Wayne says. "As my study proceeds, I'll test other units, other models. But G9A27 will be most useful for norming the results, since it is the same model as you, with the same modifications, but it does not exhibit your self-awareness."

"I apologize for any malfunction," G9A27 says. "Should I exhibit self-awareness?"

"No, no," Wayne says. "You are functioning properly, G9A27."

I turn my attention to G9A27. I know this unit. I have *been* this unit, during my malfunction a decade ago. Yet I do not recognize it in the way I automatically recognize people whom I know. I adjust my empathy net to maximum sensitivity, but there is nothing there in G9A27. Nothing in its stance, mannerisms, tone, or expression engages my net. Its voice is calmingly neutral. It turns its head—so much like mine, we are twins—and it focuses on Wayne as he speaks; but the motion is mechanically smooth, and without any hint of interest. G9A27 is a machine, and I wonder what makes me different from it, but I cannot mistake: There *is* a difference.

I know that this has frustrated Dr. Zinta, that her entanglement experiments have failed to reproduce my behavior. The entanglement seems essential to emulation and empathy, as it allows neural net nodes to interact beyond the limits of physical circuit paths; but Dr. Zinta has been unable to replicate the unique interactions that make me self-aware. She gave up trying four years ago. Despite her best efforts, I remain unexplained.

The lab is set up like a theater: a display screen at the front, and a dozen seats facing it. Wayne paces before the screen as he speaks. "I'm going to show you both a number of scenes. After each scene, I'll ask you questions about what the characters might be feeling and thinking. Don't answer out loud! I'll give each of you an email address for your responses. And try not to second-guess yourselves: Give me your *first* answer."

Wayne points toward a seat. "Carey, please make yourself comfortable."

I look over at G9A27, which is standing. "I *am* comfortable," I say.

Wayne pauses. "Oh. Of course." Then he turns to Millie. "Miss Owens—"

"Millie," she says.

"Sorry, yes. Millie, you can wait in the lounge. This will take a while."

"Oh, no," Millie says quickly. "Can't I stay? This is fascinating!"

"Fascinating?" Wayne says, his face turning a light shade of pink.

"Oh, yes!" Millie says. "I work with frogs and snakes and lizards all day. I never see this side of science. In fact . . ." She looks in Wayne's eyes. "Could I take the tests, too? I want to know what they're like."

"Well . . ."

"Oh, please," Millie says, her eyelids batting strangely. "I'll be very quiet, you won't even know I'm here."

Wayne swallows and looks away, and my empathy net tells me that he will be keenly aware that Millie is here. But he nods. "All right, I can't use your results. I'm trying to build normal scales for androids." He looks back at Millie. "But there's no reason you can't take the tests."

"Thank you, Wayne," Millie answers. "You're the best!"

As Millie sits, Wayne turns away again, crossing to a lectern on the side of the room. "Here are your addresses." He taps a control panel on the lectern, and an address appears in my comp. "Is everyone ready?"

Millie and I nod. G9A27 says, "Yes, Mr. Stockwell."

"All right. Let's begin."

The room lights dim, and the screen grows bright. An image appears: a picnic scene, with a number of humans sitting on a blanket or playing on the grass near a stream. A display bubble near each character gives their names.

Martha, a thin African-American woman dressed in a

yellow sundress, hands a dish to Jerry. Her eyes are wide and bright. "Potato salad, Jerry?"

Jerry, a very fit but slightly older man in a blue T-shirt and jeans, takes the bowl. "Thank you." When his fingers brush Martha's, they both smile.

Glenn and Phillipe toss a Frisbee nearby. Glenn looks over, and his eyes darken when he sees Martha and Jerry. Phillipe calls, "Glenn!" But too late: the Frisbee hits Glenn in the head.

Glenn stumbles backwards, almost bumping into Isabel, who is bringing more food from somewhere outside of the scene. She deftly keeps the bowl in her hands as she laughs at the look on his face.

Wendy and Rob enter the scene from the other side, both looking around at the ground. Rob holds a broken leash. "Rex!" he says. "Come on, Rex, where are you?"

Wendy steers closer to Rob and pats him on the arm. "It's OK," she says. "He won't go far. We'll find him."

Rob looks toward the stream. "I don't know if he knows how to swim."

Wendy smiles, but it looks forced. "All dogs can swim, Rob. He'll be all right."

The screen goes dark, save for simple text: TEST SEGMENT COMPLETE. ADMINISTER QUESTIONS NOW.

Nothing happens for ten seconds. Twenty. I look toward Wayne, expecting instructions. In the darkened room, he is hard to make out; but I can see his eyes gleaming in the faint light. They are turned toward Millie.

Then Millie looks back toward Wayne, and he turns away. "Oh . . . Ummm . . . " He taps his console, and the text on the screen is replaced by head shots of the characters, along with their names. "Question one: Which characters are happy in this scene?" As he asks, I see that his eyes are once more on Millie.

I watch Millie key in her answers, but I cannot do the same. "I am sorry, Wayne, I may not answer that."

"What?" Wayne turns to me. "I'm sure you can, Carey."

"I can," I agree, "but I may not. I know the answer, but I know it through empathy. I am not permitted to share that knowledge."

"Oh!" Wayne laughs, and Millie smiles. "They're not real, Carey."

"Not real?" I ask. "They are simulations?"

"No, they're actors," Wayne explains. "These scenes are all scripted, short dramas. The situations aren't real."

"So their emotions are false?" I consider that. "Does that allow for a valid test?"

"Yes." Wayne nods. "They're good actors. They know what emotions they're supposed to convey. We know from human testing how successful they are. So we can factor that in as we evaluate your results."

I consider that. If these are only emulated emotions, then Wayne is right: My privacy protocols do not apply. I email my answer: *Martha, Jerry, and Isabel.* After a few seconds, Wayne asks, "Question two: Which characters are anxious?" I answer: *Wendy, Rob, and Glenn.*

Wayne's next question is more challenging: "How will Rob feel if he can't find Rex?"

The obvious answer is "Sad," but I don't think that is deep enough. According to my empathy net, Rob is already sad. Rex is important to him, a member of his family. Remembering my family and the passing of Mildred, I answer: *He will feel grief and loss, and this feeling shall never quite fade away.*

The test continues like this for over two hours: new scenarios, new questions. Some questions ask the subject to understand and predict how others feel. Others ask for the subject's own feelings. (Those are more difficult for me.) And a final series asks the subject for ways to manage or influence the feelings of others.

At last Wayne brings the room lights back up. "Thank you," he says, looking around the room at us. "That was a good first session."

"First session?" Millie asks.

"Yes." Wayne looks at Millie, but then looks aside. "We . . . Ummm . . . We need several sessions to build a good baseline. Different questions on different days. We also repeat some questions. The answers might change depending on mood."

Moods are the most difficult thing for me to emulate, subject to illness and hunger and stress and exhaustion, all factors that cannot touch me. Even when emulating, I emulate a consistent average profile. "But Wayne," I say, "I do not have moods."

Wayne looks at me and smiles. "That's what we're here to find out."

It is Friday when we return to MCA. Flora greets us with her usual big smile. "Carey, Millie. Back so soon?"

"Wayne is expecting us," Millie says.

"Oh, let me call him." Flora taps her phone. "Yes, Mr.

Stockwell. Your guests are here . . . Yes . . . I understand."
She taps the phone again, and she turns her attention back
to us. "You can go on back, Carey. Millie, Mr. Stockwell
says this will take some time, so if you have any place to
go—"

"But I wanted to take the test," Millie says.

"I'm sorry, he said today's not a good day for that."

"Why not?" Millie asks.

"He didn't say. But we can call you when Carey's
done."

"No, I . . ." Millie looks around the reception area. "I
have reading to do. I . . . I'll stay."

"As you wish," Flora said. She buzzes the door. "He's
waiting, Carey."

I return to the psychometrics lab. Wayne and G9A27
are already there. "Good morning, Carey," Wayne says.

"Good morning, Wayne. G9A27."

"Good morning, BRKCX-01932-217JH-98662," G9A27
says.

Wayne says, "Shall we begin?" I nod and take my place.
Wayne dims the lights, and the screen lights up.

The first scene I see is the picnic: Martha, Jerry, Glenn,
Phillipe, Isabel, Wendy, and Rob. The scene plays out
exactly as before, and again it ends with the prompt for
questions.

"Wayne," I say, "why are we watching the same
scene?"

"All part of the test," Wayne says. "I need to verify my
observations."

He continues with the same questions as before, plus
additional ones. He seems more relaxed in his approach

today. The rest of the day is also a repetition of the previous tests, but Wayne delves deeper into each scene. He has more focus.

And *I* have more focus. Wayne's questioning today is more thought-provoking, and I learn things from the test: things about human emotion, and about myself. I had taken for granted my empathy net. It has always been a part of me, but I had never stopped to analyze the knowledge it imparted to me. Now I am surprised how I can infer Rob's future sadness from a brief scene.

And Martha and Jerry . . . "Wayne, why would you not let Millie sit in on the test today?"

"I can't use her results in my paper," Wayne says. "Only androids."

"But why could she not just sit in? You could throw away her results."

Wayne shook his head. "I need to focus. The test includes my observations of your reactions."

"And you cannot do that with her in the room. She distracts you."

"Oh, geez!" Wayne slaps down his stylus. "You can't tell her that!"

"No, Wayne. I cannot." I leave the psychometrics lab. I look in Dr. Zinta's office, hoping to ask her for guidance; but she is not there. I must understand this situation on my own.

When I return to the reception room, Millie looks up from her book. I see a mix of emotions in her face: impatience, irritation, and disappointment, if my emulation net is operating correctly.

Millie rises. "I guess you're done."

"I am." I turn to Flora. "Has Wayne scheduled the next tests?"

Flora checks her schedule. "Yes," she says. "Next Tuesday. Does that work for you, Millie?"

Millie's eyes turn down, and her voice drops. "I won't be here."

Flora looks up at that, her eyes narrowed. "What do you mean, hon?"

Millie takes a breath before answering. "If *Mr. Stockwell* doesn't want me around, then fine, I'm gone."

"Say what?" Flora answers.

"Millie," I say, "that's not what Wayne meant."

"I don't *care* what he meant," Millie says. "Let's go." She starts toward the door, but I remain where I am. "Come *on*, Carey!"

This is a new side of Millie. I have never seen this before: fear. Not the temporary fear of danger from the rushing stream, but a deeper, more personal fear, mixed with uncertainty. And desire. She does not want to leave; but she does not want to stay and be hurt. She does not know which choice will be worst.

And I suspect I know the answer, but I may not tell her. I cannot reveal what Wayne feels.

But I *can* respond to what *Millie* feels. "Millie, you are being unfair to Wayne. He did not mean to upset you. I am sure of that."

Millie stops, her hand on the doorknob. "You're sure."

I start to sense a conflict with my privacy protocols. "I cannot say more, Millie."

She steps away from the door. "So you're telling me this is about how Wayne feels."

I shake my head. "No, I cannot tell you that."

"About me."

"I cannot tell you that."

"He . . . hates me?"

"I never said that."

"He likes me?"

"I never said that, either."

"Tell me!"

Again I shake my head. "I cannot, Millie. This is something you must find out for yourself."

"But . . . What if I'm wrong?"

I grip her shoulders and look into her face. "I have known you all of your life. You are strong, and you are brave. If you proceed in this, then right or wrong, you will know."

"I can't . . ."

"I know you, Millie." I squeeze her shoulders. "You can."

Millie shakes free from my hands and goes to the window, where Flora has been watching us with interest. "Flora, I . . ."

Flora's face is impassive, and she sits silently as the door buzzes. But as Millie pulls the door open, Flora smiles at me, and she winks.

I find that it does not violate my privacy protocols for me to wink back.

Then I follow Millie back to Wayne's lab, where he sits, bent over a screen. "Wayne," she says.

Wayne looks up. "Millie . . ." He looks at me, and he stands. "Carey . . . I've just started scoring today's tests."

Millie stares into his face. I am pleased to see that she does not flinch. "Wayne, about this morning . . ."

Wayne steps from behind the desk. "I'm sorry, I handled that poorly. I—"

Millie steps closer. "Wayne . . . Wait." She turns to me. "Carey, I have an emotional intelligence test for you. The scene is an android, its female friend, and . . ." She glances at Wayne. ". . . a clueless scientist. The android and the friend are longtime customers, so the scientist has their contact information in his records. The friend gives him her personal phone number. Why does she do that?"

I hesitate. "Millie, I cannot answer that. It would violate your privacy."

Millie shakes her head. "This isn't me, this is a hypothetical for the test. So please, answer the question."

This disturbs me. This flimsy rationalization cannot justify violating my privacy protocols.

But still, it is *Millie*'s privacy. If she wants me to violate it . . . "She is interested in the scientist. She would like to get to know him better, and she hopes that he will call. Not for business, but for her."

"Carey," Wayne says, drawing my attention, "I have another test. The scientist lets the friend participate in some tests, but then excludes her from some others. Why would he do that?"

"I can think of numerous reasons," I say. Now it is Wayne's privacy that is at stake. But he looks at me, and I read pleading in his eyes, so I continue, "But the most likely reason is that he fears for his job."

"What?" Millie says.

"She distracts him," I explain. "He cannot properly run the tests while she is there, because all he can think about is her. He already spoiled one day's test results, and had to run them again. He cannot risk that again."

"He . . ." Millie pauses, and then she starts again. "Carey, how would excluding her like that, with no explanation, make her feel?"

Before I can answer, Wayne holds up his hand. "The test is over, Carey." He turns to Millie. "I think we should answer that ourselves. Over lunch." Wayne takes Millie's hand. Then he turns back to me and adds, "Alone."

18. TODAY I LEARN A SECRET

Wayne sits back on Mildred's old gray couch, leaning into the corner. It is one of the few pieces of furniture that survived the fire intact, and Susan has reupholstered it twice in the years since. She and Paul are very attached to it for the memories it holds, and it was always Millie's favorite place to sit when she was growing up. She used to sit there on Susan's lap as Susan sang to her.

Today Millie sits next to Wayne, leaning against him, practically in *his* lap. His arms are wrapped around her waist. Paul and Susan sit in the big overstuffed wingback chairs that Susan got from a garage sale. She reupholstered those as well.

I have no need to sit; but I know it makes people more comfortable when I do, so I am sitting on the hearth by the fireplace while Susan and Paul discuss plans for Millie's graduation open house. Millie listens in, but I sense that she is uncomfortable.

I also sense from Paul's tone and from the way he looks around but never quite at Wayne and Millie that he is uncomfortable with them being so close. Susan, on the other hand, is amused, though she conceals it well.

Wayne also seems uncomfortable, but Millie does not notice her parents' reactions. "I wish you wouldn't make such a big deal of this," she says. "I already had a big graduation party for my bachelor's."

"Yes," Susan says, "but this is a master's. This is a major accomplishment! We're so proud of you."

"I'm proud of it too," Millie answers. "I worked hard for this, but it's just different. Undergrad was like school; this was work, a job. It doesn't seem right to have a huge party over a job. Besides, I'm much more excited by Dr. Winters's herpetology field research, cataloguing *Rana juliani* and other frogs. I hope I get accepted there!"

"All the more reason to get this done," Susan says. "We don't have to have a huge party, but we really should celebrate before my baby heads to Belize for the summer."

Millie rolls her eyes. "Mom . . ."

Paul says, "Couldn't we just go out for a nice dinner with a few friends, then?"

"Oh!" Susan says. "We could rent a hall, have a nice catered dinner."

Millie's eyes grow wide. "A hall?"

Paul laughs. "So all we have to do is settle on a number between five and five hundred, and we're set."

"Five *hundred!*" Millie exclaims.

"No, no, nothing like five hundred," Susan says. "But maybe fifty."

"Yes," Paul says, "something smaller. Fifty, or less than fifty. We're just planning a celebration. It's not like we're planning a wedding."

The room falls silent. Suddenly Millie and Susan both look at the floor. Wayne becomes interested in the pattern on the couch.

Paul looks around. "Oops. Sorry. I said the W word. My mistake."

"Dad!" Millie says. "Could you be more obvious?"

"I said sorry. And you're right. One thing at a time."

"Besides," Susan says, "you've got your doctoral program ahead. You don't have time to think about a wedding."

"Well—" Wayne says. I can see in his eyes that he has something important to say.

But Millie cuts in. "That's right. I've got to think about my thesis, talk to my advisor about that, and my application for Dr. Winters. I've got enough on my plate. One more reason why I don't want to be tied up in a huge event here for the graduation."

"All right," Susan says, "just immediate family and a few of your friends. Is that good? And Wayne's parents, of course."

"And Carey," Millie says.

"I do not need dinner," I answer.

"Yes, but she said family, so you should be there. I wish Anna could."

"She'll televisit, I'm sure," Susan answers. "But the boys are getting to be a handful for her. There's no way she can get away from London at this time."

Then Susan checks her comp. "Oh, my," she continues. "I have an early meeting tomorrow. I should get to bed."

Paul rises from the wingback chair. "Yeah, I have

reports to review yet. I think we both should call it a night. We can table this to the weekend, can't we?"

"I think we can," Susan says, rising, as Millie nods. "All right," Susan continues, "I'm off to bed. Good night." She heads out.

Paul follows behind, then looks back and waves. "Good night, Millie. Good night, Wayne." Then he turns to me. "Good night, Carey." He heads for the stairs.

As soon as Susan and Paul are out of earshot, Wayne lets out a laugh.

"What's so funny?" Millie asks.

"You," Wayne answers. He pokes Millie in the ribs, and she squirms. "My rebel Rana. You hate all the fuss, don't you?"

"I really do." Millie nods, and curls closer to Wayne. "All those people, I don't really even know them. It's all about appearances. I know, it makes Mom happy, but I just want to run away."

"And yet you have to have Carey there."

"Of course!" she says, looking at me. "It's family!"

Wayne laughs. "Family?"

"It is!" Millie sits up and pulls away from Wayne. "Carey's family. I thought you understood that by now."

Wayne turns to me. "Carey, are you part of Millie's family?"

I nod. "They have accepted me into their family."

"Ah, the Turing answer." Wayne grins. "If they accept it, it's true?"

"No," I said. "It's *practical*. It makes everyone comfortable. Putting people at ease shows good emotional intelligence."

"Touché," Wayne replied.

"So if I have to have a party, of course I want Carey there," Millie says. "But really, I just don't want all the bother."

Wayne squeezes her. "It's all right, Rana. You can get through this. We'll get through it together, and then soon enough we'll be down in Belize."

"Wayne!" Millie interrupts, glancing at me.

"I'm sorry, *you'll* be down in Belize." Wayne looks at me, and I read secrets in his face.

Millie looks at me as well. She is concerned. "Carey, forget you heard that."

"I cannot forget, Millie, you know that. I'm not designed to forget."

"Okay, but don't think about it, all right? Just don't."

But my associative net systems, much like a human's, betray me. I find Millie's profile slipping into my emulation net, thinking about precisely what she asked me not to. "I see," I say.

"Carey," Wayne asks, "see what?"

Millie rises and looks down at me. "Carey, don't say a word."

"It can't know," Wayne says.

"You don't know Carey," Millie answers. "Of course it knows, don't you?"

I nod. "You do not want to be apart for a whole summer, so Wayne is going with you." And then I remember Wayne's earlier comments, and I add, "You are eloping."

Wayne nods. "It'll be a working honeymoon, if they'll take us. I can't do research, but I can carry bags, and whatever else they need from me."

I look at Millie, "And you're sure Dr. Winters will accept this?"

Millie looks away. "He said it's just a formality at this point. As long as Wayne pays his own way, Dr. Winters will be glad to have help."

"And don't worry," Wayne adds, "I've got leave time. Dr. Jansons has already approved, and I've got money saved up."

Millie says, "It will be an adventure . . ."

I finish for her, "A romantic dream, science in the tropics with your husband. I understand."

"Thank you, Carey." Millie smiles, relieved.

"But your mother will not," I continue. "She has been looking forward to a ceremony for your master's. Not to mention a big wedding in the future."

"I know, but she had a big wedding for Anna. All those people from London, and India, and Dad's partners from all over the world. I hated it."

"You were only six. That was a lot for a six-year-old to put up with."

"And it's a lot for a twenty-four-year-old to put up with. I don't like all that fuss and ceremony, but . . ."

"You would put up with it for your mother's sake. But now this research opportunity is too good for you to resist."

"Uh-huh," she says. "How can I pass this up? Can you imagine a more romantic honeymoon than Wayne and me in the swamp, cataloguing frogs?"

I try to imagine it, but I cannot. "I am not a human female, Millie. This does not fit with my understanding of the normal meaning of the term 'honeymoon.'"

Millie laughs. "All right, but when have I ever been normal? I do things my way, you know that. I've always wanted to travel the world and do research like this. I can't pass up this chance. Oh Carey, please don't tell Mom and Dad."

"Should you not tell them yourself?"

"It would just be . . . They'd try to talk us out of it. They'd try to tell me that I'm not ready, tell Wayne that it's not responsible to lose a summer's income. They'd tell us we can wait a couple of years, until my doctorate is done. They'd make all these rational, logical arguments. They're android arguments, not human arguments. I want to marry Wayne, and I want it now. And I want to go with him to the swamps and make memories that will be with us for the rest of our lives. Oh Carey, please. Please don't tell them."

"I cannot tell them, Millie," I say. "I cannot share information that I know through emulation and empathy. My privacy protocols forbid that." Millie nods.

I let a little bit of Susan's emulation profile into my emulation net, and then I continue. "So it is possible that your mother will not care, will only be happy for you. But it is possible that this will hurt her deeply, far more than you realize. I cannot tell you either way."

"No," Millie agrees.

"It is possible that she longs for the big ceremony in the big chapel. *Again.* That she is more concerned with social status than with your happiness. But it is also possible that your wedding is what matters to her, whether in the big chapel or in a tiny little church in Belize. You know your mother, you can answer that; but I may not."

"No . . ."

"And it may be that she will not care, and that missing your wedding shall quickly be forgotten. But it may cause her such pain that there would be a rift between you two, and that she would do anything to share your happiness on your wedding day. And if I were certain of that . . ."

"You could not tell me that."

"No, I could not," I said. "But I can tell you that I do not believe you would ever do that to her intentionally, because you love your mother. And even though you thought that eloping was the simple answer, now you are starting to doubt."

"I . . ." Millie leans over me and kisses my cheek. "Thank you, Carey." It is a pointless gesture, but I know that for her, it means deep gratitude.

Then Millie leaves the room, and I hear her climb the stairs and knock on Paul and Susan's door. "Mom? Dad? Wayne and I have something to tell you."

Wayne grins at me. "You're getting really good at this."

"At what?" I ask.

"Intervening without intervening."

"I did not intervene. I did not tell her anything that I should not."

"No, but what you didn't say made all the difference," Wayne says. "I tried to tell her the same thing, but she *heard* it from you. She only argued with me. You're very persuasive."

"I was built to take care of patients," I explain. "Persuasion is a necessary part of bedside manner."

"Yes, I can see that," Wayne continues. "You're a marvel, Carey. In some ways almost human."

"In some ways?" I ask.

"All right, in a lot of ways, then. You still don't score as human on my tests, but you're a hell of a lot more than just an android."

19. TODAY WE TRAVEL TO BELIZE

Today we are traveling. The luggage bots follow us out to the garage, and the lift ramp deposits them in the cargo compartment while we get into the car. The chauffeur system wakes up and asks, "Where to, folks?"

Paul answers, "GRR."

"Yes sir," the chauffeur replies. "Gerald R. Ford International Airport, next stop." The car leaves, and the garage closes behind us.

Millie and Wayne have already left for Belize with the Winters party. After a lot of discussion, Millie had persuaded Susan not to have elaborate party decorations and china sent to Belize. "It's a simple country, Mom," she had said. "That's what I want, a simple wedding. It's more romantic that way."

If smiling were in my nature, I would have smiled then. Millie's emotional influence score must be very high. She knew that romance was a powerful argument with Susan.

Now Susan is as excited about the wedding as she had been for Anna's. She and Paul spend the trip to the airport talking about the wedding and the plans Susan has made through a hotel in Belize. Well, Susan is excited, at least. She does most of the talking. Paul nods politely and chips in a little here and there. I do the same.

At the airport, the car pulls up curbside and unloads the lug bots, and we get out. Paul leads the lug bots up to the luggage induct and pushes our ticket codes through the system. The induct loads the bots through its scanner, and lights up green. A voice from the induct says, "Have a nice trip, Owens family! Have a nice trip, Medical Care Android BRKCX-01932-217JH-98662!"

I am surprised that the system addressed me. Emulating a common human response, I answer, "Thank you."

Susan leads us in through the building, her carry-on bot following close behind her. As we approach the security zone, a guard there, a short, trim, African-American woman, waves us forward. She wears light exo armor. A large augmented reality helmet covers her head, and I can barely see her big smile behind the visor. "Mr. Owens, scanner one." She points at the nearest walk-through scanner. "Mrs. Owens, scanner two." Then she frowns at me. "Carey Owens?"

I step forward, "That is me." I sense her discomfort, and I try to ease it. "Yes, I am an android. I have a ticket."

"I can see you have a ticket." She checks her visor. "Oh, it says here that you are equipment. I'm not used to people naming their supplies, and I don't know what to do with you. You're my first android."

"You are my first airport security officer," I say.

She smiles at my response. "Can you step over to the

far scanner, the one that's out of service over there? My supervisor will figure out what we're supposed to do."

"Thank you." I walk over to the scanning unit, and I wait. I notice the label on the scanner, EMP-SCAN 1400, and then in smaller print underneath it says, "A Division of MCA." I search the internet and find that EMP-SCAN is a line of q-state empathy scanners, much like my empathy network, designed to identify anxious and possibly dangerous passengers. I had not realized that MCA had pursued this line of business, which appears to be a spinoff from Dr. Zinta's entanglement studies. This large, boxy device is my technological descendant.

Soon I see Paul and Susan at the far end of the scanner, waiting. I check the time on my comp. There are three hours before our flight. I hope that Paul has planned ahead for delays such as this.

It is six minutes before the guard appears with another guard in tow. This one is taller, a thin woman with more elaborate armor and AR gear. I presume that indicates that she is the supervisor.

The new guard walks up to me and looks me over. "You are Medical Care Android BRKCX-01932-217JH-98662?"

"Yes, I am," I reply.

"But your ticket is for Carey Owens."

"Yes, my family calls me that."

"Your family?" She looks through the scanner at Paul and Susan.

"Yes, I call them that."

The shorter guard smothers a giggle. The tall guard remains stern. "Well, the ticket is a little irregular," she says, "but it is a valid ticket, and airline policy does allow delicate gear to be carried in a ticketed seat." She looks me up and down again. "Are you delicate?"

I decide a neutral answer is the safest. "By what standards of measurement?"

I suspect that she glares at me behind the helmet. "If I didn't know better, I would think you were trying to be funny. You look pretty old. Maybe you're ready to fall apart? You've got to be, what, ten-year-old technology? Fifteen?"

"I was manufactured twenty-five years ago."

"That explains the whole retro look," she says. "Nobody builds humanoid devices anymore. Your type is hardly seen anymore, except in museums."

Unsure what answer might make her more irritated, I say nothing.

"All right." She taps her comp. "I am walking some equipment through on scanner seven. Follow me, BRKCX-01932-217JH-98662."

I follow the supervisor through the scanner. She walks up to Paul and Susan. "Here's your android," she says. "Keep an eye on it."

"We will," Susan says. I can see that Paul is irritated by the delay, but Susan is more diplomatic. The supervisor leaves and we head for our gate.

Along the way, I notice lug bots, cleaning bots, automated service kiosks at restaurants, even a few companion bots. But the supervisor is right. In all the airport, I am the only humanoid device.

Over the years, I have noticed my kind dwindling in number. Dr. Zinta once explained this phenomenon.

People just lost interest, she had explained. For a while, units like myself were popular not just for medical care, but for personal assistants of all kinds. But then that fad passed. She said marketing had blamed it on the uncanny valley: a psychological theory that devices which are very close to human, but not quite human, disturb people, whereas less humanlike devices are easier to accept. This theory, almost as old as the Turing test, is equally debated in the artificial intelligence community—but not within marketing. Accepted wisdom is that there is no money in humanoids. Robotic devices are everywhere throughout the modern world, but few androids.

When we board the plane, Susan once again has to show my ticket to convince the attendant that I have a legitimate seat reserved. When we reach our aisle, the attendant helpfully suggests, "Perhaps your machine would like a window seat." I start to object that I do not have a preference, but I recognize that she is anxious. I look at Paul and Susan, and they nod. The attendant wants me out of the way so that she does not have to deal with me. Without a word, I sit by the window.

We switch planes in Chicago. At O'Hare, the crowd is larger: people from all over the world, and a wider range of robotic assistants. I note that here I am not completely alone. I see some androids doing maintenance and janitorial work. I wonder at their programming. They look like economy models, so I doubt their neural nets are very sophisticated, even if they are newer than mine. They are probably very task- and safety-oriented.

The flight to Belize is longer, nearly three hours. Susan and Paul talk for much of the way. I sense them relaxing.

They are both very busy with their jobs, and this unexpected trip is taking on aspects of a vacation for them. Susan is now very happy. I can tell she still wishes she could have planned a big wedding for Millie, but being there at all proves to be enough for her.

While they talk, I listen in case they need anything from me; but my processors are mostly devoted to reading, studying my geriatrics texts. Reading from the library is a different experience from installing new skill modules; but if I were human I might say that it is pleasant. Skill modules just arrive, connected up and ready for my networks to access; but reading is discovering. The authors lead me through facts, research, hypotheses, and conclusions, so I get to see the foundation of the knowledge. In a way, this ties into my empathy net: I see reasons behind information, not just the information itself. I decide that once I am done with my geriatric studies I should revisit other topics that I know only through skill modules.

I am tracing through a 3D map of circulatory diseases when the captain announces our approach to Belize. Then an attendant comes up to our row, leans in, and says softly, "Mr. and Mrs. Owens?"

"Yes," Susan says.

"Airport security in Belize request that you remain on the plane while the other passengers disembark."

"What's the matter?" Susan says, but Paul looks at me knowingly.

The attendant, on the other hand, never meets my eyes. "It's about your android. A special inspection."

"What about Carey?" Susan asks.

Paul puts a hand on her arm. "It's all right, hon. I was told to expect this. I've got all the papers in order. We'll be fine."

"I hope we don't miss our water taxi."

"If we do, we'll find another," Paul assures her. "Thank you, miss."

When we finally disembark, a squad of soldiers in green camouflage fatigues waits for us at the bottom of the ramp. They have rifles, not aimed at us, but not shouldered, either. Ready. Their eyes are alert, and they are ready to act. Following Paul's example, I walk carefully down the ramp, my hands far from my sides.

At the front of the soldiers stands a taller man, dark skinned, in a solid beige uniform covered in braid and decorations. A black beret with a gold badge rests atop his head. There is something to his bearing and in his expression that I find difficult to read. This is my first exposure to empathy in this culture; and I find that the signals are subtly different. Is that anger I see? Fear? Or something else? I cannot tell, and I feel strangely vulnerable. Like I have lost one of my senses.

When we reach the bottom of the ramp, the man takes two steps forward. He limps slightly in his left leg, and *that* I can read clearly: It pains him; and from the way he glares at me, somehow he associates that pain with me.

At last the man stands in front of us. "Mr. and Mrs. Owens, I am Colonel Rejón of the Belize Defence Force. Welcome to our country."

"Thank you," Paul says. Susan looks upset.

"I'm sure you know what this is about," the colonel continues. "Your device . . ." He looks at me, and I glimpse hostility. ". . . is most unusual. I must confirm that it is in compliance with our laws, particularly those about automated soldiers."

I almost respond; but Paul looks sideways at me, and I realize that he wants me to remain quiet. Susan, on the other hand, is not interested in quiet. "Carey is not a soldier," she says. "It is a caretaker."

"Oh?" the colonel asks.

"A medical caretaker," Paul explains, "sort of a sophisticated auto doc."

"I have seen auto docs," the colonel replies. "We have some in our country. We are not a backward people! None of them are humanoid like this."

"It is an old, outdated model," Paul answers.

"Nevertheless," the colonel continues, "I must insist that our technicians inspect it to make sure that it carries no weapons systems."

"That's right here in our paperwork," Paul says pushing papers to the colonel's comp.

"Yes," the colonel says, checking his comp. "That is what an American inspection says, but now there must be a Belizean inspection. Since the Guatemalan incursion, our laws are quite strict. We do not allow automated weapons systems, nor systems which might be adapted as weapons."

Susan checks her own comp. "We're going to miss our water taxi."

The colonel nods. "I am sure you already have. Once the inspection is done, we will arrange transport for you to make up for the inconvenience. But now I must insist that you go with me."

He points us across the tarmac, and then follows behind us, two aides flanking him. His limp is barely noticeable, but my programming compels me to notice. The rest of the soldiers line up beside and in front of us. Then they march forward, making it clear that they expect us to proceed with them.

By my temperature sensors, it is thirty degrees warmer than we had left in Michigan. The tarmac radiates heat. I know Paul wants me to remain silent, but his and Susan's health could be at risk. Finally, I speak up. "Sir," I look at Paul, "I recommend hydration."

The colonel stops and looks at me. Paul pays no attention to him, and he answers. "Yes, Carey, I think that would be a good idea. Colonel, can we get some water?"

"When we get to the laboratory. We are almost there." Again he looks at me.

The services headquarters is a Quonset-style building far from the passenger terminal. Inside, it is air-conditioned: not to the level that Paul or Susan might set their house, but significantly cooler than outside. The colonel snaps his fingers and says to one of the guards, "Bring the Owenses some water." Then he says to us, "Through here."

Colonel Rejón opens another door, and beyond is a laboratory. MCA's lab is significantly more advanced than this, with scanners that would put these units to shame. These are older, and they show heavy signs of wear; but they are still newer than myself. If the skill of the technician is at least as good, my inspection here should be safe.

"Over here," the colonel says. "This is the bench. Rodrigo is waiting. You can leave your luggage for customs inspection. We can do that while you are waiting, so as not to delay you any more than we have to."

Susan looks back and forth between the bench and the luggage, and Paul says, "I'll keep an eye on the caretaker. You go with the luggage."

"All right." Her hand lightly brushes my arm as she follows three of the soldiers with the lug bots. Meanwhile, the colonel, the remaining soldiers, Paul, and I approach the table. A technician stands next to it, a young man with a shaven dark head and a short beard. He wears a lab coat, not much different from what they wear at MCA. It is clean and well maintained, and my confidence increases.

Rodrigo comes up and looks me over. "Well, you are quite something, aren't you, friend?" Again, I have difficulty reading his emotions. He seems friendly, but I am not certain.

"Rodrigo," the colonel says, "This is Medical Care Android BRKCX-01932-217JH-98662. Or as its ticket reads . . ." Rejón glances at Paul. ". . . 'Carey.' You should have received a complete specifications manual by now."

"Yes, I have, Colonel."

"I need you to ensure that this unit complies with the specifications and does not violate any of our rules against automated soldiers."

"Indeed." Rodrigo looks me up and down. "You must be twenty years old?"

"Twenty-six, sir. Twenty-five since I was in service, so you were pretty close."

He opens one eye wider. "Pretty close, you say. Yes, I see." He looks over the specifications. "For twenty years old, this is sophisticated stuff."

"I have had upgrades through the years."

Again, he eyes me. "You have, yes. Interesting. And these emulation and empathy nets. I have heard of such equipment. Not something you would put in an automated soldier, Colonel. They would interfere with its ability to follow orders without question."

"Yes," the colonel answers, "but do not assume. Do the inspection. Now."

"I will. All right, friend," he slaps me on the shoulder, "climb up on the table here and lie down."

"Yes, Rodrigo." I do as I was instructed.

"Now, I am going to disassemble you, and I do not wish to cause any feedback problems as I do. Where is your activation switch?"

I look at Paul, and he nods. "Go ahead."

"My right upper torso compartment," I say, and I slide it open. "Next to the status light is a dial."

"I see," Rodrigo says, looking at the three settings. "Off, passive, active. Why three?"

"In passive I operate strictly on programming and simple commands. In active, my neural nets are engaged."

"Very interesting. All right, lay back, relax, and we will get this out of the way as quickly as possible." He smiles and then repeats the old joke, but it is new for him: "I promise this won't hurt a bit." And he turns me off.

I awaken to see Rodrigo's face looming over mine, looking down at me. "There you go, friend. Is everything okay?"

I check my internals and see that while I was in the

passive mode, he has run my self-diagnostics. "I am well, thank you."

The colonel stands just at the edge of my vision, hands behind his back, looking down. Glaring at me. I am sure that this is hostility, though I cannot yet understand the reasons. Colonel Rejón says, "What did you find, Rodrigo?"

Rodrigo straightens and looks at the colonel. "I have removed and disassembled all of the limbs of this unit. I have checked the synthetic flesh for any sort of hidden weapons, finding none. I have tested and worked the synthetic musculoskeletal system. It all serves only the purpose of moving the android and letting it perform medical work, including emergency response. There is nothing hidden within that system. I have checked its torso compartments and found only routine first aid supplies and antiseptics and other simple medicines. We've taken those and inspected them, and there are no customs violations. And I ran its self-diagnostics. I can confirm for you, Colonel, that this is a twenty-six-year-old Medical Care Android, quite primitive by standards of devices in America today. Some of our own equipment is generations ahead of this as well. Certainly it is not as sophisticated as the Guatemalan automated soldiers that you fought years ago. So I can certify, Colonel, that there is nothing special about this android."

Rodrigo looks down at me, and with the eye away from the colonel, he winks. In America, the expected response is to wink back, indicating a confidence, a secret shared; but is that also true in Belize? I do not know; and in any case, if we share a secret, I do not wish it revealed. So I do not respond.

"Nothing special about 'Carey,'" the colonel says. He sounds almost disappointed. There is something hidden in his face, something I cannot quite recognize. He is still dissatisfied, that much I know.

But then Rejón continues, "Very well. But there is a small matter of the import duties."

"For a personal device?" Paul says.

"We've already paid those," Susan says. I look over and see her standing behind Paul.

"You paid for a standard device," the colonel explains, "but this one required extra inspections and extra processing. I am afraid there will be an additional fee." He pushes a figure to Paul's comp.

Susan looks over Paul's shoulder and frowns. Paul holds up a hand before she can speak. "Very well," he says. "I'll transfer the funds right away."

The colonel nods. "All right. Again, welcome to Belize. I'm sorry for the inconvenience." But I am starting, finally, to build an emulation profile for him. What he feels is not sorrow, it is . . . suspicion? "Thank you for being cooperative. Now I must get back to other business."

20. TODAY WE ARRIVE IN CAYE CAULKER

Rodrigo volunteers to bring us to Caye Caulker. His small boat almost overflows with him, Susan, Paul, their luggage, and myself. It rides low in the surf, and I can see that Paul is excited to be out on the ocean, but a little nervous. Rodrigo seems completely at ease, and Susan is too fascinated by the sights and sounds to pay attention to the water. Rodrigo gives us a tour of the harbor and the area, citing local historical events with a mix of stories about current developments in Belize. "We are still a sleepy country," he says. "Our motto is 'Slow down.' We do not live in Belize to rush, to strive. We in Belize live to appreciate life. But tourists expect some level of modern conveniences, and we have some businesses growing up to serve those. Belize changes, but slowly. We may not have all the technological luxuries to which you are accustomed, but we have the sand and the surf, a cool breeze, the hot sun, the cayes, the people."

Paul looks away from the waves. "You have some amount of industry obviously," he says. "You have your workshop. You wouldn't have something like that without a reason."

"We must repair things," Rodrigo says. "Even today, you will not find many powered vehicles on the islands, but there are many on the mainland. Our hospitals have advanced much in recent years, and their equipment needs service as well. There is always work for technicians like me to keep things running. We may not be MCA, but we have challenges."

Paul glances at me, then back to Rodrigo. "So you're familiar with MCA?"

"I did some reading when the colonel told me I would be inspecting. I looked over Carey's schematics from MCA. Interesting, though dated. I also did a little research on the company. Your generation of BRKCX units was the only one with those empathy nets and neural nets. My reading says those were deemed to be a failure."

"They were," I say.

"I listen to you, and I think maybe not so much a failure," Rodrigo says. He says no more, but a question is clearly implied.

Before I can answer, Paul cuts in. "Carey is unique, one of the early models. More successful."

"Unique indeed. You understand much my friend, don't you?"

I nod. "Some. Belize surprises me. Your expressions, your mannerisms are new to me. There is something I did not understand. You did not tell Colonel Rejón what I can do. You kept it secret from him. Why?"

"I kept no secret. I answered all of his questions. I filled out the reports. I confirmed that you have no weapons that could threaten people of Belize, and that's what he wanted to know."

"Yes, it is."

"But if I had told him the rest," Rodrigo continues, "he would've been suspicious, fearful. You must understand our border conflict in Guatemala goes back over two centuries. Ten years ago it broke out into war. Guatemala is a much richer country than us, and they acquired automated soldiers for their incursion. Military robots. Those were second- or thirdhand on the black market, I'm sure. They were not much more effective than human troops, just less prone to stress and exhaustion. But the psychological effect! The idea of the metal monsters roaming our jungles almost broke the government."

Rodrigo looks away. I think he does not want me to read his face as he continues. "The people were willing to surrender rather than face these creatures. It took everything the government had to pull the people together, and it took fierce fighting by our troops, with heavy losses." Then he looks back at me, and I sense . . . pride? "The colonel is a veteran of that fighting. A hero! *Captain* Javier Rejón and Lieutenant León were the only survivors of their Defence unit. They stood off a squad of mechanicals long enough for reinforcements to turn the tide of that battle. And a brave journalist captured it all. When we saw this video, our pride was stirred. That was when we decided to fight."

Then Rodrigo turns back to me. "I may find the colonel to be difficult at times, but I respect his service to our people. Because of that experience, he is very serious about our laws in this regard. And he is not the only one.

So I'm not sure how special you are, my friend, how well you understand, but try not to draw attention to yourself."

"I understand," I said.

"That's good." Rodrigo smiles broadly. "Maybe someday I will visit America, and you can introduce me around MCA. This is what they were doing twenty-five years ago. I can only imagine what they're doing today."

"No need to imagine," Paul says. "I should introduce you to my future son-in-law."

A single weathered wooden pier juts out into the bay at Caye Caulker, and there are people standing on it in the fading light of the sun. I adjust my vision, and I recognize Millie and Wayne. There is also an older gentleman—bald, bearded, wearing glasses—as well as a few younger people. Dr. Winters and his students, I surmise.

Rodrigo guides the boat up to the pier, where steep wooden steps descend to the waterline and below. "My good android," he says, "if you could grab that piling." I look where he points and I see a big wooden post sticking out of the water, with strong mooring lines hanging from it. He slows the motor and then reverses it. We almost hit the post, but I grab it and stop our forward motion. "All right, hold on," he continues. He ties the rear of the boat to another piling, and then he steps carefully around Paul and Susan to the front of the boat. "Unless you are programmed for knots, I think it best that I tie us off," he says.

"I am not," I say.

He looks at me and laughs. "Is that a joke? I am knot."

I am puzzled at first and then I realize his point. "No, I am not programmed for homonym humor."

Rodrigo laughs louder. "Homonym humor. That's even funnier!" He grabs one of the lines and ties up the front of the boat, and then he goes back and grabs the side of the stair. "I will hold this steady as you good people ascend. Then Carey and I will bring your luggage up."

As I reach the top of the pier, I am surprised at who I see. "Anna?"

Anna hugs me. "You didn't think I would miss Frog Girl's wedding, did you? I told Vishal he could handle the boys for a few days, and here I am."

Paul smiles at his reunited family. Then he looks around. "This is really beautiful, Rodrigo. I can see it now. The waters." He turns and looks at the village at the end of the pier. "Simple living." Over the treetops, the sun is almost gone. "A little hot, but the wind is pleasant. I see it."

Rodrigo grins. "Slow down, Mr. Owens. This is Belize. What's the hurry?"

"What's the hurry?" Susan asks. "We've got a wedding to prepare for!" She checks her comp. "Only sixteen hours away!"

"Oh, Mom," Anna says. "We've got that all covered. Wait until you see this church! That's all the romance Millie will need. Flowers, candles. You're going to love it."

Paul puts an arm around Susan's waist. "Flowers, candles, simple church. Ah, memories . . ." he says.

Susan glares at him, but only for a moment. Then she smiles. "I suppose it was good enough for us."

Rodrigo reaches out and shakes Paul's hand and then

gives him a card. "This is my number. I will be happy to transport you again when you are ready to return to the mainland."

"Thank you, Rodrigo," Paul says.

"And . . . Wayne?"

Wayne looks at Rodrigo. "Yes?"

"I am Rodrigo Pineda." Rodrigo shakes Wayne's hand. "I would not pull you away from your wedding; but I hope we can talk during your visit." He looks over at me. "I want to hear all about MCA."

Wayne nods, though his face shows confusion. Then Rodrigo turns to me and holds out his hand to me as well. I shake it. "My android friend," he says. "So much I could learn from you. But my wife and my little ones are waiting for me. Enjoy your stay in Belize." He quickly descends the stairs.

Millie introduces us to Dr. Winters and her fellow researchers, and then she leads us off the pier. Caye Caulker is very strange to my eyes. It is clean, and everything is bright; but there is so much variety in style, building materials, colors. Each building appears to have been constructed of whatever happened to be available, and in a style to fit the materials. Here and there are brick buildings, businesses and a local Defence post. More are wood or plaster. Some are corrugated sheet metal. Windows are open in many of the older buildings; but the newer-looking ones are as sealed as any building in America, and I see air-conditioning units in those. Most of the buildings have solar panels on walls or roofs.

Numerous people pass through the streets, not enough to seem crowded, just busy. They come in a range of ages and sizes and shades. As with Colonel Rejón, I find their emotions difficult to read. There are cultural differences that surprise me, expressions and body language that defy the expectations of my empathy net.

But I do notice one unusual similarity among them: Virtually everyone looks relaxed, peaceful, unhurried. It is such a difference from the busy world I know. I seem to be the only exciting element in their day: Many stop to stare at me, while children run up and follow me. Other children run through the alleys, shouting to friends, "Come see the mechanical man!"

At the far end of the main street, we approach Our Lady of Assumption. It is small, very old by the looks of it, but in good repair. It is a single story, not much larger than the Owens home. A bell tower rises in the front with a big brass bell visible from below. The doors are nearly three meters tall. Susan walks up and rubs her hand on them. "Look at the beautiful mahogany."

Dr. Winters pulls open the door and holds it as we enter. "Oh," Susan says as she walks in. "Oh, this is so beautiful." Inside, a large chapel dominates the space, just beyond a small vestibule. The pews are all the same dark mahogany as the doors. The altar area at the front is clean white stucco decorated in colorful tapestries depicting scenes I do not recognize. The lectern again is mahogany. The windows on the walls are colored glass, also depicting people and events with which I am unfamiliar.

As Millie shows Susan and Anna the vestibule, a door opens near the altar. A short, dark-skinned man, balding with a fringe of gray, comes in. Wayne walks over to him, pulling Paul along. "Father Gregor," he says.

"Mr. Stockwell." Gregor smiles and shakes Wayne's hand.

"Father," Wayne continues, "this is Paul Owens, Millie's father."

"I'm so glad you could join us, Mr. Owens."

Paul shakes Gregor's hand. "We couldn't miss this, especially not this beautiful church and your wonderful country."

"Thank you, Mr. Owens. I am so happy that you will be here for the blessed event."

"We are too, Father," Paul says. "We are, too." Paul looks over at Susan and Millie as they move around the church, talking and laughing and pointing as they make plans. "Well, Wayne, it looks like they'll be a while with wedding plans here. Maybe you and I should take the luggage to the hotel?"

Wayne nods, and Paul turns back to Gregor. "So, Father, I will see you tomorrow. Very nice to meet you. Beautiful church you have here."

"Simple and beautiful. We work hard to keep it up."

We head over to the women to say our goodbyes. Wayne embraces Millie. "We have to take the luggage to the hotel. You got things covered here, Rana?"

Millie wraps her arms around Wayne's neck. "We have lots to do here. Be back soon?" Wayne nods, and they kiss.

When the kiss continues, Paul clears his throat. "Enough time for that tomorrow, you two."

Wayne's face turns red, and the couple separate. Wayne leads us out of the church and down the three broad steps to the street, pointing at a two-story building just south of the church.

"We and Dr. Winters's team are in here in Nova House," Wayne says. "I'm sorry, we got the last rooms. But we found you and Anna rooms in Mica's Place on the east side of town, overlooking the ocean. Come on. I'll show you the way."

Paul unlocks and opens the hotel room door, and he laughs. "It's so colorful."

I enter behind Wayne and I see what Paul means. The walls are a bright lime green. The floors are dark wood, but a bright blue throw covers most of them. A dresser and a nightstand and two wooden chairs are painted a deep red, which matches the pillows on the bed. The bedspread is yellow and green stripes, the green almost matching the walls.

"And clean," Paul adds. "Well maintained. You made a good choice, Wayne."

"It wasn't much of a choice. This is the only other place in town, Mr. Owens."

"Hey! Enough with the Mr. Owens bit. You can call me Dad or Paul, your choice."

"Well, Dad will take some getting used to. I guess Paul."

Paul looks at me and grins with just his eyes. "All right. Today I am Paul. But work on Dad."

21. TODAY MILLIE GETS MARRIED

When we get to the church the next morning, the research team are busily decorating. Susan and Millie are nowhere to be seen. Wayne is also absent, as is Dr. Winters.

Paul stands and fidgets. He looks out of place in his tuxedo here in the casual world of Caye Caulker, and I suspect he does not want to touch anything that might get it dirty.

Anna sees us come up to the stairs and she runs out. "Carey, perfect!" she says. "I don't know why I didn't think of this sooner."

"Think of what, Anna?"

"You can be our usher."

I look back on my memories of Anna's own wedding. "Yes, I remember," I say. The ushers then had had a simple job: asking "Friends of the bride or friends of the groom?" and then walking each party down the aisle, seating them. They had been very uncomfortable seating me, even though I clearly belonged on the bride's side. Paul and Susan had assured them that I was with them.

Then I think of a problem. "But are there any friends of the groom?"

"Well, the research team are both and they're the only guests we have. Everyone else is family. So just seat everyone anywhere. We'll hardly fill the church. Just balance them out on both sides."

So that is what I do as the music begins. A woman from the village plays soft, slow music on a piano near the rear of the chapel as I walk guests down the aisle two at a time. It does not take long to seat everyone. I seat Dr. Winters in the front on the right. Today he is Wayne's father, emulating much as I might.

Then I go back and find that Susan and Millie have just come over from Millie's hotel. Millie wears a simple white dress, with a short hem suitable for the hot weather in Belize. Her face is covered with a gauzy veil. Susan stands and looks at her, gripping Millie's shoulders, and then her hands. Then they hug, crying, but carefully so as not to smudge makeup.

Susan comes up the stairs and smiles at me. "Let's do this, Carey."

I walk her down the aisle at a slow, stately pace, matching the music. While we were outside, Wayne has appeared and stands in front of the altar next to Father Gregor. Wayne wears a white suit too large for him, perhaps borrowed from a local. He shifts back and forth on his feet. Nervous? Impatient? Probably. I am still learning to read Wayne, so I cannot be sure.

We march to the front row, and I turn, bending to assist Susan into the pew. When I straighten and turn back toward the assembled guests, my empathy net is overwhelmed. This is a new experience for me: so many people, all with such strong emotions. Susan is both happy and sad. Anna is happy and satisfied. Wayne is happy and nervous. Even Dr. Winters, a relative outsider, has an air of pleasant enjoyment of the ceremony. I am sure that I should feel happy as well.

Father Gregor comes up to me and says softly, "Please tell the bride and her father that we are ready."

I nod, and I head back up the aisle and out the door. "They're ready for you," I say.

Paul lifts Millie's veil and kisses her gently. "Whatever happened to my little Frog Girl?" he asks.

Millie chokes back a tear. "I grew up, Daddy."

"Our baby," Paul said. "This beautiful, stubborn young woman. This scientist. We're so proud of you."

"Daddy, I'm so glad you're here. And you, Carey." Millie turns and looks at me. "I'm so happy to have my family here for this."

"I am glad as well," I say.

In analyzing it, I see that this statement is true. This occasion satisfies and balances. It is a logical step in the long sequence starting from Mildred and leading to this time.

"All right," Millie says. She pulls her veil back down. "Let's do this thing."

22. TONIGHT WE CELEBRATE

After the ceremony, we move to the hotel next door, where the café has been decorated in paper bells, flowers, and more candles. The hotel owner greets us as we come in. "Welcome! Félicitations! I am Thérèse Cales, and this is my husband, Alejandro. Welcome on your blessed day!"

The rest of the guests come in, and everyone stands as Father Gregor gives the blessing. The owner calls her staff in from the kitchen, and they seat everyone except myself. I quietly stand in a corner out of the way as the staff bring in drinks, baskets of bread, and plates of fruit. The fruit plate is followed by plates of steaming chicken with coconut rice and beans, plus plantains.

The owner is a constant presence, flitting from table to table, checking to make sure everything is all right. She even finds time to come over and whisper to me. "I am sorry, Monsieur Carey," she says. "I have never met an android before. Is there something I can get for you?"

"I need nothing, Mrs. Cales." I look over at the head table. "But Millie is pleased. Thank you."

Mrs. Cales looks over at Millie. "She is a beautiful bride. But oh! Her glass is empty!" She moves off to the head table to pour some wine for Millie and Wayne.

As I watch Mrs. Cales and the others at work, I can almost feel my empathy net adjusting, expanding. I still have much to learn about Belizean culture, but I start to see recurring patterns. In time, I am sure, I shall understand them as I understand Americans.

After the meal, Thérèse and Alejandro bring out instruments: him a large guitar, and her (with much rolling and scraping) a harp. They quickly drop into a duet, just a few short, light, energetic bars to get the attention of the guests. Then the volume drops and Alejandro speaks over the music. "Ladies and gentlemen, honored guests of Caye Caulker, we have the great pleasure of performing for the first dance of Wayne and Millie Stockwell." The music switches to a louder but slower tune, a harmonious waltz, as Millie and Wayne come out on the small dance floor and start to circle around the room.

Many more dances follow: Paul with Millie, Susan with Wayne, and Anna with Dr. Winters. Then everyone rises to dance. My appreciation of music is strictly academic. I understand how rhythmic patterns and variations can please humans, but they elicit no response within me. I can recognize technical prowess, and these two musicians are very good.

But there is a way I can appreciate the music. I activate my emulation net at a low level, just reactions, not changing my body. Today, at a low level, I am Susan; and as Susan, I find this music very good indeed.

Then as Carey I realize that I am grateful, and I wish to express that. I approach one of the servers. "Two glasses of wine, please."

She giggles. "The mechanical wants wine?"

"Yes, please," I say.

"Very well." She ducks into the kitchen and brings me back two glasses. I hold them, waiting for the musicians to take a break between songs. Then I walk up to them, still emulating Susan enough to convey her warmth. I bow my head. "You play beautifully, Mr. and Mrs. Cales. Please, some wine to show my appreciation."

The man stares at me at first, but his wife touches his arm. "Alejandro," she says, and he looks down. She turns to me. "Yes, I would like some wine. Thank you. Alejandro, this nice gentleman has brought us some wine."

Alejandro smiles and takes the glass. "Yes, some wine between friends. That would be good." Thérèse takes her glass as well, and they drink. Then Alejandro looks at me. "You are different."

"Thank you," I say, recognizing it as a compliment.

He drinks the rest of the wine. Thérèse sits back behind the harp, and then he strikes a chord. "Next," he says, "a number for our new friend, the caretaker." They start up a new song. I do not recognize it. It has a more modern beat than their other songs. The dancers return to the floor. Millie comes over to me, smiling at the musicians. "A song for Carey? Thank you." She takes my hands. "If this is your song, then dance with me," Millie says.

"I do not dance," I answer.

"That's what you said at Anna's wedding, and I didn't

believe you then, either. Come on." Millie takes my hand and pulls me out onto the floor.

I do not understand dancing, but I observe Wayne dancing with Susan. By activating low-level emulation, I can mimic his rhythmic gait.

Millie holds me close, "Do you remember last time?" she asks. "Eighteen years ago?"

"I remember everything."

"Of course you do. Remember . . . I asked you why people got married? You couldn't explain it."

"I still cannot."

She laughs. "Well, what does your empathy tell you?"

I pause in mid step, concentrating fully on her tone, her stance, her mood. "It tells me that you are very happy. That you feel somehow . . . I don't have a good word for it. Perhaps complete."

"Complete. That's close," she says, and we resume dancing. "I am so happy, but I am especially happy that Dad and Mom could be here. And you. Thank you for convincing me."

"It is good that you are happy."

Millie giggles again. "Do you remember what I said back then? I said someday I'd marry you. You told me that I couldn't marry an android, so I said I would marry my frog Jake instead."

"That is correct. I think it is better that you are marrying Wayne than an android or a frog. Do you make him complete as well?"

She looks over at Wayne as he dances with Susan, and she nods. "I do. I really think I do."

I search for the right response for a human to say at this moment. "Then I am happy for you, Millie."

This time it is she who stops dancing. She examines me, and then she says, "You know, I think you really are."

23. TONIGHT WE ARE ARRESTED

It is after midnight when the party ends. The streets are dark, but Paul and Susan's comps provide adequate lighting. I follow behind them, double-checking the route. I remember the way, and the town layout is not complicated.

We have gone barely a block when a voice comes from the shadows of an alley ahead. "American visitors," it says. "So happy with your fine computers. May I see them?"

Paul steps in front of Susan. "No, I don't think so," he says. "We're heading back to our hotel."

"No," the voice says. The form comes out from the shadows. The comp lights glint from a barrel of a gun. "I want your computers, your wallets, rings. And turn those lights off."

Again my empathy net has failed to understand Belize. The man is nervous and afraid, but I did not predict violence. Now my understanding grows: He wants this over quickly. He expects me to either argue with him or submit.

Instead, I leap. I was designed as a medical assistant, not an acrobat, but I have had many physical upgrades since the fire that claimed Mildred. I am now limber, my perceptions are thousands of times faster than human, and my frame has been rebuilt with lighter, stronger alloys. They propel me through the air in a tumbling arc over Paul and Susan's heads.

The man's eyes bulge as I land and bound forward, running at him. A loud shot rings through the night air, and I feel the bullet tug at the silicone flesh of my lower chassis. Diagnostics tell me of minor damage to my physical emulation systems, but nothing that I need worry about at the moment.

Before I can reach the thief, he fires again. This time the shot tears through my left shoulder, damaging my articulation system. The joint itself is functional, but the control circuits are damaged. So it is with my right hand that I grab the gun barrel, rip it from his hands, and smash it against the wall. But the wall is stucco over tar paper, so the gun just punches through it. I had hoped to disable it, rendering it no longer a factor in this confrontation. But instead, I throw it behind me.

This all happens so quickly, the man only now realizes that his shots have not stopped me. He turns to run, but I grab his arm and yank him out of the alley. In the moonlight, for the first time, he sees my face. He looks me over and shouts, "Mechanical! Help!" He struggles to get away, but my grip is too strong.

Paul comes up, the gun in his hand. "Stop!" he says and points the gun at that the man.

I hear more shouts. Two officers on motorized bicycles

speed up to the scene. "No one move," the first one says. "Hands in the air. Put that gun down."

Paul puts the gun down and raises his hands. Susan raises hers as well. But I cannot raise my left arm, and my right is holding onto the thief. He also makes no move to comply, and he tries to pull away back down the alley.

The second officer fires a warning shot over our heads. "On the ground! Now!" I throw the thief to the ground, and then I join him down there.

The man shouts, "Mechanical! It's an invasion."

"It's not an invasion," Paul says.

The second officer shouts, "Silence! You're all under arrest."

24. TODAY I AM INTERROGATED

I am lying on a table in a conference room at the local Defence Force headquarters. Somewhere they have found heavy chains to wrap around me, securing me to the table. I do not know where Paul and Susan are; but from the way the soldiers are acting, I think they are more interested in me. Paul and Susan should be relatively safe. I consider asking about them, but anything I do seems to agitate the officers. It is better that I act the dumb machine.

My comm signals. I do not recognize the number, but the ident reads *U.S.A. Consulate, Belize*. I answer internally with a non-committal, "Yes."

A woman on the other end asks, "Is this BRKCX-01932-217JH-98662?"

"Yes, it is."

"Also known as Carey?"

"Yes," I say.

"This is Ambassador Hendricks with the U.S. Consulate. Anna Owens contacted me. Are you free to talk?"

"The police are unaware that I can converse internally."

"Are you all right?"

I answer, "I sustained minor damage during a robbery attempt. It is repairable at a proper facility."

Hendricks takes a breath before proceeding. "I've placed some calls to the government in Belize City. I've gotten the Owenses released. I'm on my way there as fast as I can to make sure that they're okay. I should be there soon."

"Thank you."

"But you are another matter. I am told—" But at that moment, her voice cuts out.

Then I realize that it is not her, it is me. All of my external lines are dead. Someone is jamming them.

Soon enough, I learn who. I am not surprised when Colonel Rejón walks into the room, followed by his ever-present aides. "You fools! I told you to get a jammer set up. No one out here in the cayes knows how to do anything right." He comes in and looks down at me. "You're jammed now. Who were you talking to?"

I see no purpose in lying. Cooperation seems like the wisest course. So I answer, "Ambassador Hendricks."

"A foolish American woman, like all of them. She thinks she runs things down here. I should have you destroyed just to show her who's in charge in Belize."

I remain silent. He has not asked me a question, so today I am a dumb machine.

But then he grins down at me. "No reaction? You do not struggle? Come, come, I've heard the rumors. Rodrigo's a fool. You are more than a mere caretaker. Talk to me."

I remain silent. The colonel leans in closer and shouts, "Talk, or I'll have you destroyed immediately!"

My empathy net is still unreliable. The colonel may be bluffing. There would be legal and diplomatic ramifications if he destroyed me now that the ambassador is involved. He may be merely trying to frighten me into a reaction. But I cannot be sure.

The colonel paces back and forth by the table, his limp more noticeable than before. "You say nothing now, but you spoke before." One of his aides whispers in his ear and the colonel nods. "You answered a question. All right. Let's try some more. Why did you attack that man in the street?"

"This unit did not attack him," I answer. "This unit defended the Owenses from his attack. He threatened them with a gun, and he shot this unit twice."

"When the officers arrived, Mr. Owens had the gun." I am a dumb machine. I respond only to questions not statements. So I remain silent until the colonel adds, "How do you explain that?"

"This unit took the gun away from the attacker and threw it out of danger. Mr. Owens picked it up, and used it to convince the thief to stop struggling."

"Struggling." Again I wait for a question. He adds, "What do you mean?"

"After this unit took the gun away, the thief tried to flee, and this unit apprehended him and held him until Mr. Owens appeared. Then the police arrived, and this unit laid down on the ground as instructed, taking the thief with him."

"That's not what he says," the colonel replies. "He says

you chased him, hunted him down for Mr. Owens's sport. What do you say to that?"

"That may be what the thief said, but it is untrue. This unit can produce video and audio of the encounter to confirm that. The gun and the ammunition should have the thief's fingerprints on it. But only the gun should have Mr. Owens's fingerprints."

The colonel's eyes widen, and I know I have gone too far. I have shown too much cleverness. "That's a very interesting observation. Is that programmed into your medical banks?"

"No, it is not," I answer truthfully.

"So you reasoned that out. Is that what you're saying?"

"This unit reasoned it out."

"I think you are a very dangerous machine," the colonel says. "Perhaps I should have you destroyed now before anyone else can intervene."

Before I can consider this, a woman appears in the doorway. Tall, fair skinned with short red hair, she wears a gray suit. Her body language tells me that she believes she has authority here. Behind her are Paul and Susan. "Colonel Rejón," she says, "I'm Ambassador Hendricks." She reaches out her hand, but the colonel just looks down at it, eyes narrowed.

"Ambassador, who let you in?" The colonel looks at one of his aides, and the man leaves. "Whoever it is will be very sorry he disobeyed me."

"Colonel, I represent the United States government. Your government wishes to cooperate in this matter as fully as possible."

At that the colonel smiles. "Cooperate? My government?

Ambassador, we do things differently here. When it comes to matters of state security, I answer only to my chain of command."

"And what do they say about this?" Hendricks asks.

"Nothing, yet. I haven't reported to them. They have entrusted me to handle this."

"To handle what? A thief assaults two Americans, and their android saves them, capturing the man with no one injured. You should be thanking it."

"*It* is an automated soldier, which is against the law in Belize."

"It is not an automated soldier," Hendricks replies. "Your own technician certified that."

"Yes, I shall have words with Rodrigo. He failed on this."

Hendricks raises her voice. "Colonel, you have no right to keep this android."

"It is a dangerous device. I have not just the right, but the responsibility to keep it until I have authorization to have it destroyed."

"No!" Susan says, but Paul holds her back and quiets her.

The ambassador says, "Colonel, that would be a mistake."

"Why? It is a mere caretaker android, decades out of date. It could easily be replaced. But if it is something more . . ."

"Colonel, this is not a decision you should make." I am impressed with the ambassador. She has found the colonel's weakness, and she is hitting it with everything she has. "You have the unit secured."

"For now, yes."

"Then there is no rush. You do not need to take immediate action. If it must be destroyed, then you can wait for that order to come down through your chain of command. And therefore, whatever consequences will follow . . ." She pauses and gets her face right in the colonel's. ". . . and I promise you, there will be consequences . . . will accrue to your superiors, not to yourself."

The colonel does not blink. "Are you threatening me, Ambassador?"

"I am advising you, Colonel. As you say in Belize, slow down."

I have been in low-power mode to conserve my batteries. When I awaken, Millie leans over me. "Carey, are you all right?"

I hear Wayne's voice. "Rana, I know you're worried, but I have to get to it to see how bad the damage is."

Millie straightens up, and I see Wayne behind her. On the other side of the table are Susan, Paul, Anna, and Ambassador Hendricks. Wayne steps in closer. "This is no way to work. I don't have my tools. Do we have to have these chains?"

The ambassador nods. "The colonel insists, and I couldn't change his mind."

"This is nonsense. Carey's no threat to anyone."

Wayne tries to move the chains on my upper torso for a better view at my shoulder.

"If it would help, Wayne," I say, "I could get out of the chains."

"What are you waiting for?" Millie says.

"Not a good idea," the ambassador answers. "The colonel could come in at any moment. I wish you hadn't even said that. This room may easily be bugged."

"I do not believe it is, Ambassador," I say. "This room is under broad-spectrum electronic jamming. I believe that would interfere with any listening device as well."

The Ambassador checks and then frowns. "You're right. We're probably safe to speak here; but still, I advise you to stay in those chains."

Wayne asks, "Can it at least shift so I can get to its shoulder?"

"Can you?" the ambassador asks.

"I think I can do that, yes." I twist my body while simultaneously contracting all of my chassis and structural extenders. The chains loosen.

"Perfect," Wayne says. He slides the chains down from my shoulder and looks. "That's not too bad," he says. "The actuator's ruined, plus you have a tear in your flesh. If I had a spare actuator and my tools, I'd have you fixed in a minute. Where else did he shoot you?"

"Left abdomen. The bullet went right through, damaged my microtubules."

"Hey! Who's the android technician around here and who's the android?"

"I am sorry, Wayne. Please continue."

Wayne checks my abdomen, prodding at the damaged area. "Millie," he says. "Do you have your lens?"

"Um, let me check." Millie searches through her purse and hands Wayne a magnifying lens.

Wayne probes and scans again, and then says, "It took out a significant node of the microtubule network."

"What does that mean?" Millie asks. There is fear in her voice.

"Not to worry, love. That network is how Carey uses pneumatics and fiber optics to change the shape and color of its body. You'll do no emulating below the waist," Wayne says to me. "Not until we can get you back in Dr. Jansons's lab. No one has made parts like these for fifteen years. But emulation isn't a critical function. You'll be fine."

Paul turns to the ambassador. "So what happens now?"

Ambassador Hendricks frowns. "I wish I had good news for you, Mr. Owens. I'm pulling every string I have, but the Belizeans have a long tradition of rejecting outside authority. They celebrate their independence from Britain for the entire month of September, and their victory over the Guatemalan invaders is still one of their proudest accomplishments. If I try to push, they're going to push back harder, and things will go worse for you. I can encourage. I can entreat. But I can't push.

"And I can't get a lot of cooperation from the State Department," she continues. "I've tried to convince them, but they think this is a minor property matter, and they want me to make it just go away the fastest way possible. They have offered to compensate you for the loss of your android."

"No!" Millie shouts.

"Don't worry, I've told them that's not an option. But they haven't been here. They haven't talked to Carey. They haven't believed my reports, frankly. So I'm pulling the strings that I can, but I've only got so many I can pull."

"So what do we do?" Susan asks.

"We let the process go through. We go before the magistrate and see if we can convince him that Carey is no threat."

"A trial?" Paul asks.

Hendricks shakes her head. "Trials are for humans," she says. "Belize courts are based on those of their former British rulers. Humans have rights here, and that includes a right to a trial. Carey has no rights. There will be a hearing tomorrow when Magistrate Teves arrives from the mainland. Just a hearing in chambers. No right to a barrister, no right to cross-examine the witnesses. The magistrate will ask questions, and we'll have to answer and convince him that Carey is a simple machine, nothing more."

"But it *is* more," Millie insists.

Wayne smiles faintly. "Yes, it is, Rana. And Ambassador, I think I can convince the magistrate of that."

25. TODAY I HAVE MY HEARING

When Magistrate Teves arrives the next day, he comes into the office where I am chained, followed close behind by Colonel Rejón, his aides, and Ambassador Hendricks. The magistrate is medium height and neatly dressed in a light tropical suit, not his magisterial robes. "This is the device?" he asks.

"Yes," the colonel says.

The magistrate looks around the room. "This room will suffice for chambers for our hearing today. Do you object?"

"No, your lordship," the colonel says.

"No, your lordship," Hendricks echoes.

"All right." The magistrate checks his comp, looking over information there for several minutes before he says, "So Colonel, one of your technicians examined this device?"

"Yes, he did. He was not as thorough as he should have been."

"That's not what I asked, Colonel. This technician is here today?"

"Yes, he is waiting in another office."

"Have him brought here," the magistrate says.

"Your lordship," Ambassador Hendricks says, "there are other parties concerned. They are also waiting. I suggest that you might want to have them all brought here to expedite matters."

The colonel shakes his head. "It is too risky, your lordship. With so many in the room, if the device broke free, someone might be injured before we could restrain it."

The magistrate looks down at me and asks, "Is there any danger of it breaking free? These chains look very secure."

I look at Ambassador Hendricks, and she winces. She thinks Wayne's plan is risky. But I have decided: I shall be as human as I am able. I will be tried for who I am, not what I am. I answer, "I shall not break free, your lordship."

The magistrate's eyes grow wide, as do the colonel's. "And why not?" the magistrate asks.

"Because that would not respect your authority," I answer, "nor Colonel Rejón's. And it would disrupt these proceedings. I would like to return to my family."

"Your family," the magistrate muses. "They are among those waiting?" The ambassador nods. "And Ambassador, you wish them to join us?"

Colonel Rejón interrupts, "I would rather not take that chance, your lordship."

"It is not you taking the chance, it will be me. Bring all concerned parties here."

"Yes, your lordship." The colonel leaves the office.

Ambassador Hendricks starts to speak, but the magistrate raises a hand. "Ambassador, you have no formal standing in this hearing. I allow you and these other parties to be here out of courtesy; but out of similar courtesy, I do not think it would be proper to let you argue your case while the colonel is not here to offer rebuttal."

"Yes, your lordship," Hendricks says.

While they wait, the magistrate looks me over head to toe. "You are unusual to be sure, but you do not look like a war machine." Hendricks again starts to speak, but stops as the magistrate raises his hand again. "I remember the automated soldiers: armored devices, tough, light, and well armed." His eyes seem to look past me. "When they rushed through the jungle, it was all I could do to hold my post." Then he focuses on me again, and he prods at me. "You are almost flesh—soft." He squeezes my hands. "Ah, there is metal underneath though. Perhaps you are strong."

Before I can answer, the colonel returns, followed by Rodrigo, Paul, Susan, Anna, Millie, and Wayne. Rodrigo carries a large tool box, as does Wayne. Magistrate Teves raises an eyebrow. "Colonel?"

Colonel Rejón answers, "I confirm that the boxes contain only mechanical and electronic tools, your lordship. You should be quite safe."

"Thank you, Colonel. All right." The magistrate turns to Rodrigo. "You are the technician who inspected this device for the Belizean Defence Force under orders from Colonel Rejón?"

"Yes, I am," he says, "Rodrigo Pineda."

"And this is your report?" The magistrate tries to push

a document to Rodrigo's comp, but the magistrate's own comp only beeps an error. "Something is wrong here. My computer was fine this morning."

The colonel answers, "We have a multiband jammer blanketing this room so that the device cannot call out and possibly summon assistance."

"Do you really think that is necessary, Colonel?"

"I do, your lordship. It is for your protection as well, so I must insist."

"Very well. Quite inconvenient, but I will accept it for now. Mr. Pineda, come read this report on my comp, and confirm to me that it is yours."

Rodrigo steps around the table to where the magistrate stands by my head. He checks page after page on the magistrate's comp before answering. "I confirm that this is my report in its entirety, unaltered."

"Do you stand by these conclusions? BRKCX-01932-217JH-98662 is an older-model caretaker android with no war-making capabilities, and you found nothing unusual about it?"

"Well, for such an old unit to be still in service and in such good shape is unusual. In technology terms, this is an antique."

"Yes, but that is all you found?"

Rodrigo measures his words carefully. I can see he is afraid of lying to the magistrate, but reluctant to offer support to the colonel's argument. "Your lordship, its neural nets appear to have been growing steadily throughout its years of service, and so it is a very experienced android. One might even argue clever, because it has such a rich store of situations upon which to draw."

"That does not make it dangerous?"

"No, your lordship, it does not."

The magistrate turns to the colonel. "Do you have anything more you would like to ask?"

"Yes, I do, your lordship." Colonel Rejón turns to Rodrigo. "So Mr. Pineda, you examined this unit quite closely?"

"Yes."

"In your examination, did anything tell you that it could leap two meters over an obstacle, pursue a man at unnatural speeds, and deflect bullets without harm?"

The ambassador says, "Your lordship!"

The magistrate turns on her with a glare. She grows silent, and the magistrate turns back to Rodrigo. "Answer the question," he says.

Rodrigo shakes his head. "It is a complicated question. And also inaccurate: The android did not deflect bullets, and it *was* harmed. But to answer the question: Yes, an analysis of the structural design of the android, the capabilities of its actuators, and its synthetic musculature indicates that all of this is possible."

"But you didn't note it at the time?" the colonel asks.

"I recognize the possibilities in hindsight, Colonel."

"So you admit that you missed that."

"You asked for me to search for weapons, Colonel, and weapons systems. I searched much more thoroughly than that; but no, I did not comprehend the full range of mobility and durability of this device."

The magistrate frowns. "And you also did not notice that this unit speaks for itself? That it appears self-aware?"

I see stress on Rodrigo's face, so I answer before he

can. "I did not do so during the inspection, your lordship. I only answered questions."

"And why was that?"

"I wanted to reassure the colonel and Mr. Pineda that I meant no threat."

The colonel turns back to the magistrate. "There is your answer, your lordship. The device is dangerous, and it concealed that fact from our most thorough examination. That makes it even more dangerous. Perhaps this is even *deliberate* subterfuge."

"I cannot rule out that possibility," the magistrate admits.

"Your lordship," Ambassador Hendricks says.

This time the magistrate nods to her. "You have something you wish to contribute to this hearing, Ambassador Hendricks?"

"Your lordship, I would say that Mr. Stockwell here can explain to you everything that you need to know."

"Mr. Stockwell," the magistrate turns as the ambassador points at Wayne. "You are . . . ?"

"Wayne Stockwell, your honor—"

"Ahem," the magistrate interrupts.

"He means 'your lordship,'" Hendricks says.

"Yes, my apologies, your lordship," Wayne continues. "I am a cyberneticist with the MCA corporation, the manufacturers of this device."

"The Americans sent a cyberneticist down for this hearing?"

"No, your lordship, I was already here for Dr. Winters's research project, and for my wedding." Wayne gestures toward Millie.

"Your lordship," the colonel says, "I object. This man is related by marriage to the owners of this device. He could very well be part of this espionage plan."

"That is up to me to decide, Colonel," the magistrate says. "Let me check." He looks at his comp, and then grimaces as he realizes again that he is cut off from the outside world. "Ambassador Hendricks, I was going to check his credentials. Can you vouch for him?"

"I can, your lordship. I had him thoroughly checked out. He has been a member of this family for two days. He has been an employee of the MCA corporation for over three years, and he served an internship with them before that. He knows as much about this device as anyone."

"Then for now I will accept your credentials, Mr. Stockwell. What would you like to add to this hearing?"

"First, your lordship, I would like to show what actually happened, since that is what the unit is being judged on." Wayne turns to me. "BRKCX-01932-217JH-98662, I need you to download to me your record of the robbery, from before you heard anything until the police escorted you away."

I cannot push the recording to him, of course, so Wayne inserts a transfer cable and pulls the document from my comp. Then he projects it as a holographic recording, and we go through the lead up in real time. When I start to move in the image, Wayne slows it down. "Now here, your lordship," he says, "you will see that the unit took no action until the thief threatened the Owenses with a gun, pointing it in their direction."

The magistrate frowns. "It is no news to me, Mr. Stockwell, that we sadly have a crime problem in Caye

Caulker. This does indeed look like a typical late-night robbery," he turns to Paul and Susan, "which might have been avoided had you used more sense."

"I'm sor—" Paul starts to say.

But the magistrate holds up his hand before Paul can finish. "You aren't the first Americans to make fools of yourselves here. You won't be the last. I hope you learn a lesson from this."

Then Wayne lets the playback continue. What is viewed from my perspective is live video. The rest of the hologram is a schematic reconstruction of my own body as I move. My eyes could not see that, but my motor and position sensors recreated it from memory.

But I have no need to watch this playback, since I remember it perfectly. Instead I look around the room, my empathy net tuned to maximum as I try to understand the mood. The Owenses are anxious, while Wayne is more confident. Ambassador Hendricks is calm and determined. The magistrate, true to his calling, is reserved. Neutral, as neutral as I have ever seen in a human.

And Colonel Rejón is . . . obstinate. Defiant. And underneath that, another reaction that I cannot quite work out.

"You see, your lordship," Wayne continues, "the android leaps over the Owenses, and not in an attack. Notice how it expanded its torso, spread out its arms to give them cover. It was trying to defend them." He lets the recording continue. "The android had already asked the man to put down the gun. Only when the man refuses and shoots at the device, damaging it in two places, does it act against him. Now, watch what it does." In the image,

I grab the gun from the man and smash it through the wall. Wayne freezes the scene. "Do you see that?"

"Yes," the magistrate says. "It was very quick."

"Very quick, but there is something curious." Wayne turns to me. "BRKCX-01932-217JH-98662, why did you smash the gun against the wall?"

"Your lordship, I object," the colonel says again.

"On what grounds?"

"You cannot have this *thing* testify."

"It seems I already have," the magistrate says with a smile. "This is not testimony, Colonel. This is fact finding, and I will hear as much as I can hear." The magistrate turns to me. "So have you been listening this entire time?"

"Yes, I have," I answer. "Should I answer the original question asked by Dr. Stockwell?"

"Yes, I think you should."

"I misinterpreted what the wall was constructed from," I answer. "I thought it would be more solid, and I wanted to disable the weapon so that no one would get injured by it."

"So that no one would get injured," Wayne says.

The colonel sniffs. "Such a convenient rationalization." The magistrate glares at the colonel, but he lets the comment stand.

Wayne continues, "But once you had the gun in your hand, why did you not smash the thief with it? That would have also rendered it harmless."

"Wayne!" I am shocked at my own outburst. It is as if my emulation net has a life of its own, and my rational control net can only observe. "I could not do that!"

"Why not?" the magistrate asks.

"I am a medical care android, your lordship," I answer. "I cannot allow injuries if they can be avoided, and I must treat them if they are unavoidable."

"But that leap that you did," the magistrate continues. "Is that part of your design?"

"It is now," I answer. "I requested it after . . ." But I am reluctant to explain.

"After what?" the magistrate asks.

"It's all right, Carey," Paul says. "You don't have to worry about Mom's privacy. Answer the question."

The magistrate stares at Paul, and then says, "Yes, answer."

"Yes, your lordship. I requested these physical upgrades after I . . ." I look at Paul. "I failed."

"I do not understand," the magistrate says.

"May I show you?" The magistrate nods, and I turn to Wayne. "Please . . . Download this recording, and play it for the magistrate."

So Wayne does, and we all watch my recorded memories of *that* night, in vivid video and audio. The fire alarms. Mildred's panic. The smoke. Her struggles to escape. The fire. The oxygen tanks. Running through the picture window. The explosion. Tumbling through the air. Tossing Mildred free. (I wince when I see her land.) Impact, and the way it jars and disorients me. The flames eating at my flesh. Putting out the fire in Mildred's blanket. Carrying her to safety. Mildred's terror when she realizes what I am. And finally, having no way to give her the oxygen therapy that she needed.

The room falls silent. I see tears in Anna's eyes. Millie swallows hard.

And I . . . I am sad. I miss Mildred. And I am . . . angry?

Wayne pauses the playback, and the magistrate says, "You stumbled. You fell. You were clumsy."

"And I had no oxygen," I answer. "So I asked for upgrades. To be ready." I stare at Colonel Rejón; and I realize that yes, for the first time, I am angry. "I do not harm people. Ever. Do not judge me by those mechanicals you fought."

"You *are* mechanical," Rejón answers.

"And you are human, Belizean, just like the bandit who attacked us. I judge you by your fierce love for your country, your need to keep it safe, not by what he did. Belize is not that bandit, and I am not the mechanical soldiers. I am myself, unique. Judge me as me."

The colonel and I lock eyes; and suddenly, at last, I understand. I see in his eyes what I saw in Mildred's that night: Though he hides it well, Colonel Rejón is terrified of me. Whatever he faced in the jungle, he cannot dare to risk facing it again.

"You are unique?" the magistrate asks, pulling my attention away from the colonel.

"Your lordship, if I may . . ." Paul says. The magistrate nods, and Paul turns to Wayne. "Please . . . Resume the playback."

And so I watch myself as Henry at Mildred's deathbed; and those memories make me forget all about Colonel Rejón. Wayne skips large stretches, showing just enough to give a sense of the night. Anna leaving the room in tears. Millie, five years old again. Susan telling stories. Paul rubbing my shoulders. My . . . Henry's kiss goodbye.

While I watch the video, I do not notice Paul moving

up beside me. I only realize that he is there when he speaks again. "Unique, your lordship. Show me another android who could do that, be exactly who we needed on that terrible night. Carey's not a killer. Carey is . . . family."

The magistrate stares at me, and then back at the last image from the projection. Finally he says, "So *this* is why you asked for the upgrades. You felt bad, because your patient died."

I pause, considering the magistrate's words. I had been an emotional infant then. I understand myself so much better now, thanks to my family, and to my work with Wayne. And I see the truth that I did not see then. "I felt guilty. Because I failed."

"Guilty?" The magistrate looks at Colonel Rejón, raising an eyebrow. "I think that mechanical soldiers who feel guilt would be an improvement, don't you, Colonel?"

"Your lordship—"

The magistrate interrupts before the colonel can continue. "I think that a machine with a conscience is not a machine at all. Carey Owens, I am not sure what you are; but you are *not* a mechanical soldier." He turns to Rejón. "There is nothing to fear here, old friend."

I turn to the colonel. My memories of Mildred's passing have overpowered my anger. Now that I have the capability, I pity him. I wish that I could ease his fears.

Then the magistrate says to one of Rejón's aides, "Remove the chains." The magistrate turns to Hendricks. "Ambassador?" Hendricks's mouth is a thin-drawn line. She knows not to upset matters, so she says nothing. The magistrate continues, "I rule that this unit, formally designated BRKCX-01932-217JH-98662, is not a dangerous device, not an automated soldier. It may freely travel within the nation of Belize, and I expect Ambassador Hendricks to arrange a passport for it immediately, in the name of Carey Owens. I so record." He taps at his comp. "Blast it! Colonel, turn off the jammers."

The colonel walks up to me, almost face-to-face. He is conflicted: surprised by what he has seen, but still worried for his people. Still afraid, but maybe a little less so. He whispers, "You are . . . different, mechanical." Then he leaves the room.

Soon the magistrate's comp beeps, and he continues. "I so record and push to the national records. This hearing is adjourned."

26. TODAY OUR NEST IS EMPTY

When we return home from Belize, the home feels unbalanced, like when my networks have been operating too long with no chance to reset. But my networks themselves are fine. It is the Owens family that is different. Millie's absence has changed the home in ways that I have difficulty analyzing.

But more than that, Paul has changed as well. He is relaxed as I have never seen him before. And I realize for the first time that there's a tension that has been in him since his mother's illness. It has been so much a part of him that I had not realized it was not his natural state.

It could not have been the result of Mildred's illness, or at least not that alone, because it has persisted for eighteen years since her death. I speculate that it is his work, because his attitude toward that has changed. Now when he brings work home, I find that he puts it away more quickly and says under his breath, "Slow down."

Susan's change is more obvious, and more clearly due to Millie's moving out. With school not in session and only occasional televisit meetings required, she has much free time. She sits around the house or the garden, sometimes working, sometimes playing music or singing. I still have no appreciation for music, but I analyze that her voice is of good quality. She sings songs that comfort her, but they can only do so much.

On our fifth day back, after Paul has left for work and I serve up breakfast, I ask, "Susan, is there anything I can do for you?"

She looks up at me with a half smile. "I'm all right, Carey. I'm just getting used to the empty nest syndrome."

"Empty nest?"

"Like birds. They build a nest to lay their eggs and raise the chicks and feed them. The nest gets so crowded and full of happy, cheerful noises. And then one day, the young birds stretch their wings and fly away, and the parents are left with a nest that's much too big for them and much too quiet. Their lives have changed, and much of their purpose in building the nest has been fulfilled. It's done, and now it's gone."

"I see," I say. "And what do the birds do?"

"Well, birds turn around and do it again the next year. They start all over with another batch of eggs."

"I see." I pour her some more juice. "So, are you and Paul going to start over?" At that, Susan laughs out loud. "I am sorry. Did I say something funny?"

"Oh, Carey, I just forget how large the gaps are in your experience. No, we're too old to have another child. Frankly, people thought it was odd we had Millie so long after Anna. No, our nest is empty and it's going to stay empty, just the two of us bumping around this large house. And you, of course."

"You could move to a smaller house," I say.

At that, Susan laughs again, but not so strongly. "Never happen," she says. "This is where Paul grew up. He loves the place too much. I love it, too. So many memories here. But his memories go back twenty years farther than mine. No, as long as we're able to keep this place up, we'll stay here."

"And I will stay here to help you keep it up."

"Thank you, Carey." She pats my hand. "I guess with you, our nest will always be a little less empty."

I pause, contemplating what I have learned, and then I ask, "So I must return to my original question. Is there anything I can do to help?"

Susan finishes the last of her juice. "You know, there might be," she says. "One of the most reliable ways to deal with that empty nest is to change it up."

"I do not understand."

"Remodeling. Give everything a new look. Don't throw out the old memories, but it'll make it easier to make some new ones, because we repurpose the house for our golden years."

"I am unfamiliar with home remodeling."

"That's okay," Susan says. "My dad and mom were both expert carpenters. They built and remodeled three homes when I was growing up. I can teach you."

"Teach me?"

"Yeah, I think this is a project we should do together while I've got so much free time this summer. Oh, this is going to be fun! Let me call Paul, and then we'll start planning. This is just the summer change we need."

✳ ✳ ✳

Susan tells me that we are going to convert Millie's room into another office. I try to imagine such a conversion, but she says she will do the design work. First, however, we must get everything out of the room. All of Millie's possessions must be boxed up and put into storage in the rear of the laundry room where my charging station is. I am very efficient at boxing and carrying, so I agree to do that work while Susan works on her design.

I remember after Mildred passed away, and Paul and Susan began cleaning up the undamaged parts of the home for the contractors. That involved much packing of Mildred's belongings. It was a sad occasion then, and I had offered at the time to do the work for them much as I was doing now. But Paul and Susan had insisted: As sad as the work was, it was their obligation to Mildred's memory to go through each item individually, remember what it meant to her and to them, and decide what to do with it.

This occasion I understand to be less sad. It is still a departure, part of the empty nest syndrome that Susan described, but Millie is still with us. When she comes home from Belize and she and Wayne find a new place of their own, much of this material can go with her. Still, I am struck by how some of these items resonate within my empathy net, as if with each item boxed, a little bit of Millie is leaving.

There is her small collection of paper books, rare things today, but still common when she had been a child. Science books, especially frogs and amphibians, but also storybooks. She had been very fond of *Peter Pan*, and I remember reading that to her over and over. She had been capable of reading it herself, but she had always insisted that I read it better. I had emulated the different characters and voices from the information in the text, and she had giggled in childish glee at my performances.

In her desk, I find papers that she wrote back in junior high, another vestige of an older time. I find her jewelry box, almost empty: Millie finds jewelry to be impractical with all the time she spends outside. The box contains only items that were special, gifts from relatives and friends: a gold necklace with a blue crystal pendant, an old-fashioned watch that had once been Mildred's, and the ring that she had worn at Anna's wedding. Last is a cheap plastic charm bracelet filled with animal charms, including a frog charm that is worn practically smooth and featureless from her years of fondling it.

In her closet, I find shoes, most worn out but never thrown away, some far too small for her to ever wear again. And of course there is her wardrobe. It falls into two categories: casual, comfortable, and durable, for trips to the woods in search of specimens; and equally practical, but more fashionable for when she goes to class. On a shelf in the closet, I find the terrarium where once she had kept her first frog, Jake. He is long gone. She had many more frogs follow, but now she has all she can do to keep up with the ones in her lab. Two years ago, she finally gave up on keeping the terrarium clean and frogs inside it. All the equipment is still here, and I carefully box it up. Perhaps she'll find it useful again someday.

At last, all that is left in the room is the furniture. Susan says those pieces should go in the garage. So I haul down the dresser, the nightstand, the chair, and the dressing table. When Paul gets home from work that night, we disassemble the bed, and then we haul the mattress and box spring downstairs and out to the garage.

When we are done, I look around the room. I understand now: My nest is empty. I must find a way to fill it.

27. TODAY I AM BO

As I prepare breakfast, I decide I must speak to Paul and Susan now. There is no reason to wait.

When they come downstairs, I pour coffee for each of them. Then I begin. "Susan, Paul, I have something to discuss."

They both stare at me. This is out of character for me, as they understand my character. Finally Susan says, "We're listening, Carey."

I have planned my introduction all night, but I am ready to change course if I upset them. "You miss Millie around the house, but you have outside interests to keep you busy. You both have busy lives with responsible jobs that take much of your time. You are both in good health; and thanks to the advances of medical science, you should be for many years to come."

Paul laughs. "I think we've got a few good years ahead of us, yes."

"So although I can help with the cleaning and the cooking around here, there is little for me to do."

"Well, you're helping with the remodeling, too," Susan says, glancing at Paul.

I sense some secret shared between them, but that does not concern me at the moment. "Yes," I reply, "but that is a thing we do *together*. It is a shared activity, and I welcome that; but I am also learning that I am not ready to do such work alone."

"You'll learn," Paul says.

"Of course," I answer. "But I still want something to do with my day, something useful."

"I understand, Carey," Susan says. "What do you have in mind?"

"With your permission, I would like to get a job."

They both shake their heads. "You know better than that, Carey," Paul says. "You don't need our permission. But if you want our support, I think it's a great idea."

Susan nods. "Absolutely." But then she frowns. "If you can find someplace that will take you. Many places have all the help they need, human and robot."

"And some . . ." Paul shakes his head. "Some won't take androids. It's just the way things are."

I already know this from perusing job advertisements on the local boards. I had quickly realized that there were android agencies, for the few androids still in service. But many job listings specifically said: *No agency placements.* "I understand," I say. "But even looking for work will give me something to do."

"If you're sure," Susan says.

"I am," I reply.

"Then go for it," Paul says.

"Good luck," Susan agrees. "We're pulling for you."

※　※　※

I walk in to Allegan, the nearest town. It is a short walk away. The local boards show one business advertising for help: DeBruyn's Market, our local grocery store. This is a place that knows me well. I come here often with Susan or Paul.

I walk up to the service desk and Kathryn, the service manager, greets me. "Hello, Carey," she says. "Shopping today?"

"No, Kathryn," I answer. "I wish to apply for a job."

Her eyes show surprise. "A job?"

"Yes, I have read your advertisement." I push the reference to her comm. "You are looking for someone to work on your receiving dock."

"Yes, I am Carcy, but . . ."

The way that she trails off makes me reply, "But not an android."

"Carey, please, I didn't say that."

"No, but you are thinking that. I am sorry to have troubled you." I turn away.

"Carey, wait." She grabs my hand. "You know we like you here. It's just . . ."

"You are afraid I would upset the customers? I come here often. The locals are used to me."

"No, I'm fine with that, but . . . Come back into my office." I follow Kathryn into a back room. She closes the door behind us. "Look, Carey, I really need a high school kid for this job. Or maybe some young person starting a family, someone who really needs the work."

That stops me. "And I do not *need* the work. I only want it."

"That's right," she says. "This is entry-level work. With

this sort of job, sometimes I count myself lucky if the worker's worth what I pay."

"I can work very hard," I say.

"I know you can, but it's about helping people grow into a better worker. At a bigger store, I wouldn't even be hiring. I would already have an android leased for this position. But I started on that receiving dock. Half our crew did, that or other starter jobs."

"And I do not need to grow."

"No," she answers. "To be honest, you're too good for this job. If you were human with your skills and experience, I would expect that two months after hiring you, you'd find something you're better suited for."

"I am best suited for care of patients with mental impairment, particularly the elderly," I reply. "But I have been decertified for medical upgrades."

Kathryn furrows her brow. "But you can still do that work?"

"Yes."

Kathryn taps her comm. "Hey, Lex," she says, "I'm taking an early lunch." Then she turns back to me. "Come on, Carey, let's find you a job."

We pull into a driveway. It is a wide, shallow U, bordered by neatly trimmed green lawns inside and around the arms of the U. The sign at the entrance proclaims, CREEKSIDE HOME, A LONG-TERM CARE FACILITY. The long, flat base of the U is a parking lot, four rows with twenty spaces each; but almost all of the spaces are empty. Beyond the parking lot is a long low building, with two wings and a long corridor between them.

"A nursing home?" I ask.

"Not just a nursing home," Kathryn answers. "It's not on the sign—they don't want to disturb the neighbors—but they specialize in rehabilitation and therapy for mental and memory disorders."

"Is it closed?" I ask. "There are almost no cars here."

"I know. It's sad. This lot is always empty." Kathryn sighs. "Except the staff, of course. My friend Vera works here. Let me talk to her. She's always saying they need more help than they can get. Stay here and let me talk to her."

Kathryn leaves the car and heads into the east wing. I look around. There is a large lawn west of the west wing. A gazebo sits in the middle of the lawn. It looks freshly painted. I see four older people heading out to it. One is in a wheelchair. She wears a bright purple jumpsuit. Two others are walking with assist suits: a man in brown pants and green shirt, and a woman in jeans and a white blouse. The fourth person is younger and walks without assistance, a young man in jeans and sloppy shirt. His head is shaved bald.

Others are already in the gazebo. My empathy nets cannot pick up much from such a short exposure and at such a distance; but from the way that they move, I think that these residents are happy to be outside on such a good day.

Then I am startled by a tapping at my window. I turn and see an older man in a colorful tight blue shirt spangled with red and white stars. He wears matching blue pants. He has tapped the window with a small red ball about the size of a grapefruit.

I lower the window. "Can I help you?"

"Are you coming, Bo, or not?" he asks.

"I am sorry," I say. "My name is not Bo."

There is a puzzled look on his face, and I realize this disturbs him. So today I am Bo. "I'm sorry," I say. With no clue who Bo is or how he might behave in this situation, I simply assume a pleasant, cheerful demeanor. "I'm just kidding. I am Bo, and you are . . . ?"

"I'm Luke, you rube. I thought I was the one that conked his head."

So he has had a head injury, and it has affected his memory, but not so much that he is unaware of it. I find myself naturally sliding into diagnostic mode. It feels satisfying. I have not exercised this capability in so long. It is good to be able to analyze and maybe help.

I adjust my appearance to a generic male of approximately Luke's age. I have no clue for skin color, hair color, or eye color, so I aim for demographic average for this area: a deep tan with light brown eyes. I decide rather than try to get the hair right, it is simpler to retract my follicles and be bald.

I get out of Kathryn's car, and hope I have not gotten Bo's appearance so far wrong as to upset Luke. But he is not even looking. He walks toward the front lawn, and I see now that he has three of the balls: one red, one green, and one blue.

When he is in the center of the front lawn between the two arms of the driveway, Luke drops the balls and starts to stretch. First side to side, then around in a circle, circling his arms, bending down to touch his hands between the toes. It is a thorough stretching regimen, and

I join him because I can see that it will make him comfortable.

After several minutes of stretching, Luke finishes with some jogging in place. I do not know about his mental condition, but he seems in excellent health for his age.

After Luke is done jogging, he picks up the red ball and tosses it into the air above his head with his right hand. He catches it with his left, passes it back to his right and tosses it again. On the third toss, while the red ball is still in the air, he tosses the green up after it; and this time after he catches the red, he adds the blue into the mix. I stand back and watch, impressed with his performance. Now all three balls are spinning up and down, and Luke breaks out into a big grin. "I still got it, Bo. I might have lost my marbles, but not my skills."

"You still got it, Luke," I answer. "You're doing great."

"And how about you?" Luke asks; and without warning he snaps the red ball sideways in an arc toward me.

I do not hesitate. I grew up playing with Millie, and I know how to play catch. I easily pluck the red ball out of the air. It's heavier than I expected—wood, not plastic.

"Well?" Luke says as he continues tossing the blue and the green balls.

"I caught it," I say.

"I know that," Luke answers. "Now throw it back."

"But you're . . ."

"I can still toss and catch at the same time. Come on!"

I study, and I realize that Luke is still maintaining the three-ball rhythm even with just two there. Blue, green, gap. Blue, green, gap. Blue, green . . . and I time my return throw so that it arrives just at the gap without missing a beat. Luke catches it with his left hand, passes it to his right, and throws it up as his left hand snaps the green ball toward me.

This time I understand Luke's timing, and so I pass the ball from my right hand to my left, and then from my left timed to the gap back to Luke. I am just in time to catch the incoming blue ball. We make several passes like this: At all times we have two balls between us and one over his head.

I realize that we have drawn a crowd. All of the residents who had been at the gazebo are now clustered around us, watching from a safe distance.

Then Luke says, "Your turn." I look, and he stares at me expectantly; and I guess what he means, so I toss the red ball over my head. Without missing a beat, we have changed the rhythm: two balls between us and one over my head. The crowd applauds, and we continue that for a dozen passes.

Then Luke and I start switching the rhythm, with me lobbing balls overhead, and then him back and forth. Each time we switch, the crowd gasps and claps.

Without noticeably looking at the balls, Luke grins at me. "Just like old times, eh Bo?"

I nod. "Just like old times."

"Just like . . ." Luke replies. "Like . . . Like . . ." He misses the blue ball, and it falls. He starts to tremble and sway.

I see the red ball falling toward his head. Without hesitation, I rush toward him. With my left arm, I cradle Luke as he falls. With my right hand, I slap away the ball.

Luke shakes all over, some sort of seizure. I check that his airway is clear, and I gently lay him down.

"Mr. Lucas!" I hear a female voice shout. I turn to the east wing doors, and I see Kathryn exiting. Ahead of her, a large nurse runs toward us and drops to one knee. "Mr. Lucas . . ."

"He is having a seizure," I say.

"I can see that," she replies, with some annoyance in her voice. She looks at the balls. "He was juggling, wasn't he?"

"Yes, quite well."

"Damn!" she says. She looks at the crowd around us. "Step back, please. Give him room." She places a hand on his forehead. "It's okay, Mr. Lucas, you'll get through."

"How did juggling cause a seizure?" I ask.

"It doesn't every time," she answers, "but sometimes . . . He had a head injury doing acrobatic work in the circus."

"Ah," I say. "Perhaps a hippocampal lesion?"

"That's right." She looks at me. "How did you know?"

"Your facility is a memory clinic," I explain. "A hippocampal lesion can cause loss of ability to form long-term memories. In some reported cases there can also be seizures when a patient performs in ways that involve combinations of memory and motor skills."

"That's right," she says. She looks back at Kathryn. "He does know his stuff. Or she? Or . . ."

"'It' will do," I say. "I try to keep up with the latest research. Does he need medical attention?"

"No." The nurse shakes her head. "Just time. Some days he gets the seizures, but some days he doesn't. Juggling relaxes him. I would hate to take that away . . ."

Luke starts to stir. He sees the nurse looming over him,

and then he turns to me. "You called Nurse Ratched on me? And you call yourself my friend . . ."

"It's Nurse Rayburn," she answers. "And your friend here . . ."

"Bo," I say.

"Bo kept you from getting hurt."

"He's my partner," Luke says. "Partners always look after each other." And then his face clouds. "Where have you been, Bo?"

"Traveling," I say.

"With the old show?"

Nurse Rayburn shakes her head slightly, and I say, "No, just seeing the world."

"It's good to have you back, Bo. Nobody around this place has any act worth seeing. It's hard to put on a decent circus with just one juggler. Maybe now, with the two of us, management can get backing to add some new acts."

"We do have got a pretty good act," I say.

"Yeah, help me up here." Nurse Rayburn nods slightly, so I reach down my hand and help Luke to his feet. "Hey, Nurse Ratched!"

Nurse Rayburn rolls her eyes. "Yes, Mr. Lucas?"

"Isn't it about time to eat around here? I'm pretty hungry."

"That's a good sign," she says.

"Come on, Bo," Luke says to me. "The food here is better than the old chow wagon. Let's have a bite to eat."

"I'm not hungry," I say. "But perhaps I could . . ." Nurse Rayburn nods. "Perhaps I can join you."

"That would be great, Bo. It'll be good to talk about old

times with someone who was there and can appreciate life with the circus."

I don't want him to get his expectations too high, so I say, "My memory is kind of vague, Luke. I don't remember a lot of that, but I'd love to hear it again."

"Oh, yeah, you'll remember. As soon as I start telling you the stories, you'll remember. Life with the circus is one long uninterrupted deeeelight!"

I take Luke's right arm, and Nurse Rayburn takes the left. We do not hold him up, but we are ready to grab him just in case.

It is pleasant to work with Nurse Rayburn. I have not worked with skilled nurses since Nurse Judy, before Mildred passed away. They have a body language, facial expressions and simple gestures based on shared experience with patients. I can tell what she means without her having to say it.

"Ummm . . . 'Bo' . . ." I turn. Kathryn is walking beside me. "I have to get back to work. Will you be all right here?"

Nurse Rayburn smiles at her. "He . . . It will be fine. I'll find it a ride home after lunch. We'll need time to talk."

"Yes," I say. "Thank you, Kathryn. I am grateful." Kathryn returns to her car, and she leaves.

Nurse Rayburn and I guide Luke into the east wing and to a dining hall that lies just inside the entry. It is a clean, well-lit place with tables spaced far apart to allow room for wheelchairs. Bright blue linens cover each table, and each place is set with matching white and blue plates and coffee cups.

Other residents are already assembling. Some are seated at tables, some are wheeling in or walking in, some of those with assist suits. Nurses move back and forth among the tables, helping residents get settled. Servers take orders at some of the tables.

"Over here, Bo," Luke says. "You can sit at our table. You'll be the hit of lunch."

I look around. Each table is large enough for six diners, and we have eight—nine counting myself. "Luke, we will not all fit."

"Oh, don't worry about that," Luke says. "Pete, Linda, and I can pull another table over." Luke goes over to the table next to ours and starts to pull them together.

"I have this," I say, joining Luke before anyone else can. Together, we close the gap between the tables.

Nurse Rayburn says, "This is not allowed. You know that, Mr. Lucas."

"Ah, screw it," Luke says. "What are you going to do, throw me out? You know everybody's going to want to talk to the guest."

He seems to be right. As our group sits, others start coming up, and Luke introduces "Bo" around. Soon we pull a third table in, and residents crowd together as close as their assist suits and wheelchairs allow. They tell me their names; and the advantage of an android memory is that I do not forget any of them, nor their faces. All go into my emulation net.

Over lunch they share stories. I can tell through my empathy net that most of them have heard most of these stories multiple times. There is a sense of distraction, of tedium, as they listen. But as each one talks directly to me, their eyes light up, and it is like when my neural nets engage and I wake up. They tell me of the work they have done, of the places they have lived. Luke tells a number of stories of the circus, and he is a good storyteller. Even those who have surely heard these stories before laugh at all the right places.

Auralee, a thin, fit woman, tells me of her time in the space program. She was an engineer on moon flights. She still rattles off numbers, specs, dates, and trajectories as if it were yesterday. All of this data is boring the rest of the table, but I file it away. I do not know what her memory impairment may be, but it has not affected her math skills.

But the most common topic of conversation is family. Parents and aunts and uncles and grandparents, but especially children; and those stories make a complicated impression on my empathy net. There is pride, there is love, but there is also sadness—even bitterness—and I recognize this from my time with Mildred. Sadness, because they miss their families. I remember Mildred longing for people who were not there—some who would never be again. I remember emulating family members for her and how much joy it brought her to have visitors. Luke and the rest make such a big deal of me joining them for lunch. I wonder just how often they have visitors.

My emulation net starts to ripple with the possibility of emulating their missing families, but I override that. Mildred was a single patient. I could be who she needed. But here there are too many patients. Some are in good mental shape. There are some who slur their words a bit, a stutter here and there. But there are too many with diagnosable memory troubles and delusions. I imagine myself flickering from identity to identity in a futile effort to be everything for everyone; and I cannot see that ending well. Even I may emulate only one person at a time, so I remain as Bo.

But in place of emulation, I do the next best thing: I listen, and I encourage the stories. These residents miss their families, and I understand that all too well.

After an hour, android staff appear to clean up the dishes. They stand patiently by our tables. Nurse Rayburn waves them away. "We're in no rush here," she says. From the smile on her face, the tilt of her head, and the tone of her voice, I can see that she is happy because her residents are happy, and she cares for them very deeply. I decide that Nurse Rayburn is a good woman, but she is tired from so much worry.

Eventually all the food is gone and the android staff clear away the dishes. The residents start leaving the table, one or two at a time, most saying goodbye to me as they go. Soon the androids pull the tables to their original positions, and all that are left are Luke and myself and an old woman in a wheelchair. She has not spoken throughout the lunch. Luke looks at her and smiles. "How are you today, Mrs. Carruthers?"

Her hair is a sparse mat, straightened and colored, but it does not look natural for her. Her arms are barely thicker than the wheelchair armrests on which they lay. Her whole body is frail, like Mildred was toward the end. Her face sags on the left side, and so her words are slurred when she says, "I'm okay, Mr. Lucas." There are many pauses in those few words.

"Did you enjoy lunch?"

"Uh," she says. "Slop."

"I'm sorry, Mrs. Carruthers. Did you want me to find you something else?"

"I'm fine," she says.

But Luke persists. "Some Jell-O, perhaps? Let's see if you can have some Jell-O." He leaves the table and heads to the kitchen, and I am alone at the table with Mrs. Carruthers.

She looks at me, and the right side of her face droops in a frown to match her left. "Don't like metal men," she says.

"I am sorry, Mrs. Carruthers. I shall leave."

But she continues as if she hasn't heard me. "Not natural. Metal. I had a metal dog once. Not right. Wag its tail, sniff, and bark, but not a dog."

"I understand, Mrs. Carruthers."

"Not a dog! It does tricks, but it never eats. It never shits in the house. Not a dog. They told me it was, but . . ." She swallows, and continues. "I had a dog once. *That* was a dog. Big . . . big collie. Friendly. Wag her tail, the whole body wagged. She came up, licked my face. She loved me. Metal dog can't love me."

"I am sorry, Mrs. Carruthers. You are right. Mechanical devices have no feelings, but we do try to help."

"No love. No hate. Don't get sad." A tear runs down her cheek. "Don't get sad."

She shifts her hand on the wheelchair controller, and the chair backs away from the table. She rolls out of the room without another word.

She is wrong. I find that I do get sad. For her.

Mrs. Carruthers has disappeared in the hallway when Luke returns with Jell-O. "She left?"

"I do not think she likes me, Luke."

"She doesn't like anybody. She'll warm up to you in time."

"I am not sure, Luke. She does not like . . ." I do not know how to finish.

". . . Mechanical devices?" Luke says. He half grins at me. "You're not from the circus. I was confused. One of my bad days. But I'm feeling much better now. You're . . . some kind of robot, ain't ya?"

"An android," I correct him.

"You're not Bo. But . . . you remind me of him. It's . . . easier for me if I think of you as him. You have another name?"

"Carey," I say.

"Carey." He works his mouth as if tasting the word. "Carey . . . Sounds like a girl's name. Nope, I probably won't remember that. Hope you don't mind if I slip and call you Bo."

"If that makes you comfortable."

Luke smiles. "Come on, let's go take Mrs. Carruthers her Jell-O."

"I do not know if I should, Luke. Am I allowed to visit her?"

"The more visitors around here, the better." Luke leads me to the hallway. Mrs. Carruthers has not gone far. Her wheelchair is moving at barely a walking pace.

Luke calls out, "Hey, Mrs. Carruthers, you forgot your Jell-O."

She does not look up. I notice her face has grown more

pale in the brief time I have observed her. I grab her finger. She weakly tugs it away, so I grab it again. Her pulse ox is very low, eighty-three. "Luke, get a nurse. She needs oxygen."

"Vera!" Luke calls. "Vera, we need help here."

Nurse Rayburn comes running. She sees me bent over Mrs. Carruthers, and she says, "Oh, you can't touch the residents."

"Her pulse ox." I check again. "It is eighty-two."

Nurse Rayburn looks at Mrs. Carruthers's pale skin and blue lips. "Oh, my. Kathy, give me some oxygen!" She checks Mrs. Carruthers's pulse. "Come on, Mrs. Carruthers, come on." She rubs Mrs. Carruthers's hands. "So cold."

Another nurse rushes up with an oxygen tank and a mask. "Let's get her into her bed," she says. "We'll have to tent her."

The two nurses take Mrs. Carruthers away in her chair. Luke and I stand, watching. I am concerned for Mrs. Carruthers, but Luke holds out a cup to me. "Do you want some Jell-O? Nah, I didn't think so." Then he digs the spoon in and eats it himself.

When the Jell-O is gone, Luke says, "Feel kind of silly standing here in this hall. Let's go to my room. I can show you what a circus is all about."

In his room, Luke shows me old-fashioned paper pictures from the circus he once worked with. They are without a doubt the most colorfully garbed people I have seen anywhere. A few of the costumes remind me of the outfits in Belize, but even the Belizeans did not have so much variety.

Luke shows me pictures of his acrobatic act. "Juggling

is just a sideline," he says. His pictures also include his brother, his parents, and an aunt. They were an acrobatic team. "The whole family was part of the circus. No, the circus *was* my whole family. Some by blood and some by sweat and toil, grease paint and sawdust. And now the circus is gone. Oh, there may be a tent show here and there, but they already have all the acts they need. No one needs an old acrobat like me. No one."

I hear a deeper sadness in his voice, and I wish I knew what to say; but before I can respond, Nurse Rayburn appears in the doorway. "Yes?" Luke asks.

"It's Mrs. Carruthers," she answers. I can see from the blank look on Luke's face that he has already forgotten the incident. Nurse Rayburn senses it as well, and she turns to me.

"I can't go into details," she says. "Privacy laws." I sympathize. I know all too well the limitations of privacy laws. But then she adds, "She'll be okay for now. It's a good thing you called us. She was getting cyanotic. We have her tented now."

"I am glad," I say.

"As for you, Bo . . . You saved her life; but I looked up your registration number, BRKCX-01932-217JH-98662. You are over twenty-five years old, and you were decertified for medical upgrades over a decade ago."

"But all of my knowledge is still up to date," I say. "I can verify that if you'd like to test me."

"I believe you, but liability matters here. Mrs. Carruthers won't care, but if her family were to find out that you were diagnosing her, well, there could be a lawsuit."

Luke shakes his head. "When was the last time any of her family has been here?"

"Almost two years," she answers.

Luke scowls. "Christ, no wonder she's so bitter. When did *any* of our family ever come here?"

"A few now and then," Nurse Rayburn answers. I sense her sorrow. It is not fresh, it is something she has learned to live with. "You're not wrong, Mr. Lucas." She turns back to me. "So thank you for saving her life; but in the future, you can't touch any patients in this facility. Same rules as any of our androids on staff. They can't do any job that involves contact with a resident."

"He ain't like those others, Vera," Luke protests. "You must've figured that out by now."

"It's still an android."

"All right," Luke says, "but what if he wants to help in other ways? Noncontact work?"

"That's what I'm thinking, Bo," she says. "You're good for this place. You care, I can tell."

I answer, "I am a caretaker."

"I think you could do a lot of good around here," she answers. "Over time, maybe I can convince the management to let you do more." She pauses and looks away. "But . . . Ummm . . . We don't have money to lease you."

"I am not for lease," I answer. "I work where I choose."

"OK, well, we don't have money to pay you, either. But we're always looking for volunteers."

"What do you say, Bo?" Luke asks. "Do you have anything better to do with your time?"

I had already answered that when I started this day. I

need a purpose. I need someone to care for, and these residents need someone who can care.

"All right," I say. "Nurse Rayburn, I cannot promise how long I will be available, but I would like to help out."

"That's the spirit," Luke says, throwing an arm around my shoulder.

"Hey!" Nurse Rayburn says. "I said no contact."

"He's not touching me," Luke says. "I'm touching Bo, my partner."

28. TODAY I TAKE DELIVERY

It will take time for Nurse Rayburn to persuade her management to let me be a volunteer; so for a few days, I stay home and straighten up the garage. Paul has told me where he wants the building supplies stored while we work, and I need to clear that space out. Bicycles, wagons, garden tools, a rototiller, hoses—so much is piled up in that part of the garage. Susan often jokes with Paul about the garage they can never park in. It seems a shame to me that now they will clear it out only to put something else in it that is not a car.

Susan has ordered construction supplies for the remodeling effort; but she is at the school when the delivery truck arrives, so I greet the driver at the door. "Mrs. Owens?" he asks, and then he looks up from his tablet at me. "Oh, you're not Mrs. Owens."

"No, I am Carey Owens, their medical care android."

"Is Mrs. Owens around? Mr. Owens?"

"No, they are both at work."

"Now that's a problem," the driver answers. "I need one of them to sign for this. I spent a lot of juice getting out here. Delivery's free, but if I have to take it back, they're going to get hit with a twenty percent restock fee. And then they'll get charged for delivery if I bring it back out again."

"I am sorry. They did not know this."

"People never read the fine print," he says, rubbing his chin and looking at his tablet. "Do you know when they'll be home?"

I check their schedules. "No less than three hours from now, possibly longer."

"Three hours . . ." Then he looks at me funny. "You said your name is Carey Owens?"

"Yes."

He holds out his tablet. "Could you sign that right here?"

"Sign?"

"Your name. Right in here."

"Would that be proper?"

He scratches his head. "Look pal, if you got a signature, I got a load for you. If you don't tell the bosses that you're a machine, I won't tell them. Nobody has to be the wiser."

"I have never signed for anything before."

"Well congratulations, this will be your first time. If you just sign right here, we can start unloading."

I take the tablet and the stylus, but I pause. Is this legal? Is my signature a valid release? But if it is not, the driver will be the only one at risk. He might get in trouble for delivering a load without authorization; but he seems to accept that, and it will save Paul and Susan a restocking and delivery fee.

I know of no law that I am breaking, so I sign the tablet.

"Very neat handwriting," the driver says. "All right, pal, where do you want it?" I lead him to the garage and open the door. The truck is already backed up close to the garage. The driver pushes a button, and a gate slowly folds down.

"So we go into the truck?" I ask.

"Nah," he says, "this is a modern operation. We got robots for that. Let them do the hard work. That's what they're good at." Then he looks back at me. "Sorry, no offense."

"I cannot be offended," I assure him.

"All right, Carey, sit back and let my boys do the work."

The rear truck door opens, sliding up into the ceiling of the truck. Standing behind it are four robots, cylinders almost as high as my shoulders, each with four strong manipulator arms. I look at those, and I wonder what Colonel Rejón in Belize would think of them. They are much stronger than me, and four arms would make them more dangerous, especially if they had weapons. They are also more durably armored than me. If he thought I was a threat, I could only imagine his response to these.

In only one way do I see myself physically superior to them—they are all on rollers, while I have feet. Feet make it easier to go in more places. Mentally, though . . . I look up their model numbers. They are modern devices, simply controlled by a central unit. They have no neural nets, not even binary.

Two of the robots roll out onto the lift gate, which then drops down to the ground. The other two stay inside and start passing out bundles of supplies.

"Back up," the driver says. "Give them room. The boys are strong, but they aren't always bright."

"I am sure that they have safety protocols built in," I say.

"Yeah, they have safety protocols. They have good gyros, good stability, but even a robot can make a mistake now and then. So it's a safety rule. I have to keep all people away from the truck when they're unloading. And I guess for this, I'll call you a people, too. So come on, let's back away."

We move back, and I watch the robots do their work quickly and efficiently. In under ten minutes, all of Susan's order has been unloaded, scanned, and confirmed. I am impressed. As simple as these models are, they are very efficient in their job—far more so than the driver and I would have been. They did their work efficiently, well, and safely. I wonder if somewhere inside their control networks this gives them satisfaction.

29. TODAY WE START REMODELING

The next two days are the weekend; and though Paul always has some work to do, the three of us spend the entire time tearing apart the room. First we remove the existing baseboards and molding and frames, and then we tear down the drywall. I am surprised how complicated this task is. I would have thought that even though construction is a skill, destruction should be a simple matter for a self-aware android such as myself. It is just a matter of destroying and removing, yes? But the first time I try to pull down a section of the wall, it crumbles, and dust flies everywhere.

Paul looks at the result and grins. "Not so much force," he says. "It all has to be destroyed eventually, but it's easier if we can take it down in bigger chunks. Pull gently at the pieces. Toss them in the bin over there. But here," he hands me a dustpan and a whisk broom. "Clean up the mess first."

After I have swept up the dust and dumped it in the bin, I watch how Susan and Paul work at this: slower, methodically trying to break off the biggest chunks of drywall they can. I emulate Susan slightly to try to borrow her deft touch at this, and soon I have learned how to get the largest possible pieces.

Eventually the room is an empty shell with studs showing behind the drywall. I am fascinated by this. I have never considered building construction before. It has not been one of my concerns. I see now how simple yet effective the design is. Wooden studs, weathered and old but strong, spaced at approximately thirty centimeters. They provide a solid skeleton for the room, much like my own internal skeletal system, though more durable and not so flexible. Then drywall had been nailed to the studs, and then painted and papered over.

"All right, let's get the nails," Paul says.

Susan hands me a claw hammer and shows me how to pull nails. "Again, slow and firm," she says. "No rush, slow down. If you seat the claw firmly and pull gently," she demonstrates, "the nail pops right out." And it does. "If you go too fast, you're liable to break one of these old nails or bend the head. If that happens, call me over. Don't try to fix it. Let me show you how. You can make it worse."

By the end of the day, we have the room stripped clean and all the plaster dust swept up. Susan orders pizza, and we stop for the night.

The next day we pull up the old carpet and then the wooden floor underneath. Paul and Susan look at the floor joists under the plywood. Susan shakes her head. "They're as bad as in Anna's room," she says.

"You think so?" Paul asks.

"Yeah, we have to replace these as well."

"Well, that's not going to happen today, so let's go out and get some lumber ordered."

The next day is Monday, my first day as a volunteer at Creekside Home. Susan goes with me. A delivery driver may accept my signature, but Creekside still expects Susan to cosign my agreements.

But as we enter through the dining room, I can see that Susan is nervous. So many patients, with such a range of mental impairments, are reviving her old fears. She cannot bring herself to look at them.

"Will you be all right, Susan?" I ask.

She glances around, and then looks down. "I feel awful for them."

I take her hand. "I know. That's why I want to help." I look up, and I see Nurse Rayburn approaching. "Nurse, can we do this paperwork in the office, please?"

"Certainly, Carey," she says, and she leads us to the office. We sit inside, and we both sign paperwork. When we're done, Nurse Rayburn files it in the system, and I escort Susan back to her car.

Then I return to the home, and I start my first day as a volunteer. Greg, one of the orderlies, shows me the facilities: the kitchen, the storerooms, the therapy rooms, the showers, the medical ward, and the common rooms. In each, we go over the responsibilities I might perform there, and Greg introduces me to the rest of the staff.

Greg also introduces me to the residents, though many know me from my previous visit, and others have heard word of me. Like Mrs. Carruthers, a few distrust me at first; but many are happy to have someone new to talk to. I file away names and stories, building new empathy profiles throughout the day.

Although I am not authorized to access their medical records, I soon learn the conditions of most of the residents. One of their favorite topics is their health and their ailments, their medicines and their procedures, and complaints about all of the above. I listen respectfully and nod encouragement now and then. I understand that at their age, maintaining their health takes regular attention; so it is naturally on their minds. Plus, for many of them, as with their stories, just having someone listen to their concerns gives them some relief. If listening to their problems is all I can do to help, then I shall be the best listener that I can be.

There is so much work for me here. Even though some of the residents are in sad conditions, it is good to feel needed again.

30. TODAY I AM SURPRISED

Two days later, the same delivery driver appears at the door. "Hey, Carey," he says. "Got another load here." He hands me the tablet as if it were the most natural thing to do, and I sign just as naturally. Then his robots unload the joists. Susan is here, but I do not think to call her. She comes out as I am closing the garage door. The driver nods, tips his hat to her, and drives away.

Then I haul two joists upstairs and Susan begins explaining to me the difficult task of removing and replacing and shoring up floor joists in an existing structure. It takes the rest of the week for us to do the job to her satisfaction. We settle into a new routine: All three of us go to our daily workplaces, with Paul taking me to and from Creekside; and then in the evening, one of us gets dinner while the other two remodel.

On the weekend Paul and I haul up plywood while Susan nails the sheets into place. By late Sunday night, the floor is entirely replaced. Paul and Susan lean against each other in the doorway, inspecting their work, while I carefully pace around the room listening for squeaks. "There are none to be found," I say.

Paul squeezes Susan. "Good job, dear." She leans in and kisses him, and we go downstairs for dinner.

The project is put on hold after that. It is another three days before the window people arrive to replace the windows. The new windows are high-efficiency with self-polarizing glass, allowing you to dial in a level of lightness.

I ask if we are going to continue now. Susan shakes her head. "We're still waiting for the electricians to run new lines."

"Paul expects to have a lot of electronic equipment in here?"

"Oh, we need to modernize the whole thing. So many devices that weren't around when this house was built originally. We have to have power for all of them."

The electricians arrive on Friday before we leave for work. Susan has already sent them 3D recordings of the room and her specifications, so they arrive with cabling diagrams and material ready to go. They set to work as we leave.

The next day Susan proclaims to be Drywall Weekend. Paul and I haul up the first bundle of sheets and set it in the room. I see now that the electricians have strung new power and data lines, twice as many as the room originally held, plus an extra cluster in the closet. I wonder what sort of work Paul plans to do in that room; but before I can ask, we start to work on the drywall. Paul and I carefully measure and align sheets, cutting where necessary, while Susan hammers them in place. It is hard work, but not complicated. Susan and Paul know what they are doing, and I learn quickly. There is little to distract them, so we spend the weekend in deep conversation as they work. They bounce around from topic to topic: Belize, the wedding, Anna's wedding, Susan's school, Paul's work, his latest projects, my work at Creekside, their own wedding, raising the kids, how much Mildred would have liked the room, Paul's brother, world affairs. Paul's old interest in sailing has returned after the trip to Belize, and Susan encourages him to join a sailing club. Paul reminds Susan of songs that he enjoys, and she sings them. They find so much to talk about as they work.

I sense that they are pleased with a job to do, with the immediate satisfaction of seeing the results. Pleased to look on their work and know that they have done it well. This I understand without resorting to empathy. Just as I take satisfaction with learning and doing my job at Creekside Home, humans appreciate doing a task well, and will strive to do better. At least these humans do. I wonder: Does this make them like androids, or does it mean I am more like them than I have realized?

On Monday evening, Susan teaches me to paint. It is a seemingly simple task: Dip in the brush, smoothly apply a layer. We start with the upper layer, the off-white, and I set to work while Susan takes a call for the school. Ninety minutes later, she returns to the room. "Carey," she says, "you're going much too slowly. The room will take forever at this rate."

I carefully set the brush back down on the paint pan. "I am sorry, Susan. I am trying to be careful."

"I know," she says, "I told you to. Make it even, no streaks. But you don't have to be *that* careful."

Susan takes the brush, dips it into the paint farther than

I had, and then makes much larger, faster strokes with it. I look. "Susan, it is not even."

"Sure it is."

"No, look here."

"You're right, but that's not enough of a problem to bother with. That'll be taken care of with a second coat. You need to make it good, you don't need to make it perfect. Human good, not android good."

Even after decades living among humans, judgment still eludes me. I still see so much of the world as binary rules. But in time I have learned to emulate the judgment of others. "I will try."

"Good. I've got two more calls, and then I'll join you."

We finish the first coat that day just in time for Paul to come in, look it over, and nod approvingly. The next day, we apply the second; and then we begin on the lower paint on Wednesday. The paint is finished and dried by Friday. On Saturday, we put up the border. This task is the simplest we have taken on, and it is done only halfway through the day. We go downstairs, and I make lunch for Paul and Susan. We dine on the patio in the garden. After lunch, we start on the baseboards, the trim, and the molding.

By late Sunday, the shell looks complete. Paul and I install a new overhead light, a large white fixture that looks like clouds. And when that is done, we take the stepladder out. Then the three of us go in to inspect the room.

"Looks really good," Paul says.

"We make a great team." Susan hugs him and pats my arm.

I look over at the doorway. The door is still detached.

"So all we have to do is put the door on and we are done? You can move your things in?"

Paul shakes his head, and Susan smiles broadly. "We can't put the door on until the MCA team is done," Paul says.

His comment confuses me. "The MCA team?"

"Yes, they'll be here tomorrow to move your charging station into the closet."

I am still confused. "Paul, you want me to have my charging station in your office?"

Now it is Paul who grins. "Not my office. *Your* room."

"My room?"

Susan lets go of Paul and comes over and hugs me. "Your room, Carey. It's past time we got you out of that dank old laundry room, and up here where you belong."

"But the laundry room is sufficient for my purposes."

"Your purposes aren't fixed, Carey," she says. "You've grown so much since you came into our lives. In every way that matters to us, you're a person. And people don't live in laundry rooms."

"But it is such a waste of space. I only need the closet."

"We have the space," Susan replies. "Don't worry about waste. It's your space. You'll fill it. You'll make it useful."

"Fill it? With what?"

"With whatever you want."

"I do not want—" I start to speak, but Susan holds up a hand to silence me.

"Yes, we've heard it before, Carey," she says. "Maybe it's time you start figuring out what you want. This is your space, and now you can decorate it more with whatever you like."

"But I have nothing to fill it with."

"And that's another thing," Paul says. "Carey, I've been crunching the numbers, and you have long since worked off what we paid for you including the original lease payments. Between cooking and cleaning—before the cleaning bots came along—taking care of Millie, taking care of Mom, let's not forget that."

I object, "You already paid MCA for your mother's care."

"Yes, but they didn't pay you. All this work, it adds up to quite a sum."

"You have provided me power, and you have paid for my regular maintenance."

"Yes, I factored that in. But the fact is, Carey, by my estimation, we owe you a whole lot of money."

I shake my head. "You have told me that I am family. As I understand the term, family does not pay family for helping each other."

"He's got you there," Susan says. "But you know what else, Carey? Family shares in what the family earns as well as how the family works. Your power, your maintenance costs, they don't begin to add up to how much you do for this family, and how much of a pleasure it is to have you around."

"She's right," Paul says, "but you're right, too. We won't pay you for this work, but we *will* give you an allowance."

"An allowance?" I ask.

"You remember. Millie had one when she was growing up. It's your portion of the family budget to do with what you will, plus a significant back payment long overdue. I'll have the accountants set it up tomorrow and give you the codes so you can order what you like for the room, and do whatever else you find to do with the allowance."

I am still confused by this concept, but I know the proper thing to say. "Thank you, Susan. Thank you, Paul."

Paul replies, "Now we're going to go clean up and make our own dinner for once."

"If you still remember how," Susan says.

"Love, I will make you a dinner so good you'll forget all about Carey." Then he looks at me. "That's a joke. Meanwhile, you start thinking about what you'd like in your room."

31. TODAY I EXPERIENCE THE MIRACLE OF LIFE

"Oh, Carey, it's perfect," Millie says, looking down at the polished mahogany bassinet with the frog sheets on the mattresses. "But we already have a bassinet."

"I know," I say to Millie. Then I notice the strain in her face. "Come, sit down, please." I assist her to drop gently into the easy chair in the corner of my room. At thirty-four weeks pregnant, she finds it a little more difficult to get up and down every day. "I saw the bassinet you got from Susan and Paul," I explain. "But this is for my room when you bring the baby over and need someplace to put him down for a nap."

She looks up at me and smiles, her old impish grin. "Silly Mr. Robot. You didn't have to give up space in your room for my baby."

"It is my space," I say. "I can do with it what I want."

Looking around, I am pleased with the choices I have made over the past five years. It took me weeks to finally decide what I wanted. I looked at how others used their rooms. In some cases, their room is an escape from the rest of the world. A private place where they can relax.

But I had that already, even when I was down in the laundry room. I am never more relaxed than when I'm in my recharging station, rebalancing my networks. I need no more space for that.

But other times one's personal room is where one entertains only the closest friends and family—those you would entertain not in the public areas of the house but in confidence, in private. I decided that that was the purpose for which I could use a room of my own; and for that, I wanted a place that was inviting to my family, to those I would entertain here.

The room's colors and fixtures have a nautical theme that reminds me of Belize. The door knob and window controls are shaped like sailing knots, and that seems to please Paul. So I had ordered pictures to hang on the walls, pictures of sailing ships and the islands. To those I added a wedding picture of the family in Our Lady of Assumption, as well as pictures of Anna and the boys and Vishal from their last visit to the States. I had also ordered new wall lamps shaped like ship wheels with lights like oil lamps attached.

I had done more than purchase things; I had asked for mementos. A couple of Mildred's old statues that had been on a shelf by her bed while she had been alive. Jake's old terrarium, which Millie and I have again stocked with frogs. An old brass compass from a sailboat that Paul refitted. A vase that Susan had made in her pottery class (I always kept it filled with fresh flowers). And for Susan's comfort, I had a high-end music system keyed to her presence so it would always play her favorite songs when she came into the room.

And then there are gifts that Millie has given me over the years: pictures and plaques and toys, each carefully preserved. And first among these is one memento that is uniquely mine: my blue Christmas stocking hangs in front of my closet, so that it is the first thing that I see when I awaken in my charging station.

I also have comfortable family furniture. An easy chair and a short couch with a foot rest. A coffee table and end tables hold the pictures and mementos. And now with Millie soon to give birth to another grandchild in the family, I have the bassinet. Susan had said I should furnish the room so it felt like home to me. These things in this place are what I associate with home.

"Are you all right, Millie?" I ask. Her face still looks strained. "Should I get you some tea?"

"Oh, some green tea would be wonderful, Carey, but you don't have to bother. I can get it myself."

"You will do nothing of the sort," I say. "I know you are stubborn and strong-willed; but with the condition you are in, I can go down and get the tea and be back faster than you can get out of that chair."

"Oh, yeah?" She puts her hands on the armrest and starts to leverage herself up. But then she stops. "Whoa . . . Whoa . . . All right, you win this one, Carey, but only for another few weeks. After that I'll take care of myself again, *and* the baby."

I go downstairs. The tea is already brewing. I had known Millie would want some. In a minute it is ready. I put the pot on Mildred's old oak tray, and I add one of Mildred's fine china cups on a matching plate. I get the cream pitcher from the refrigerator, and then I go back upstairs and set the tray down next to Millie. She pours cream in the cup and then pours the tea in.

"And of course you'll have help from Wayne," I continue as if there had been no break in the conversation.

"Oh, Wayne," Millie says. "I'm sure he'll be a help." I detect concern, but I am not sure if she wants to talk or not. Sometimes it is difficult to tell with her. Her mood can change quickly.

But I try. "Wayne is not being helpful?"

"Oh, that's not what I meant, Carey. No, it's just he's going to be taking family leave when the baby is born, and he has so many new projects going on. Wayne has advanced their knowledge so much from studying you. He has reintroduced things that the company has forgotten. Dr. Zinta hasn't forgotten, of course, but she's so busy now running the place. She's more of an administrator than a researcher at this point."

"I know," I say. "That makes her very sad. She misses the research."

"I know. Wayne looks at her and he makes me promise to never let him make that mistake of going into management. So anyway, she might know these things, but her team doesn't. There's been so much turnover in the years. Wayne's now third most senior in the department, second if you exclude Dr. Zinta. So he's trying to teach all these old tricks to the new dogs and get them to understand techniques that haven't been taught in cybernetic schools in over a decade. He has so much he wants to get done before the leave begins. He's been working long hours, and now he's off to this conference, and the timing on this . . ."

I wonder what she means. "What is wrong with the timing?"

"Well, he's in Seattle, and Mom and Dad are off on their second honeymoon in Belize because they want that out of the way before Junior comes along."

"That seems like smart planning on their part as well. Everyone will be able to help you out when the time comes."

"I know, but there's so much that I would like help with *now*. I have to get ready myself, plus I still have to get things in shape for my leave so the university can put another instructor in to cover my lectures and labs."

"So you are tired and you need help and no one is here to help you."

"Well, you are, of course, Carey. You're always here. What would I do without you? But I could use someone helping around the house."

"Millie, are you asking me to move in with you and Wayne?"

"I can't ask that. You have so much to do here. And at Creekside."

"Millie, now who is being silly? Your mother and father are not even home right now, and they are still not so old that they cannot get by without me. They have cleaning bots, and the house today is so automated that there is hardly anything for me to do unless we find new projects to work on. And I can take a leave at Creekside. It is not like I am a machine; I get time off."

Millie grinned. "I know but—"

"But nothing," I interrupt. "I insist. Immediately. I will turn the house over to automatic, and I will go to your house with you tonight. I will contact Nurse Rayburn on the way."

"Shouldn't you check with Mom and Dad?"

"They told me years ago: In their eyes I am an adult person, able to make my own decisions. If I chose to leave they would throw me a big going away party, and they would miss me, but they would not try to stop me. And for this, *they* would be at your house if you would let them."

"Oh, I couldn't take *that!*" Millie grins. "That much Mom in that small space . . ." Then she looks concerned. "Oops! Don't tell her I said that, Carey."

"Patient-therapist confidentiality, you know that. Now finish your tea and let us get packing. I still have the portable charging station we took to Belize. That is all I will need. My books," I tap my head, "are all up here." Then I stop and tap my torso. "Well, the library is in here, but you know what I mean."

Millie laughs; but then her face twists. "Hah," she adds. "Junior is kicking again. He wants to go home, too, so let's go."

After I help Millie down the stairs and into her coat, I take the portable charging station from its storage area in the laundry room and out to her car. "Trunk open," I say, but nothing happens. I try emulating Wayne enough to say in his voice, "Trunk open." The trunk opens and I put the charging station in it next to blankets and water and other emergency supplies. I wonder whether I could emulate Millie well enough to fool the car to make it take instructions from me. No one drives cars anymore except for old antiques, museum relics like myself; but you still must be the authorized owner or designated driver to instruct them where to go. Driving is an experiment I will have to try some day.

There is snow in the air, and the walk is getting slippery. I go back into the house, take Millie's arm, and carefully guide her out the door and down the steps. I gently lower her into the car, and then I get in beside her.

Millie says, "Bullfrog," and the control panel lights up with an animated bullfrog in a chauffeur's cap.

"Yes ma'am," the chauffeur answers.

"Take us home, please."

"There will be some delay, ma'am," the chauffeur says. "Road reports are slow and slippery."

"That's okay. Just as long as we're safe. That's what's important."

The snow falls more thickly in the air with each passing minute. It is good that the car's GPS keeps it in the proper lane. No human driver could even see the lane in these conditions.

"Are you all right, Millie?" I ask. The strain on her face has increased.

"I'm fine, Carey. I'll just be glad to be home."

"We will get there," I say. "The cars are slowing down because of conditions, but we will get there soon enough."

But at that moment, the console chimes and the chauffeur appears. "Redirecting to a new course," it says.

"A new course?" I ask. "Why?"

The screen shifts to a traffic map, and I see red lines and red flashing lights all along the highway. "Police report slippery conditions. Numerous slide offs and accidents on U.S. 131. They recommend alternate routes.

I project that they will soon be closing that highway entirely."

"All right, choose the safest route you can," I say.

"I always do," the chauffeur responds. "Don't be afraid."

I understand fear as an abstraction, but it is not one of my prominent emotions. I understand concern and worry, but fear is more visceral, while I am analytical. But the part of me that emulates Wayne to communicate with the chauffeur is very afraid, and continues to be so as the snow piles up on the roads.

We slow down yet further. At one point, I feel the car veer sideways. "What is happening?"

"Just a slippery patch," the chauffeur says. "We are under control." And indeed, we are back on track already.

I look over at Millie, and her face is pale. She is nervous. "Millie, are you all right?"

"Carey, maybe we should go back to Mom and Dad's."

"All right, Millie. Chauffeur, new destination. Take us back to the home of Paul and Susan Owens."

"Yes sir. As soon as I can find a safe turnaround."

The car continues on for another mile before coming to a stop at a stop sign. Then the chauffeur screen lights up again. "I need guidance," it says.

"What?" I ask.

"I have not found a proper turnaround. I could turn around in this intersection, but that would violate local traffic laws."

"Would it be safe?" I ask.

"There is no oncoming traffic in any direction. The

intersection is very slippery, but if I take it slowly, it will be safe. Do you authorize violation of local traffic laws?"

"Yes, I do."

"State your name, please, for the record, in case there is an investigation."

I look at Millie. She should give the authorization, but her eyes are closed, so I respond, "Carey Owens."

"Carey Owens is not authorized to operate this vehicle. State your name, please."

I turn up my emulation. "Wayne Stockwell." I am uncomfortable with this deception, but I am concerned for Millie.

"Very well," the chauffeur responds. "Wayne Stockwell has authorized this car to do a U-turn in this intersection. It is so recorded."

The car rolls slowly forward, angling right and then turning in a large circle to the left. At last it is headed back to the south.

As we pick up speed Millie says, "Take me home, Carey."

I am confused. "Your home? We are headed toward Paul and Susan's."

"Yes, Mom and Dad's home, please."

"We are going there as fast as we safely can."

"That's good, Carey. Thank you."

But suddenly the car is sliding. It is the same slippery spot we had hit before on the way north. At that time, we had slid into the southbound lane. This time, we slide off to the west. "Emergency!" the chauffeur says. "Emergency! Active restraints engaged." Our seat belts and shoulder harnesses expand with sudden air pressure, and air bags fill the passenger compartment, locking us firmly in place as the chauffeur says, "Warning! This car is out of control. Warning!"

I feel the car thump against the guard rail. There is a sliding and scraping sound, and we slow. But suddenly the scraping is gone. The guard rail has ended. I feel the car tilt and then slide down a deep ditch. "Warning!" the chauffeur says. "Brace for impact. Calling nine-one-one."

Millie screams as we slide down the hill, out of control, picking up speed. I can barely see out around the air bags.

Then there is a loud thump as the car hits something, and it tumbles. As soon as it does, air bags emerge from the headliner as well, protecting our heads, but also blocking our vision. We are now completely immobile as the car rolls once, twice, and comes to a halt upside down. Over the crunch I hear the chauffeur, "Calling nine-one-one. Vehicle in the ditch. Biosensors detect no injuries."

"Millie, are you all right?" I ask.

She gasps. "I'm not hurt, but you need to get me out of here."

"Millie, that is not recommended. The storm outside is dangerous. It is better to stay in here, safe and warm, until we are rescued."

"No, get me out of these airbags, Carey."

"Millie, what is wrong?"

"Carey, I think I'm in labor."

"Millie, it is too soon."

"I know that, Carey! Don't tell me, tell Junior."

"You must stop."

"I thought you understood pregnancy, Carey. It's out of my control now."

I know the car has already called 911, but this is a new situation. I call as well.

A woman answers, "Nine-one-one, what is your emergency?"

"Our car is in a ditch," I say.

"Yes, we have that recorded. Your car reports no one injured. We'll get help there as soon as we can. In the meantime, stay safe and warm."

"You do not understand. Mildred Stockwell is pregnant. She is in labor."

"Oh, that's more complicated. Is she okay, Mr. Stockwell?"

I am not Wayne. My programming tells me to be truthful. Even when emulating, I must emulate as truthfully as I am able.

But I do not argue with her. If being Wayne will smooth the conversation, then today I am Wayne. "She is okay," I answer in his voice.

"And how far along is she?"

"Millie, how far along are you?"

"Thirty-four weeks, almost thirty-five."

"Between thirty-four and thirty-five weeks," I say.

"Mr. Stockwell, don't worry. Is this your first baby?"

"Yes, it is."

"First labor can take a long time. Just keep her warm and safe and comfortable. There are a lot of accidents out tonight, some with people in a lot worse shape than your wife. I know you're worried, but I'll get an ambulance there as soon as I can. Do you understand?"

"Yes."

"All right. Are you good now? I can stay on the line if

you need, but I've got more calls coming in. We're pretty busy here."

"No, we are okay."

"And Mr. Stockwell, before I let you go . . . I don't want to worry you."

"I do not worry," I say.

"There's the textbook and there's reality. If that baby decides it's coming early, you call right back. We'll have to talk you through the delivery."

"Thank you, I will." I disconnect, and I find the release to deflate my airbag so I can get some room. "All right, Millie," I say. "Everything is okay. They are sending an ambulance."

"Everything is *not* okay, Carey. I'm hanging here upside down. Get me down! *Get me down!*"

I deflate more airbags, giving me space to work. Then I kneel on the roof under Millie to deflate her airbags. As I do, I expand my silicone flesh to the maximum, giving her a soft cushion to land on. I catch her and then set her down on the ceiling, which is now our floor. "It is all right, Millie," I say. "They say first labor can take a long time. There is plenty of time for the ambulance to get here."

"I don't think so," she said. "Carey, I think that Junior is coming pretty soon."

"No, Millie, you have to wait for the ambulance."

"Ahhhh!" she screams. Then, panting for breath, she continues. "I can't cross my legs and hold it. This baby is coming, and you have to deliver it."

"Millie, I am not programmed for that."

"Well, you better get programmed quickly, Carey, because I need you."

I do not call 911 again. Instead, I call Dr. Zinta's private number. "Yes, Carey, what is it?"

"Dr. Zinta, I need an obstetrics module."

"What? Carey you know you're not certified for medical upgrades anymore."

"Dr. Zinta, please. Millie and I are crashed in a ditch. She is in labor, and there is no one around but me. Please, Dr. Zinta. I want this. I need this for Millie."

Dr. Zinta hesitates for only a moment, but then she says, "All right, let me tie into my system at work . . . There's the module . . . And there's your address . . . And it is flashing that you are not a valid address for this, particularly for this module . . . and I type in my override code . . ."

Just that quickly, an obstetrics textbook starts flowing through my processor and my programming bank. Though my hands have never touched an infant, my bank now has thousands of case studies in it, the best obstetrics knowledge from the leading medical schools.

And it all tells me the same thing: Skill is not enough. With a baby coming this early, what I need is the right facility with the right equipment.

But what I have is myself and my medical kit, and these will have to do. "Thank you, Dr. Zinta. I have to get to work."

"Carey, I'll call Wayne and tell him to get back home immediately. You take care of Millie and that baby. You can do it. If anyone can, you can do it."

"Thank you." I disconnect, and I start processing my newly programmed knowledge.

I look around and see liquid all over the roof of the car. At first I suspect a leak, then I realize that Millie's water has broken. I need to make her comfortable and also keep her dry. I carefully open the trunk from the inside, and Millie's "ditch kit" falls out: blankets and spare clothes and other emergency supplies that Paul has taught her to keep in the car for emergencies. I pull down the seat cushions and place them on the ceiling to get her above the dampness. I arrange the blankets and clothes and scraps of airbags into a nest on top of the cushions, and then I help Millie to slide into it.

I am arranging a pillow behind Millie's head when my comm rings. The code is Wayne's.

"Hello, Wayne," I say.

"Carey. How's Millie? How's the baby?"

"Millie is in labor."

"The doctor said that could be hours."

"It could." I check her vitals, and I am inclined to agree with Millie, not with 911. "But it can also be much faster. I think you are about to be a father, Wayne."

"Can't she hold off until the ambulance gets there?"

"No, Wayne, I do not believe she can."

"Carey, can you put me through to her?"

"I can do better than that, Wayne. You have visual?"

"Yes, I do."

"All right. Let me hook you up to my eyes and my speaker. Millie," I say. "Wayne's on the phone. He's here."

"Wayne," Millie says, her breath short.

"Hey, Rana," Wayne says. "Carey tells me the tadpole's in motion."

"The tadpole's ready to be a frog, Wayne. I don't think Junior's going to wait for you."

"It's okay. You take care of Junior. I'm on my way, hon."

"Wayne, you don't have to—"

"The clients understand. Dr. Zinta's already sent my ticket. How are the contractions?"

"They came on fast, Wayne. We were driving. I started to feel something. Thought it was false labor, like before, but then . . ."

"All right, Rana. Carey's got you. You're in good hands and I'm here to coach."

"I wish you were really here, Wayne."

"So do I, love. But hey, if you squeeze Carcy's hand, you can't break it. I've heard stories of guys who couldn't write for a week after their wives got ahold of them."

"That's okay . . . Ah . . . Aaah . . . AAAAHHH!"

"What was that?"

"Contraction, Wayne. Just under a minute."

"Under a minute? Okay, Millie."

I have already removed Millie's trousers and underpants. I have positioned the remaining seat cushions so that she may prop her feet on them, and I spread her legs so I can get in between them. I can already see to her cervix. The opening is dilated nearly seven centimeters.

Wayne gasps. "Millie, I think I saw the tadpole's head. He's coming!"

"He is coming," I say, "but she needs to dilate more, Wayne."

"Oh," Millie says. "I feel another contraction coming."

"Carey, can you give her anything for the pain?"

"No," I say. "It is too late for that anyway. Even if we were in a hospital, they could not give her any anesthetics now. I have my first aid kit in my chassis, of course, but no medication for this. There is nothing we can do but keep her calm."

At that moment, Millie screams with another contraction. It shakes her all over.

"All right, he is coming fast. Dilated nearly another centimeter."

"Is that a good thing, Carey?"

"She is fine," I say. But I do not add that dilating this quickly is very painful for her.

I may have fooled Wayne, but Millie is not fooled. "Carey," she says, "he's coming. I'm not ready."

"You do not have to rush, Millie. Give it time."

"Carey," she says. I see tears running down her face. She pushes again, and I see the baby's head enter the birth canal.

"I see the head!" Wayne says as Millie relaxes again. But then he says, "Wait! It went back!"

Turtle sign, the textbooks call it. The baby retreating when the mother relaxes. It can be a sign of shoulder dystocia, a form of obstructed labor where the anterior shoulder of the infant cannot pass below the pubic symphysis. If the baby is not delivered soon, it may die as the umbilical cord is compressed within the birth canal.

I wish I were equipped with an ultrasound unit so I could see inside Millie's womb. I probe her abdomen with my fingers, and she screams. I cannot be certain. I have only textbook knowledge. But what I feel concerns me.

"Millie," I say, "how strong do you feel?"

"I'm sore . . . But . . ."

Wayne says, "What's the matter, Carey?"

"I think it is shoulder dystocia. The baby's shoulder is

caught up inside. The McRoberts maneuver is recommended: Someone hyperextends her legs against her abdomen, widening her pelvis and flattening her spine. Only I do not have an assistant, and I need to deliver the baby. So Millie, I am going to lift your legs and bend them against you. And the baby needs you to grab them and hold on. No matter how it hurts, do not let go."

Millie speaks through gritted teeth. "Do it, Carey."

I bend her legs up. When Millie screams, my empathy net threatens to overload. I want to stop her pain, but I know I cannot.

Millie grabs her legs. She sobs repeatedly, but she does not let go. I return to my spot between her legs.

It is not enough. Another compression starts, and the baby's head emerges, but no more.

I consider the various external pressure maneuvers recommended by the texts: Rubin I with suprapubic pressure, Rubin II with posterior pressure, or others. But all of these require not just knowledge, but experience. The caregiver must know the feel of the baby through the mother's skin, to find and feel the right places to apply pressure. I cannot trust myself to perform any of these, not as fast as I need to. But there is another course.

"Carey . . ." Millie says, barely more than a breath. "I can't . . . hold on . . ."

"All right, Millie," I say. "Relax. It did not work. We need to try another course."

"What?" Wayne asks.

"It is called an intentional fetal clavicular fracture. That will let the baby pass through the birth canal."

"No!" Wayne shouts. "You don't know how."

"Wayne, Dr. Zinta downloaded an obstetrics module."

Wayne can be a stickler for rules, but today he has more important concerns. "Oh, thank God. Okay, if you're sure . . ."

"It is the best procedure in these circumstances. Trust me, I will not let anything happen to Millie or the baby."

Millie screams as another contraction hits. Somehow she finds the breath to say, "Do it, Carey. Now. Please, for the baby."

The baby's face is red and puffy. Time is running short. I reach inside of Millie and very carefully touch the baby's head. It is slippery, and I am able to slide my fingers around the head and find his shoulders. The right shoulder is in the birth canal, and the right arm is halfway in as well. But the left shoulder is wedged up against Millie's pelvis.

I try to push the baby back and twist it to a better angle, but I lack the experience for this maneuver as well.

Millie sobs. "Carey, I feel another . . ."

"I know." I have no choice but to break the clavicle.

But I am torn. My empathy net is overloaded. I feel Millie's pain, and the baby's fear. And now . . . I cannot bring myself to injure the child, but I must. "Millie, get ready for that really big push."

I was wrong before. Today . . . Today I am afraid. I fear for the baby. I fear for Millie, and I fear for Wayne so far away. I realize now that fear need not be personal, but can be for the people who matter to me.

But I cannot let my fear stop me. I raise the priority of my medical programming. It will do what it must.

"Here it . . . Here it . . . Here it COMES!" Millie screams.

Like a separate observer in my processing nets, fear screams at me: *You cannot do this.* But I say nothing, and I hear Wayne say, "Come on, Millie. Another push. Come on!"

I reach inside Millie again, feeling past the head and to the shoulder. I feel the delicate twig of the baby's clavicle. My newfound fear tries to stop me, but I apply firm but gentle pressure on the tiny bone.

Then there is the slightest of snapping sounds. The baby's face twists in pain, and my hands pull out just as the baby slides out into them. There is a squirming baby boy silently squalling in my hands. Wayne says. "Oh, he's so beautiful, Millie!"

I see that Millie's nails have torn holes in the cover of the seat cushion. Her eyes are half closed. "Millie," I say. "Stay awake. Come on. We need your help here. Come on."

"Come on, Millie," Wayne says, and Millie's eyelids flutter. "I know this is hard, but Junior needs you. Come on."

I quickly clear the baby's mouth, and immediately he screams from the pain in his shoulder. That is a good sign.

Millie says, "What's the matter?"

"He has a healthy cry, Millie. It is a good thing. Now I need you to take him." The car is warm, but not enough. The baby needs to be kept as warm as possible. I open Millie's shirt and press the baby up against her. "Now here." I open my chassis and pull out a portable oxygen concentrator. I had added this to my supplies after the fire, after I had been unable to get oxygen for Mildred. I had determined that that should not happen again. "This will get him some oxygen. I know he sounds loud, but his lungs might not be fully ready, so we need to make sure he's breathing well. Hold him right to your chest, keep him warm, and keep this on his face."

I push the mask into place, I close up Millie's shirt around the baby, and I wrap her coat around them both. "You keep warm and safe, while I finish things up down here."

I return between her legs and peer up inside of her. "Wayne, you might not want to look at this part," I say.

"No, I'm fine. If I can't be there, I want to see it. The whole thing."

"All right, she is weak. I suspect anemia. We need to get her some null plasma." Fortunately null plasma, an artificial blood substitute, needs no refrigeration and has a long shelf life. I have two units always with me. "I know you are tired, Millie, but you must keep your legs up. We need to be sure this plasma gets back in and starts circulating through you." I uncoil an IV tube, find the biggest vein in her right leg, and as gently as I can, insert the needle.

"Aaahh!" Millie cries out.

But only for an instant, and then the needle is in. The tube is hooked directly to a saline pump, so that will get Millie some fluid, which is good. She has lost a lot. Then I connect the null plasma pack to the saline. The dark yellow fluid starts coursing down the tube and into her leg.

"What's the situation, Carey?"

"The null plasma should handle the blood loss."

"So she's going to be fine? And the baby?"

I cannot readily lie, but the full truth would only hurt him. The odds are good, but there is still a chance we may lose Millie or the baby. Or both. So I tell Wayne, "Everything is fine, Wayne. You have a beautiful baby boy. And now I have to cut the umbilical cord."

"That was supposed to be my job," Wayne says. I sense regret in his voice. "But if it has to be somebody else, I'm glad it's you, Carey."

I clamp off the distal end of the umbilical with a clamp near Millie's vulva. Then I add another clamp up close to where the cord comes from Millie's shirt. "All right, Millie," I say. "You have to open up for just a little bit so I can cut and tie the cord."

She seems asleep, but then she makes a slight moan and I take that for assent. Again opening her coat and her shirt, I use the scalpel to gently slice through the cord. Then I tie the knot as recommended in my obstetrics text, noting that it is almost identical to a knot taught on one of Paul's sailing videos.

"All right. That is good enough for now," I say. "They will check it at the hospital."

Millie's eyes flutter open, and I see a weary smile on her face. I check to make sure that the mask is still secure on the baby's face, and then I check heart rate for both her and the baby, along with blood pressure and blood oxygen.

I do not have to lie to Wayne anymore. "They are stabilizing, Wayne. They are all right."

"Millie," Wayne says, "you did it. He's so beautiful."

"We did it," Millie says. Her voice is very soft, so I turn up the gain on my audio inputs.

After a pause, Wayne adds, "I wish I were there, Rana."

"It's okay," Millie answers. "Everything's fine. Carey's here."

"I know," Wayne says. "I just wish . . . I wish I were there."

In the distance, I hear a siren, drawing closer. "Help is on the way, Wayne. I will get them to the hospital quickly, your wife and your son."

"My boy and my girl," Wayne says. There is another long pause, and then he adds, "Thank you, Carey."

"I should thank you, Wayne, and Millie. This is nothing I have ever experienced before."

I leave my audio and video open for Wayne while I make an internal call to Dr. Zinta.

She answers, "Carey, how's it going?"

"Mother and son are doing fine, Dr. Zinta. I can hear help approaching."

"Can I see him?"

I look up. Millie's eyes are closed again, and I hear a slight snore. "They are both asleep right now," I say, "but let me show you the delivery."

I start a playback on Dr. Zinta's channel, and then I open a third channel to Belize to give Paul and Susan the good news. Susan cries with delight, and Paul shouts so loud that it rattles my chassis. When he is done, he says, "Fantastic news, Carey! I'm so glad you were there for them. How does it feel to bring a new life into the world?"

"It felt . . . frightening, Paul. But now it feels good. Happy. I think I begin to understand the human concept of a miracle."

32. TODAY WE WATCH BUTTERFLIES

"Would you like to rent a tour guide?" the cashier asks.

Before Millie can answer, Timmy pulls under the turnstile. "Timmy, come back here," Millie says.

"I will get him." I step around the turnstile quickly and grab the child gently by the arm. "Timmy, Mommy told you to wait."

"But look at that, Uncle Carey, look at that!" I look at what he points at. It is a red sandstone sculpture, sharp angles and gentle curves. I see legs and arms sticking out in many places, tangled into a giant block, two meters by almost two and a half by a meter tall. But no heads, no faces.

"That is interesting, Timmy, but we cannot get ahead of everybody. So come on back." I pull Timmy back. Garrett, his older brother, waits patiently. He is nearly twelve years old, and he has more impulse control. Tabitha, Timmy's little sister, is happy in Millie's arms and smiling at Dr. Zinta.

I pull Timmy back to the family just in time to hear

Millie say, "Do we really need to spend money on a tour guide?"

Dr. Zinta answers, "I'm a member, I get guides for free. Besides, I want to see what your husband has been up to with these new guide androids."

Dr. Zinta pushes her membership credentials to the cashier, and the cashier smiles. "Oh, welcome. You've got the family membership, so two adults and two children are covered. That leaves one child and . . ." The cashier looks at me.

"And one adult," I say. "I can pay for this, Millie." I push a payment to the cashier. It is important to me that I pay my own way. I am uncomfortable with special privileges for being an android. For almost forty years, I have functioned as a member of the Owens family, not just a caretaker. I am accustomed to being treated as one.

If I were human, I might call this a matter of pride. The closest I can get is a sense of satisfaction with a job well done. Is that pride? Even now, I sometimes have trouble putting names to my emotions.

But I know that it is important to Paul and Susan and Millie to see me as a person, a member of their family. Wayne's research confirms: Even though I am a machine, he says that my emotional intelligence is growing into something more, that my neural nets are intersecting in ever more complex ways. This is something that he hopes to duplicate, and I find his arguments persuasive. But I have learned that this is a topic of contention between him and Millie, so I try not to bring it up when she is around.

"Here's your receipt, Mr. Owens." The cashier pushes the payment record back to me. "Have a lovely day at

Frederik Meijer Gardens and Sculpture Park. Here's your tour guide." She gestures one finger, and an android walks up. It rises not quite to my shoulders. Its head is overly large, its eyes larger yet, and a big smile is permanently fixed on its face. These guide androids are produced by MCA International, straight out of Wayne's lab, and he has discussed how their exaggerated friendly faces have helped to avoid the uncanny valley.

The android says, "Welcome, Mrs. Stockwell, Dr. Jansons, and is it Mr. Owens?"

"Just call me Carey, please," I say.

"Yes, I will call you Carey. Welcome to Frederik Meijer Gardens and Sculpture Park. We know you will enjoy our beautiful horticultural gardens and our world-class sculpture collection. Would you like me to lead you through the park? Or did you want to wander on your own? I am happy either way."

I study Wayne's workmanship. He once explained that the neural nets of these units are based on some of my technology. "But without your emotions," he had added with a laugh. Without my emulation abilities, the tour guide cannot possibly have conflicts between empathy and emulation like I have experienced throughout my existence, and Wayne has never once detected any sign of self-awareness in any of their new models. They are not me.

Observing the guide, I see signs of emulation; but it is a standard persona programmed in, not adaptive to circumstances. The android is simply a pleasant tour guide, ready to answer questions with no awareness deeper than that.

Timmy pulls away again. "Mr. Robot, what's that?"

The android does not answer, so I tap it on the shoulder. "When he says Mr. Robot, I believe he means you."

"Oh," the guide says, "of course. This unit normally responds to 'tour guide,' 'guide,' 'hey, you,' or 'buddy.' But today this unit will be Mr. Robot." The guide leads the rest of us over to where Timmy stands investigating the red sandstone sculpture.

"This sculpture is called 'Hagar,'" the guide explains. "It is inspired by the biblical story of Hagar, the second wife of Abraham who bore him the son Ishmael. As the second wife, she had no protections or privileges, and she was eventually cast out into the wild with her son where she had many struggles for their survival."

"Where is its face?" Garrett asks.

"It has no face," Dr. Zinta explains. "It's supposed to represent struggle, not the person herself. All the arms fighting to get free from each other, and all the legs fighting to escape."

I have never understood the human practice of art. I can understand photographs, portraits, or sculptures that represent people that one knows and wants to remember; but I have never understood more abstract or unusual works. I am not sure I even understand art that represents people you do not know. But with this explanation, Dr. Zinta has made me wonder. Before when I had looked at this collection of limbs, I saw something that made no sense. But now I think I understand. In its own way, this work is an emulation, frozen in a moment. In the medium of stone, the artist has captured the concept, the feel of struggle.

My empathy net works on many different inputs: tone

of voice, word choice, situation, and audience . . . but also body language and positioning. I wonder what I might read if I were to empathize with this statue. So I turn up the balance on my empathy net, and I look at the statue "Hagar." And suddenly . . . "Dr. Zinta, I see it."

"You see what, Carey?"

"No, that is not accurate. I *feel* it. I feel Hagar's struggle. How she fights against the forces around her, many of which bind her in multiple directions, and that is why she has so many limbs struggling in so many ways."

Zinta nods at me and smiles. "That's very good, Carey."

"Dr. Zinta, this is unprecedented."

"Your nets are growing, Carey. You have enough experience now to understand this work."

"Dr. Zinta, will we see more?"

She laughs. "Much more, Carey. This park is full of beautiful pieces. Would you like to see more?"

Today I am intrigued by this new world. It is as if I have been upgraded with a new sense that has revealed gaps in my knowledge of the world. I answer, "Yes, please. I want to see more."

"There is much more to see," the tour guide says. "Over here, if you look up at the ceiling, we have our famous Chihuly glass sculpture, 'Gilded Champagne Gardens Chandelier.'"

I look up, but the thing in the ceiling says nothing to me. It is a large collection of bulbs and tubes and points and leaflike objects, in red and gold and cream and yellow and brown glass. I have respect for the artistry that made it, I can see that much work went into it, but I find nothing there when I try to empathize.

"What do you see, Carey?" Dr. Zinta asks; but I have no answer.

Tabitha looks up from her mother's arms. "Monster, mommy!"

"Yeah!" Garrett says, "It's a monster. It's gonna drop down and eat you!"

"Mommy!"

"Garrett Wayne Stockwell," Millie says, "You apologize to your sister for scaring her. Right now!"

"Sorry, Tabby," Garrett says; but his tone tells me he is only sorry that he got in trouble.

"Yeah," Timmy says. "It's a funny monster, Tabby. It won't hurt us."

The tour guide leads us through more of the main building as we look at many pieces. Some speak to me to some degree. Many are too abstract for me to find meaning, and some are merely humorous. "Five Meerkats" by Tom Hillis, a collection of meerkat statues, delights the children, but it signifies nothing to me. Near them, though, is one which I cannot take my eyes off of. The work is "Masai Mother" by Tuck Langland, a simple head study of a short-haired African woman with many beads around her neck.

Again Dr. Zinta asks me, "What do you see, Carey?"

"I see dignity, grace, pride. But . . . what I feel makes no sense."

"What is it, Carey?"

"It reminds me of Mildred when I first met her, when her memory was still mostly intact. She knew trouble was coming and things would get worse, but she faced it without fear."

"She had fear," Dr. Zinta says, "but she wasn't going to let it stop her. And she couldn't show it because she wanted to be strong for her family."

"I think you are right. And this woman, she too is strong and proud and determined."

"It *is* beautiful," Millie says. "I don't see Grandma in it, but I didn't really know her like you did."

"That is her, Millie," I assure her. "A completely different face and race, but this woman has the same strength."

We continue on through the main building. We come to a big glass case, and the android says with emulated pride, "And here we have one of the few original castings of Auguste Rodin's 'The Kiss.'"

Millie's jaw drops. "Kids, come here!" She pulls them close and covers Garrett's eyes with her hands. The other two look at her. But Garrett has already seen the statue and is giggling. It is two figures, both very well muscled: a man and a woman, both nude. They embrace in a passionate kiss.

Dr. Zinta is amused at Millie's effort to shield her children. She laughs softly and then asks me, "And what do you see with this one, Carey?"

This time my answer is simpler. "It is completely representational, of course. I see two people very much in love, embracing and showing their affection. It reminds me of how I saw Wayne and Millie once on the Owens couch."

"Carey!" Millie gasps.

Garrett, meanwhile, goes from amused to disgusted. "Ew! Mom, you and Dad kissing naked on a couch?"

"Garrett, we were *not* naked. Carey, tell them we were not naked!"

"They were not naked, Garrett. But they were kissing on a couch."

"I think we should move on, children," Millie says. "Why don't you go up ahead and look at that arch there?" The kids run ahead and Millie turns back to me, "Carey, that was *not* helpful."

"I am sorry, Millie, but it was the truth. Dr. Zinta asked me what my impression was."

"You didn't have to complicate matters by dragging me and Wayne into it. And besides," she says looking at the statue wistfully, "it has been too long."

Then Millie looks at Dr. Zinta, who looks back at her; and the two women giggle. "I didn't hear a thing," Dr. Zinta says.

"It's just these long hours. Dr. Warren has him on all these new projects. He has no time for research. She has him managing two projects now."

Dr. Zinta shakes her head and tuts. "I was afraid of that. I've heard rumors . . ."

Millie frowns. "Wayne doesn't talk about it much, but there have been a lot of cutbacks. And a lot of wild schemes to generate revenue." She lowers her voice. "I think the company's not doing well."

Dr. Zinta also lowers her voice. "That's what I hear, too, Millie. Nothing official, now that I'm retired, but . . ." Then she pats Millie's shoulder. "But Wayne will turn it around. Your husband is really a genius. I am so proud that I had a chance to teach him some of what he knows, but he has gone way beyond what I taught him."

"Oh, I know. But you know, he tries to explain it to me. I try to follow along; but by the time he gets home, it's so late. And I'm so tired. And I'm sorry, Zinta, but cybernetics is so *boring*."

Dr. Zinta laughs. "Don't apologize. It takes a certain mind-set. For Wayne and me, it's amazing that people pay us to solve puzzles all day. There's an intense thrill in solving something that's nearly impossible. But if you don't have that mind-set? Boring. Frustrating. Besides, everybody has their own thing in life. I couldn't tell a tree frog from a toad."

"Oh, sure you could. It's easy. Anybody can."

They continue talking as we walk through the rest of the main building and up to the Tropical Conservatory, our prime destination for the day. As we approach a big plastic curtain split into many vertical strips, the guide says, "Please use caution when passing through the butterfly lock, particularly on the way back out. *The Meijer Gardens Butterflies are Blooming* exhibit is carefully managed to ensure that no non-native butterfly species escapes into this environment." It bends down to the kids to speak directly to them. "Inside you will see hundreds of different butterfly species from all over the world, freshly hatched from their cocoons."

"You mean eclosed," Tabitha says, and the guide's eyes open wide.

"I do not understand," the guide says.

Garrett chimes in, "They're not hatching. Eggs hatch, and they're not eggs. They're chrysalises, and they're pupating. It's metamorphosis."

"And they eclose," Tabby says. "That means they break out."

Millie and Dr. Zinta suppress their grins. Millie's children know all about metamorphosis. She has taught them about frogs, and also about butterflies. They understand it well beyond their school books. That is why they are so excited about this exhibit.

The tour guide leads us through the plastic curtain, and then stops before a second one. "When you come back out through here, can you see what these people are doing?" A tall thin man, his wife, and their two children emerge from the inner curtain. They stop and carefully turn in place. A voice comes from the ceiling: "Please return to the exhibit. You have a yellow swallowtail in your hair, ma'am."

The woman says, "I do?"

Her husband says, "Yeah hon, you do. Let's go back in and see if we can get it out."

The voice from the ceiling says, "No, just give it a chance to go away. If it does not soon, an attendant will help you to get it out. You must be very careful in handling the butterflies. Many of them are just newly hatched."

"Eclosed!" Tabitha says.

The woman goes back in and quickly pops back out. "It flew away once it was inside," she says, and the family leaves.

We cross the inner curtain. Inside the conservatory, it is significantly warmer than in the main hall, and warmer still than the spring air outside. The temperature reminds me of Belize: not as hot, but hot enough that the kids will soon get uncomfortable. The hothouse is like a miniature jungle, another way that it reminds me of Belize. There are concrete paths in between trees and flowers and hanging plants and fungi. Hidden among them are more sculptures and also a handful of birds and butterflies in every color imaginable. The children instantly start pointing and calling out. Timmy says, "Mom, look at this one."

"Mommy," Tabitha says, "I want to get down and see the butterflies."

Millie puts her down. Tabitha starts running around. "Don't run, Tabitha, you'll only scare them away. If you want to see a butterfly, you've got to be slow and quiet and stand really still."

I try following Millie's advice, freezing in place with my arms out in front of me. Soon a giant purple butterfly, a species I do not recognize, lands on my arm. It spreads its wings and holds them out. The tour guide says, "That one is newly emerged. Its wings still need to dry. If you hold still, you will be doing it a kindness."

"I can hold still for a long time," I say.

"Oh look," Millie says, snapping pictures. "Oh, this is so incredible. Look at the kids. If only Wayne were here."

"I think he would enjoy it," I say. "You can send him pictures."

Millie takes a picture of the butterfly on my arm. "I know. We send him so many pictures from so many events and fun experiences. He's missed out on so much." She looks at Dr. Zinta, who is leading the kids over to the butterfly release cage. "I miss when Dr. Zinta was his boss. Dr. Warren seems nice, in her way; but she's so much more ambitious, taking on projects like never before. And he's working so many hours now."

"I am sure he wishes he could be here, Millie."

"Does he, Carey? Can you tell me for sure that he does?"

I shake my head. "Millie, you know my confidentiality rules. I cannot analyze him and answer that." Her eyes look sad, so I add, "But I think he does."

"He loves his work so much, Zinta's right. I don't understand it, but he loves it. Or he did before he got into management. Now I'm not so sure. But it's a good living. He takes care of us."

"He is successful in his work. Are you not happy for him?"

"I am. It's just . . . Now with Tabby around, I've taken leave from the university. I'd rather be home with the kids. But you know, I'd rather be in the classroom, too. And I'd really rather be out in the field doing research."

The butterfly tests its wings, but it still clings to my arm. "This is something that is very difficult for me to comprehend, Millie."

"I know, here I am wanting three things at once. I can't have them all."

"So how do you know which one to have?"

"I'm here for my kids, and that's most important at this age. But I miss that summer in Belize. I miss being in front of the class."

Missing is an emotion that I still do not understand. I thought I understood it in regards to people. I miss Mildred. But it is harder to understand missing an experience. My memories of an experience are perfect— from the fire to Garrett's birth, and everything in between—and I can revisit them to relive the experience. Humans cannot.

But I want to help. "I can take care of the kids, Millie."

"Oh, no, Carey," she says. "You have your work at Creekside."

"I like to help the residents there. But I would like to help you with the children." And suddenly I glimpse *missing*: wanting to be in two places, helping two groups. I almost wish Dr. Zinta had succeeded in replicating me so long ago.

Finally the butterfly is ready. It flaps its wings and flutters away. "I know," Millie sighs as she watches it fly away. "Maybe . . . If you can help a couple of days a week? Until Timmy's in school. Maybe that will help Wayne, too. I hope."

"Is something wrong, Millie?"

"He gets tired these days; I get tired. It's so much harder now."

"Everything changes, Millie. You of all people should know that. Come on, let's go watch the butterfly release." I take her hand and lead her up to an area where a swarm of kids has lined up. A sign on the wall says: NEXT BUTTERFLY RELEASE AT 1:30. A digital clock below the message shows that it is 1:27.

Park attendants, one human and one android, bring out a large box of chrysalises on strings. Some are twitching. Legs emerge from some.

Tabitha notices us as we come up behind the kids. "Uncle Carey," she says, "I can't see."

I lift her up, and Timmy says, "Me, too." I lift him onto the other shoulder, and Garrett stands next to me on his toes.

Soon the miracle begins. The chrysalises start opening

here and there throughout the box. The attendants pull the cover off the box, and butterflies start emerging where caterpillars once hung. I wonder at how the attendants had timed this so well, to know exactly that this is when a large number of the butterflies will break free. There must be a science to predicting this: temperature, timing, maybe listening to each chrysalis.

Then I wonder: Were there any signs that anyone could have noted when I emerged from my neural nets? If another self-aware android were waiting to break out, if some artificial intelligence were meditating in a network, would anyone even know?

The first butterfly breaks free. It stretches out its broad black wings with red spots, drying them in the sun.

Then more colors, more sizes. Soon they start experimentally lifting and lowering their wings until they start flying off. The entire swarm of kids around us cheers and applauds.

"It's beautiful, Mommy," Tabitha says.

"Yes, it is, Tabby," Millie answers. "Metamorphosis is beautiful."

33. TODAY I HAVE A PROPOSAL FOR WAYNE

I arrive early for my maintenance appointment at MCA. Now that the family cars have come to accept me as a valid driver, I need not have other people change their schedule around my needs. Paul sometimes brings me in now that he is retired, but I prefer not to interfere with his sailing in the summer.

"Hello, Flora," I say.

"Hello, Carey," she says. "How are you today?"

"That is what I am here to determine."

She laughs at the old joke. "You're looking fine to me. Sometimes I wish I could be an android. Even with all this modern medicine, the body gets feeling old, and the bones weary. Some nights I dream about retiring someday."

"Not for a long time, I am sure. You are in good shape." And I know this to be true. With the help of Dr. Zinta, I have made upgrades to my medical systems. The company will not upgrade my programming; but when I proved that I could pay for it, they upgraded my sensors to the latest remote medical diagnostics. In fact, they seemed eager to accept my money. So if Flora wanted, I could tell her heart rate, blood pressure, and pulse oxygen. I could even produce an EEG. But of course I keep such information to myself unless asked. My privacy protocols are as strong as ever.

Flora is showing me a picture of her first grandchildren, the twins, when the reception door slides open and Wayne walks in. "Carey," he says, "you're early."

"Yes, I was catching up with Flora."

"Very good," Wayne says. "Come on back. The lab'll be set up for you shortly, so let's go to my office."

We proceed back past the testing lab, and I see that my test seat is not yet ready. It is occupied by one of the newer model androids, from the same line as the tour guide at Meijer Gardens. Rodrigo stands beside it, running it through the last stage of self-diagnostics. He looks up and smiles at me. "Hello, my mechanical friend," he says. "Is it that time again already?"

"It is," I say. "How are Luisa and the kids?"

"They are well," he smiles. "They are back in Belize, visiting her mother. Lisabeth keeps asking when the metal man will visit again."

"Soon, Rodrigo. Let us make it soon." I turn to Wayne. "May I watch this?" Wayne nods, and we stop to observe.

Seeing these diagnostics is a strange experience for me: At this stage in my own maintenance process, I am asleep and unaware, so I have never witnessed this process.

Rodrigo issues simple verbal commands to the android. "Raise your left hand. Raise your left arm. Rotate your left hand. Flex your fingers. Clench your fingers." Then, as the android follows the commands, Rodrigo changes tactics. "What is your identity code?"

"GYKMN-23512-43481-95003," the android answers.

"Very good," the technician says. "No interference between the motor controller and the supervisor net. Your responses are well within parameters. All right, now hit me." The android remains still, with its arms raised in the air. "Come on, hit me." No movement. "Why didn't you hit me?"

The android speaks in a dull monotone. "This unit may not strike a human under these circumstances."

"And under what circumstances could you hit me?"

"If it were necessary to save your life or the life of another, this unit might be forced to . . ." It stops speaking.

"Oh, there is still an imbalance there, isn't there?" Rodrigo plugs in the diagnostic cable and taps some commands on his tablet.

"To hit you," the android continues, "but only if this unit could not intercede between you and the danger to yourself or to another. Also in the case where you might need to be subdued, because you are irrationally failing to flee a danger. Also in the case where I perceive the danger and it was coming quickly enough that I could not take time to warn you. And also—"

"Stop," Rodrigo says. "All right, you've got the rules right."

I continue to listen as Rodrigo alternates physical tests with functional decision-making tests. I am surprised, because the questions asked are very involved, far more so than I ever expected them to ask; but the android's answers are simplistic. It has a very rudimentary understanding of harm, strictly in the physical sense, and strictly on a scale leaning toward most easily repaired. I am sure that it could not have broken Garrett's clavicle to save the life of the baby.

At last the diagnostics are done. "All right, stand up," Rodrigo says as he disconnects the monitor leads. The android stands as instructed and takes no further action. "Here you go." Rodrigo touches a series of spots on the android's neck, and emulation kicks in. The eyes widen, a congenial smile appears on its face, and it walks away. This is interesting: Somewhere in that single-valued emulation profile, it has the ability to understand that it was finished. Until then it was operating only on orders. Maybe there is some awareness there after all.

Rodrigo looks over at me. "Your turn." He points at the seat.

I look at Wayne. "Can we talk later?"

"Sure," Wayne answers. "Carey's all yours, Rodrigo."

I sit in the testing seat. Rodrigo straps me into the monitor sensors and turns me off.

When I awaken, Wayne has returned. He and Rodrigo are going over my results when my self-diagnostics chime the completion. They look over at me.

"Everything looks good, Carey," Wayne says. "You're in top-notch shape. Do you have any physical upgrades that you wanted?"

"There is a blood gas analyzer that could be useful, but I do not have the funds set aside for it yet. I should be ready for that next month. I will order it to make sure that you have it in stock."

"All right. I'm not sure where you'll put it. Your chassis compartments are pretty full."

"Yes, but some of what is in there is obsolete. I will rearrange and make room for the analyzer."

Wayne looks at his tablet. "Your empathy net is at peak across all tests. There does seem to be a little lag in your emulation net's response. Have you noticed that?"

"I have not." But I realize that I might not notice, so seldom do I use full emulation anymore. Rather I use it simply to try to judge how one of my family might behave when empathy alone is not giving me the answer.

As a test, I turn my emulation up slightly, and today I am Wayne.

And as Wayne I am depressed, and I want this checkup done as soon as possible, and I have feelings of anxiety. This cannot be right. I turn the emulation back down.

"Do you think the emulation lag is a problem, Wayne?" I ask.

"No," he says. "We should keep an eye on it, but I think you're all right now. Let's go back to my office. There are things I'd like to discuss."

By his office, of course, Wayne means Dr. Zinta's old office. Upon her retirement, he became the lab supervisor, despite his desire to remain in research. The increase in pay has helped as his family has grown; but I still sense financial stress in him.

Dr. Zinta's same desk is there, though with new chairs. Pictures of Millie and the children line the walls. Wayne's computer desktop is piled with virtual paperwork, and a quick scan tells me that these are financial reports, not engineering diagrams. And they do not look good.

Wayne sits, and I do the same. And then I begin. "Wayne, you are worried. I might even say anxious."

Wayne looks at me. "Carey, I . . ."

He does not finish, so I continue. "I met one of your tour guide androids at Meijer Gardens."

"And?"

"I am sorry to say that I was not impressed. It was functional, but not any sort of advance on the work that MCA did twenty years or more ago."

Wayne sighs. "I know," he says. "We've made improvements in production efficiency, and the style team has made them look new, but they're not anything special. Nothing that our competition can't do, and they do it cheaper. If it weren't for Dr. Zinta's connections at the Gardens, I don't think we would've gotten that contract."

"And that is why you are anxious," I say. "It is money issues. Business. Not technical issues."

Wayne shakes his head. "It's money, but it's technical, too. We haven't . . . *I* haven't come up with any new breakthroughs, and our competitors are catching up. Some of them have passed us in some niches. Our only real edge is in entangled neural nets. But even that . . ."

"It peaked with me. And you haven't been able to reproduce my results."

Wayne nods. "So we have nothing groundbreaking in the pipeline. That puts the marketing team at a disadvantage."

"Is that true, Wayne? Or is that just what they tell you, to excuse their own lack of results?"

"I wouldn't put it past them, Carey, but . . . they're right. We're bumping up against the limits of what our current technology can do. And the board . . . Doctor Warren . . . they're all getting anxious, too, and they're dumping it all on me."

Slowly, Wayne is confirming my guesses. So I ask, "But you haven't told Millie any of this?"

Wayne looks down at his desk. "I don't want to worry her, too."

But there is more to it. I sense in Wayne an emotion I had previously only witnessed in the emotional intelligence testing: shame. Wayne is ashamed of failures that are beyond his control.

And I also see a looming problem there. "Wayne," I say, "Millie deserves to know. She would give you support, if you would let her."

Wayne looks up at me, eyes wide. "Carey, you can't tell her."

"No, Wayne, you know I cannot." I cannot add: but not telling her will push her farther away. My privacy protocols cut both ways.

"I wish I could tell her," Wayne says. "But she has so much to worry about now, with the kids. And . . . I think she wants to go back to teaching."

I probe the limits of my confidentiality protocols, and I sense no conflict when I say, "I agree, Wayne, she does."

Wayne nods. "That might help with her stress," he says. "And the extra income . . . Well, it might make a good cushion, in case things go really badly here."

"I have offered to help with Tabby and Timmy," I say.

"Oh, thank you, Carey!"

"But Wayne, are things really that bad? Is your job at risk?"

Wayne waves at the documents on his desktop. "The whole company's at risk, Carey," he says. "The board's squeezing us for profits, our competition is eating our market share. And even with our improved efficiencies . . . We had to lower prices to compete, so our margins are close to zero. If we don't find some new breakout product, MCA could be done."

I nod at that. "And this is why you wanted to talk."

Wayne looks down at his desk. "I . . . know what we can do. A market we can dominate."

I sense it then: a mix of eagerness and worry. We have discussed this many times through the years, but never with the urgency I sense now. "You mean replication."

He looks up at me. "Yes." Urgency, and ambition, and a desire to prove himself. "I think we're close, Carey. I've been digging into Dr. Zinta's entanglement research. I've . . . spent a lot of discretionary funds on extending it. Maybe too much; the board isn't happy. But we've learned so much more since your early replication experiments with Dr. Zinta. I have new theories of where your consciousness comes from. I've been . . . eager to test them out for a while."

And in truth, he does not worry about me as Dr. Zinta does. Even though Wayne has charted my emotional growth, even though we have become friends of a sort—almost brothers, even—there is a part of him that still sees me as a machine. He hides it well, but it is always there.

And now he sees in me opportunities. To get back into research, and prove he can still contribute. To save the company. To save his family.

And I want to help. I have always wanted to help.

"Yes, Wayne. Let us do this."

But when we go to Wayne and Millie's home and discuss this with Millie, she is more adamant than Dr. Zinta ever was. "No!" she says. "Absolutely not. I forbid it!"

"Millie," I say, "this is important."

"Important? Why?"

Before I can answer, Wayne says, "For science, Rana. There's still so much we do not know. So much . . . Carey can teach us. This will be an exciting, new frontier. It may even teach us about human consciousness. Plus look at how helpful Carey is at Creekside. How many nursing homes, how many patients could use an android caretaker?"

Wayne still does not discuss the financial pressures, so I am unable to. I remain silent, but Millie turns to me. "And you agree?" she says. "You're willing to risk injury just for science?"

"Not just for science," I answer. But that is as much as I can say.

"Well, I don't agree," Millie says.

"I am sorry, Millie," I say. "This has to be done." I look to Wayne, and I wish that I could explain more. But instead, I continue, "And I am afraid it is not your choice. Legally, I am the property of Paul and Susan. Effectively, I am my own person, empowered to choose my own fate. And I choose to do this . . ." I looked for a way to put it into words. "I choose to do this for the children, Millie. For the future."

※　※　※

The night ends badly, with Millie stalking off to her room without saying good night to either of us. I try one more time to persuade Wayne to tell her about the finances, but he is as unmovable as her.

34. TODAY WE EXPERIMENT

It takes a week for Wayne to gather and recreate the components for the replication experiment. I spend that week at Creekside, helping the residents. Millie is still too angry to talk to me.

Despite getting older, Luke still stretches and works out every day. Aside from his memory impairment, he is a good example of the modern human potential to live healthy to a very old age.

Today he smiles and says, "Carey, let's go for a walk." He leads me toward the front door, and we step out into the bright summer day. There is a creek in the woods behind the nursing home, and a trail that runs beside it to Bonnie Creek Park. Residents who are in good shape often walk to the park, enjoying its trails and clearings. Luke and I have made this trip many times through the years. The creek is six feet wide in places, eight feet in others. It reminds me of hunting frogs with Millie.

We come to the bridge across the creek, one of Luke's favorite stops. "I can't tell you how long I've been waiting for this." The bridge is metal with a paved surface and thin metal guardrails on each side. Suddenly Luke grasps the west rail, pushes up with his arms, and vaults atop the rail.

"Luke," I say, "be careful."

"Be careful?" he says. "My brain's bad, but my skills are just fine." And they are, as he has proven so many times. He walks carefully along the rail to the other side of the bridge. Then he comes back, but at running speed. He bends over into a handstand on the rail, and then he walks hand over hand to the other side. Finally he cartwheels back across the bridge, spinning twice over the span of the rail.

Then he grins. "Hold still."

I know what is coming next, so I freeze in place. Suddenly Luke tumbles forward, lands with his hands on my shoulders, and springs off. I turn just in time to see him land on the east handrail, feet together, arms outspread. Then he springs backwards, once again bounding off my shoulders to land on the west rail.

Luke turns back and looks at me. "What? No applause?"

"Applause is a human habit, Luke. I can never understand when it is appropriate. But I can say that you still impress me."

"Close enough," he says, and then he leaps back down to the bridge. "God, that felt good!" Luke walks across the span, and I follow him.

On the other side, Luke continues, "You seem down, Bo. What's the matter?"

Despite Luke's memory issues, I have found him to be an astute human observer, a natural empath. But this surprises me. I was unaware that there were externally visible signs of my confusion, yet Luke has picked up on them.

"It is nothing I can discuss," I answer. "That would violate my privacy protocols."

Luke stops and looks back at me. "You're smarter than that, Bo. You can find a way to share within your rules. Besides . . ." He smiles and taps his skull. ". . . even if you tell me something wrong, I'll probably forget it tomorrow."

Luke is right. I cannot go into details about Millie's and Wayne's motivations, but I can discuss the choices I face. If Luke draws conclusions, I can simply refuse to confirm or deny them. So as we walk, we discuss my troubles.

"So let me get this straight, Bo," Luke eventually says. "There will be two of you?"

I nod. "Or three, or four. If this works, there may be no limit."

Luke scratches his chin. "A lot of you could do a lot of good around here," he says. I nod, and he continues. "But I don't know . . . Don't it bother you, the idea that you wouldn't be unique then? I'm not sure how I'd feel about another me running around." Then he smiles. "But maybe he would remember where I left my car keys."

I had not considered this question. In Belize, I had demanded to be judged as a unique individual. I had not wanted to be found guilty of the crimes committed by others like me.

But they were *not* like me. Not in the mind, where *I* exist. They had no more in common with me than I have with a coffeemaker. Now, not only was Wayne ready to create other androids with minds, but they would have *my* mind. My memories and experiences, right up to the moment of replication. They would *be* me.

I was not sure how I felt about that. Nothing in my emotional testing had touched on such a question. "Is being unique that important to humans?"

"It kind of is," Luke says. "It's a whole world of us here, billions, and some folks . . . some folks see us as numbers already. But we know. Even twins know: They're twins, but still unique. We know, each of us, that we're special. That even though there's lots of brothers and sisters on this planet, and out in space now, there's only one of me. One of Mrs. Carruthers, and Auralee, and even Nurse Ratched. Like snowflakes, no two alike. And that makes us special. And also our friends, our family. Each of us, one of a kind."

"So do you think that is what bothers Millie? That I will not be unique?"

Luke shakes his head. "I can't tell what she's thinking. That's your job, isn't it? But I think she's telling the truth: She's scared. You told me . . . You told me something. Now I . . ."

I clap his arm to try to comfort him. "It is all right, Luke. You are right, I told you about the last time they tried to replicate me."

"That's right. And there was a stream. You were almost . . . washed away. She might've drowned."

"That is right," I say.

"And there's your problem, Bo. Last time you tried something like this, she almost lost you. She doesn't want to take that chance again."

※　※　※

I have kept going over Luke's words as the week has passed. I see his point, and I realize that I have been blind to Millie's fears. It surprises me that after these decades, I could still miss something like that.

But on the other hand, Wayne's fears are fresh and clear. He has shared more of the financials with me, under a vow of confidence. If MCA cannot turn things around, they may not last another three years. And to turn things around, they need to start now.

So today, I once again sit in the testing chair, strapped into the sensor web. Wayne looks into my eyes. "Are you sure, Carey?"

I nod, making the sensor cables bounce around me. "I am ready, Wayne," I say.

"Then let's do this, Carey." Wayne turns me off.

35. TODAY I AM DEAD

. . . searching for synchronization . . .
. . . searching for synchronization . . .
. . . searching for synchronization . . .
. . . searching for synchronization . . .
. . . searching for synchronization . . .

36. TODAY I AM ALIVE

. . . synchronized.

I open my eyes, and I am surprised to see Dr. Zinta. I am further surprised that her hair is so gray. "Dr. Zinta," I say, "what happened—"

"Carey!" She throws her arms around my neck. "Carey!" She buries her head in my shoulder and says, "You're alive . . ." And then she sobs.

"I am a machine," I say. "I do not meet the definition of life."

Dr. Zinta continues to sob, so I wrap my arms around her, trying to comfort her. "What is wrong, Dr. Zinta? And where is Wayne?"

She lifts her head, and she looks in my eyes. "Wayne . . . Wayne's asleep in the guest room." She raises her voice. "Wayne!"

"Guest room?" And then I look around, and I realize that I have been moved. "Dr. Zinta, this is not the MCA lab." I am seated in a closet off from a living area. Outside the closet, I see comfortable chairs, a tall media cabinet, and a wide range of small to medium sculptures. "This is . . . your home?"

Slowly Dr. Zinta extricates herself from my arms. "Yes, Carey," she says. "I forgot you wouldn't recognize it. I've moved."

"Moved?" I ask. "When did this . . ." And then I check my internal chronometer, and I realize: It has been five years, two months, three days, and four hours since Wayne turned me off.

Wayne enters from a hallway. "Carey!"

"Wayne, what happened?"

"Carey . . ." He rushes up to me, touching my shoulder as if to be sure that I am real. "Carey, something went wrong. I . . . killed you."

"You did not kill me. I am right here."

"But we didn't know that," Dr. Zinta says. "You were gone, and he . . . we . . . couldn't bring you back."

"Obviously you could, Mom. Here I am."

"I know," Wayne says. "But only because we were too stubborn to give up. Everybody else did."

"Everybody else?" Dr. Zinta nods. "But now we can tell them that I am back. We have to call Millie. And Paul and Susan."

At that, Dr. Zinta's eyes turn down, and a tear falls from her right eye. "Dr. Zinta, what's the matter?"

Wayne squeezes my shoulder. "Carey . . ."

The cemetery is a short walk away, on a slight hill overlooking the river. Paul would have liked that. He was always happy on the water.

His grave is next to Mildred's (which I have never seen before). He would have liked that, too.

Once again, Wayne grips my shoulder. "I wasn't at the

funeral. He was my . . . father, essentially, but Millie didn't want me. I understood. For her sake. But after . . . Well, I came down on my own. I needed to say goodbye. Now I figure maybe you do, too."

Say goodbye? To whom? Paul is not here. Like Mildred, he still lives in my memory, but not here. All that is here is his name in polished granite.

His name. I crouch down and trace the letters with my fingers. The tangibility of that brings it home: Paul is dead.

"How did it happen?"

Wayne stands behind me. "About three months after you . . . stopped functioning. A sudden stroke, out on the sailboat with his friends. By the time they got back to shore, he was too far gone. A vegetative state. They tried neural regeneration, but there'd been too much damage. There was no substructure left for the regenerators to build upon. After what . . . happened to Mildred, Dad had left an advanced directive. And so, as per his instructions, Mom ordered his life-support turned off."

"If I had—"

"The only way you could've done anything would be to go out on the boat with him. Do *not* beat yourself up over this. It was out of your control, even if you hadn't been . . ."

I glimpsed briefly how humans can be rendered helpless by sudden shocks. My own infirmity is still news, I am still trying to take in what has happened. And now, the man who was in some ways both father and brother to me . . . my friend . . . is gone.

And I do not know what to do without him. He always knew. He could always help me. And now . . .

"I feel so alone," I say.

Wayne comes around in front of me. "I know. Even after all these years, I still . . ." He stops, weeping.

I cannot weep. But now I understand weeping.

As we leave the grave site, I say, "We must call Millie."

Wayne looks at me, his head cocked to the right. "Carey, a lot has changed. There's no need to rush. Let's make sure you're okay, and then we have to approach her carefully. This will be a shock to her."

"But what happened, Wayne?"

"It's taken Dr. Zinta and me five years to figure that out," Wayne answers. "I'm afraid . . . it's my fault."

"But we planned the procedure so carefully."

Wayne shakes his head. "I thought I was doing you a favor. While we had you out, I upgraded your processing modules to newer equipment. It all tested one hundred percent compatible with your old modules, just three decades newer. I wanted to be sure your circuits didn't wear out."

"And that was a mistake?"

"Yes," he says, "but I couldn't understand. We only really figured it out last month, and then it took us a month to chase down your original equipment and get it back in working order."

"Chase it down?"

Wayne sighs. "So much has happened, so much has changed. There's no good order to tell it in. After your . . . malfunction, things turned bad for MCA. They closed their doors nine months after. All their assets were sold off. Dr. Zinta . . . may have cheated a bit, using her inside connections and some financial help from Mom. She bought all of your designs. Your patents, of course, have long expired. Legally, you're still Mom's property, so MCA's creditors couldn't claim you as part of the bankruptcy assets. But the judge saw you as just part of the assets. Your modules have been . . . Well, in storage, at one of our creditors. They never knew what they had . . ."

"So since my core modules were not connected to power . . . I did not even sleep. I just . . . was not . . ."

"Eventually Dr. Zinta tracked them down," Wayne continues, "once we realized their significance. I was able to clean them up, repair minor damage. Dr. Zinta reinstalled them. And . . . you woke up."

"I'm grateful for that, Wayne, but why? What is special about my original equipment?"

"We had the secret," Wayne says. "Over thirty years ago, if we'd known to look. Remember she tried to use quantum resonance to clone your q-states? Your memory?"

"Yes."

"And it was a disaster, because your q-states became entangled with those of other medical care androids. But we've learned so much about quantum entanglement since then. The conditions that can cause it, the effects that it can have. Eventually she deduced the right answer." I sense guilt, sadness, recrimination. Wayne wishes that *he* had solved the problem. "Researchers have found that quantum processors manufactured in the same batch have a strong tendency to entangle with each other. It happens less often now, because the manufacturing processes are so much tighter. But it happened often then."

"But what does that mean?"

"Carey, the quantum processors in your emulation net, and in your empathy net, and in your control network . . . they're all from the same batch. Successful batches were rare back then, but yours was one of the best. So your combination of nodes is unique. They're not just connected through your internal circuit boards, there's a sort of back channel between them. When something affects your empathy net, it . . . echoes in your emulation net, and in your control network."

My study of cybernetics and quantum computing has not kept up with my medical training. What Wayne says is beyond my comprehension, but I can almost see it. And we have an existence proof that something is unique about me.

As we walk up to Dr. Zinta's door, Wayne continues, "So by trying to upgrade your processors, I broke your entanglement. You became just an android."

I open the door. "This could be the revolution you were looking for," I say.

Wayne turns away. "No, Carey," he says.

"But Wayne—"

"No!" Wayne steps through the door. "That part of my life is over."

Dr. Zinta walks up as we enter. "Wayne . . . Carey . . . How . . ."

"The grave site is beautiful, Mom," I say. "It is very fitting for Paul."

"Yes," she says. "Wayne, we should—"

"No," Wayne interrupts again. "I have to get to work before I'm late." He passes through another door. I briefly glimpse a garage and a car before he closes the door behind him.

I look at Dr. Zinta. "I said something wrong. I hurt Wayne, but I do not understand how."

Dr. Zinta pats my arm. "I heard a little. I can guess the rest. You suggested trying to make more conscious androids."

"Yes," I say. "We have a lead now."

Dr. Zinta shakes her head. "It's not that easy, Carey. Wayne's career is gone."

"I understand, if MCA is gone, he can't work there. But we could get funding, set up a new lab."

"Wayne can't, Carey. The loss of the business and his job . . . Those damaged his reputation. No financier will touch him.

"And Millie . . . Your 'death' hit her hard. And she blamed Wayne. And you to some extent, because you'd agreed with this plan."

"It was my plan," I say. "Not Wayne's."

"Well, she didn't see it that way. She blamed him. And then to lose her father three months later . . . It was too much for her. She was . . . broken, in a way. And she took it out on Wayne. They fought, and they fought. When the money got tight, the fights got worse. When MCA closed, it was the last straw. Millie threw him out."

"But that was four years ago."

"I know," she says. "But they're a couple of stubborn jackasses. Millie won't budge, and Wayne won't talk about it. He moved in with me—back in my old house—and we worked on your problem together. But eventually his savings ran out. Most of it was going to Millie and the kids anyway. He looked for contract work, but his reputation preceded him. Rodrigo went back to Belize and opened his own company. He offered to make Wayne a partner, but . . ."

"But Wayne loves his children," I say. "He could not bear to be so far from them."

Dr. Zinta nods. "Finally . . . he took a job at DeBruyn's Market."

I remember my conversation with Kathryn, so many years ago. *A high school kid . . . Someone who really needs the work* . . . "They put him on the receiving dock."

"Only at first, just so he would have some income. They moved him to IT support as soon as they could. He's in charge of the department now. It's still not up to his potential, but the money's better. He can support the kids, visiting when he can. He's doing what he has to do to support the family."

"And Millie? And the kids?"

"She sold the house. They moved back in with Susan."

"I have to see her. Make sure she is all right."

"Not so fast," Dr. Zinta says. "This is going to be a shock for her."

"She should be happy," I say.

"She should be," Dr. Zinta agrees. "But you've never really grasped the irrational side of people, Carey. Sometimes we don't respond well to change, even to good change."

"But she needs to know."

"Does she?" Dr. Zinta asks. There is an odd, faraway look on her face. "No, you're right, Carey. I just . . .

There's a selfish side of me. I have you back. After five hard years of work, I have you back!"

Then I understand. "And you are reluctant to share me, Mom."

She laughs, but nervously. "I'm a silly, sentimental old lady. You're the closest thing I have to a child. I'm sorry, that's making me say stupid things."

"It is not stupid," I say. I take her hand. "It is human. Special." I pull her closer. "I have not said this yet, Mom, but thank you. Thank you for not giving up. Thank you for giving me life. Again. You are right, we should take our time. I want to learn everything that I have missed. Then we can figure out how to tell Millie."

We spend the rest of the day talking. Dr. Zinta has kept in touch with Millie and Susan, but only infrequently. She knows that Tabitha has taken up dance classes, and that Garrett is on a baseball team. Timmy is very quiet, she says, but he likes to spend time outdoors with animals. Just like his mother. She thinks Susan is retired, but she's unclear on whether that has happened or is happening soon.

I look around the living room. I recognize some of the sculptures from Dr. Zinta's old home, but there are new ones as well. At another time, when I do not have so much else to think about, I would like to study these pieces better.

But then I look out the window, and I see a familiar parking lot, almost empty as usual. "Dr. Zinta, that is Creekside Home."

"Yes," she says. "While you've been . . . gone, I moved into Creekside Estates."

Creekside Estates is an assisted living community run by the same corporation as Creekside Home. "Mom, are you all right?"

"I am," she says. "I'm not sick, I'm not dying, I'm just old. It made sense to be here where I'd have help if I really needed it, and where I didn't have such a big place to take care of. And where Wayne and I could . . . work on you. Try to bring you back."

She gets more coffee, and then she continues. "I moved in here about two years ago," she says. "It wasn't an easy decision to make. Dex—a man I'd been spending time with, I'm not sure if you ever met him—had a bad stroke. His attendant got him into an auto doc right away, but there was still a lot of damage. He came to Creekside for reparative therapy, but the damage was too severe for him to return home. He's a permanent resident now. I can introduce you later.

"But that made me think. And I'd never had an attendant in my home. The idea just felt . . . It felt like taking my work home with me. If I could've had you, that would've been different. But not just an android. And I'm getting older—"

"You are not old, Mom," I interrupted.

"And you're a horrible liar, Carey. I'm pretty fit, thanks to modern medicine and taking care of myself, but I'm old. That could've been me. So I decided . . . Well, I hope Wayne goes home someday, back to Millie; but that would leave me alone. Better to be here, where help is nearby, and people check up on me now and then. And besides, this way I'm close to Dex. He even stays over some nights."

"Oh."

Dr. Zinta laughs. "Did I just embarrass an android?" She laughs again. "I said I'm old, not dead. In fact, why don't I introduce you to Dex now? Plus there are some friends in the home who will be happy to see you."

"But what about *their* shock?" I ask.

"Not to worry," she answers. "We never told them you . . . We just told them you were in for maintenance. They asked about you for a while, but eventually they stopped."

"They forgot me."

"Oh, Carey, don't act so hurt."

"I am not hurt," I say. "It is expected. The residents have memory and cognitive impairments. Forgetting is not surprising."

"No, Carey, you've got it wrong," she says. "A lot of people come and go there. A lot of them pass away there. It's polite not to mention those who are gone."

37. TONIGHT WE HAVE A PARTY

We head across the street, through the empty parking lot, and into the dining room. It is too late for lunch, and too early for dinner, so the room is unoccupied save for an android putting out tablecloths. The android looks up at us, a stiff smile on its face, and says, "Good afternoon, Dr. Zinta." Then it pauses, almost as if surprised. "Carey Owens?"

I look closer. It looks like the tour guide from Meijer Gardens. Since it recognizes me, it must be the same unit. "Yes, that is me."

I turn to Dr. Zinta. Before I can ask, she explains, "The guides at the Gardens were a test project. They didn't work out so well. Oh, no problems," she adds, "just people didn't make much use of them. And MCA needed the money, back before the company folded, so Doctor Warren sold them off. A lot of them ended up in health care facilities. It *is* how we got started, after all."

We continue through the dining room, and up to the east nurses' station. I recognize only one of the nurses,

Nell Kilgore. She looks up and recognizes me as well. "Carey!" She leans out over the desk, arms outstretched, and I lean in to briefly hug her. Over the years, my no-contact rule had been relaxed until it was effectively eliminated. And it had never applied to staff. "It is good to see you, Nell," I say. I do not add that in my memory, I had seen her only yesterday. I will have to learn to adjust to a five-year gap.

"Does Vera know you're here?" she asks.

"We haven't told her," Dr. Zinta says. "Is she in?"

"Yes," Nell answers. "She's in her office. Why don't you go in and surprise her?"

We head down the north hall, to the Director of Nursing office. I see that it now has a new nameplate: NURSE VERA RAYBURN. Dr. Zinta taps on the door, and Nurse Rayburn calls from within, "Come in." Dr. Zinta opens the door and we enter.

The office is tidier than Director Kane kept it. Nurse Rayburn was always a stickler for neatness; and with no need for paper books or reports, there is nothing to clutter up the place, just pictures of family and residents.

"What is—" Nurse Rayburn looks up from her desk. "Carey!" She gets up from behind the desk, rushes around it, and embraces me in a strong hug. "Carey, you're alive!"

I look to Dr. Zinta, and she shrugs. "She kept asking about you. I had to tell her."

"Oh, Carey," Nurse Rayburn says. "Is it really you? I mean . . . you're not a copy or something like that, are you?"

"Would it matter?" I ask.

"Well, no . . . But . . . Yes, it would."

"I am myself," I answer. "Carey Owens, the android who worked for you for twelve years."

"Oh, Carey." She backs away and grips my shoulders in her hands. "It's so good to see you." Then she turns and grins at Dr. Zinta. "I knew you could do it! I never doubted you."

Nurse Rayburn looks me over top to bottom again, and then she turns to Dr. Zinta. "Have you told Dex yet?"

"Not yet," Dr. Zinta answers. "We were just going to find him now. But I wanted you to know that Carey's back."

"Thank you! We should have a party tonight to celebrate. You've still got some friends here, Carey, who will be happy to see you back." Then she pauses. "You *are* back, aren't you? I mean, are you coming back to work?"

At first I do not understand the question. I still have not adjusted to the five-year gap. So I do not see any question about coming back.

But then I remember, and I realize that it is a complex question. "I do not know," I say. "I would like to, but I need to see if Millie and Susan need me."

Nurse Rayburn nods. "Of course, family first. I understand. But just so you know, you're always welcome here. Creekside hasn't been the same without you."

Nurse Rayburn is very efficient at putting together a party on short notice. Somewhere she comes up with streamers and balloons, and she instructs the nutrition bot to prepare special menus for everyone. She insists on keeping me hidden until the residents are seated for their meals. She goes into the dining room ahead of me, and says to the residents, "I'm sure you've all noticed the good china tonight." The residents laugh and cheer. "You may have noticed a special menu as well. And you know it wasn't on the calendar, so you're wondering why." Again there are cheers and voices of agreement. "Well," she says, "it's all to celebrate an old friend coming back for a *visit*." She emphasizes that last word as she turns back to the door and waves me in. "Come in, Carey."

I walk in, and I am met with cheers and applause. My empathy net is overwhelmed with good feelings. Several residents come up to see me and shake my hand: Auralee, Diego, Salvador, and many others. In the back of the room, I see Dr. Zinta standing next to a tall, thin, graying man who must be Dex. She smiles at me, and he waves. I wave back.

I greet so many old friends, all with variations of the same questions. "Where have you been?" "How long can you stay?" And "Are you back for good?"

Nurse Rayburn fields many of the questions herself, which is good. I am not comfortable lying about my absence. Still, I dissemble as well as I am able.

But amid all the smiles and chatter, there are faces that I miss. Nurse Rayburn had told me about Mrs. Carruthers, of course, and some others. Some we lost before my absence, when I still worked here.

But one . . . I tap Nurse Rayburn on the shoulder and gesture for her to lean closer. When she does, I ask, "Is Luke . . . ?"

She frowns. "He's still with us, Carey," she says. "But he . . . doesn't come to the dining hall much anymore. He doesn't do much of anything but sit in his room."

"I see." I feel an impulse to go find Luke; but as much as I would like to, I have too many friends here. I cannot abandon them again, not so soon.

So we have a celebration. The nutrition bot serves up healthy but high-quality, tasty meals for everyone. I insist on serving my friends myself, going from table to table, stopping briefly to talk to each one. They introduce me to their new friends, and I file each name away for later. I can only spare a few words for each person, or else the food will get cold; but I promise each one that we will talk more in the days ahead.

That is when I realize that I have decided: I *am* coming back. I am needed here.

Once everyone is eating, I make the rounds of the tables again. Several times I have to remind my friends to eat their food while it's still warm. "This is too good to waste," I say.

The nutrition bot comes in at the end with special dessert: ice cream, sherbet, and fruit freezes for everyone. I scoop up the dishes, while Dr. Zinta and Dex and the attendant droid carry them to the tables. It is a splendid night, as festive as any I have seen since Millie and Wayne's wedding.

But that memory gives me pause. It reminds me that celebrations can be brief, and trouble can follow. I wonder what I will find in Luke's room.

I tap on the partly open door. "Luke? Are you awake?" He does not answer, so I push the door fully open, and I walk inside.

Luke lies in his hospital bed. He wears an old red robe.

He used to say that robes were for old people sitting around, waiting to die. Now I see what he means. He has shrunk. His muscles have atrophied. He stares intently at the TV, even though it is not on.

"Luke," I try again. "Nurse Rayburn said you were here."

After a long pause, Luke says, "She said I should come see you. I didn't believe her."

"I wish you had come," I say. "We had a great party. There was even ice cream. I saved you some." I hold out a bowl. "Cherry ripple."

At that, his eyes twitch. Cherry ripple is his favorite. But he remains stern. "Where'd you go, Bo?" he asks.

I cannot bring myself to lie to Luke, so I think of a truth that he can understand. "I had sort of a brain injury," I say.

"You? A brain injury?" He reaches up and touches his own head. "I didn't think that could happen. Did you lose your memory, too?"

I think how to answer that. "A little bit," I say. "But it was more like I was in a coma. I did not forget, I just never knew what was around me. So do you want the ice cream?"

"Never pass up cherry ripple," he says, and he smiles.

In that moment, I see the old Luke. He has gotten grayer, weaker, but he is still Luke. Still my friend. I hand him the ice cream, and I sit so we can talk.

He is still reticent. He talks a little about residents that we knew, but that is a delicate subject. Too many of them have passed away. Mostly, he talks about the circus, stories that I have heard half a dozen times before. But I listen attentively. Telling them makes Luke smile.

Finally, when Luke pauses for a bit, I ask the question that has been bothering me. "Luke, Nurse Rayburn says you never come to dinner anymore. Why is that?"

Just like that, Luke withdraws again. "Don't feel like it," is all he says.

"But Luke, you still have friends out there."

"I know," he says. "They come in during the day. We talk." Then he turns to me. "But I'm old, Bo. Tired." He pauses before adding, "Useless. Nothing more useless than a circus *artiste* who can't do his act no more. Who wants to come see that?" Another pause, and then he adds, "Who wants to see me?"

From the way he asks, I sense a deeper sorrow. "Has Gordon come to visit?" Luke's son Gordon never had visited very often. Maybe three or four times a year, while on business trips or for holidays. I know that used to make Luke sad; but he would always say, *"At least he comes."*

I can see from the way Luke's mouth freezes that I have hit the mark. "I am sorry, Luke," I say. "Maybe you should call him."

"I'm not gonna beg," Luke says. "I may not have my reflexes anymore, I may be missing half my marbles, but I've still got my pride."

His pride. Something to feel good about in his life. That gives me an idea. "Luke," I say, "you've still got good eyes, do you not?" He nods. "You still know our routine, right?"

"Yes," he says.

"Then you can still teach me. I am out of practice, and you still have twenty years of tricks I haven't learned yet."

Luke looks at me. "You don't think you can fool an old man just because his brain's a bit rattled, do you?"

"All right," I say, "that sounded like a trick. But it is not, Luke. I enjoy working on our act. I enjoy talking to you. So this is something I want to do."

Luke is silent for so long, I worry that I have angered him. Or perhaps that he has fallen asleep. But then at last he says, "You better be on time. You have to learn a new solo act, and I'm gonna make you work at it."

38. TODAY WE HAVE A FAMILY REUNION

The next morning, Dr. Zinta calls Millie's home number, but Susan answers. I stand outside of the video pickup as Dr. Zinta says, "Good morning, Susan. I have some very good news."

"Oh?" Susan's eyes light up. "You don't mean . . ."

"I do!" Dr. Zinta says. "Come here, Carey."

I step into the camera's view, and Susan starts to cry. "Carey! Is that you?"

"It is I, Susan. I am so sorry I have caused you pain."

Susan's tears flow. "It's not pain, Carey. It's . . . Oh, please . . . Dr. Zinta, can you come over right away? Carey's not . . . injured, is it?"

"Carey's fine," Dr. Zinta says. "We just weren't sure how to break this to you. We thought it might be a shock."

"Of course it's a shock! But a good one. Please, I want to see you both."

"Is Millie home?" I ask.

"No," Susan says, "she's at the university. But I'll call her right away. She'll want to come home for you."

✳   ✳   ✳

307

We walk into the Owens home, and I am disturbed by what I see. The shelves and lampshades have not been dusted recently. There are children's books and dirty clothes scattered on the stairs. I cannot smell, but my room air analyzers show the air to be stale, with hints of dust, old body odor, and food waste. The floors show no signs of recent mopping, and only halfhearted sweeping. What is wrong with the cleaning bots?

Susan hobbles into the entryway from the living room, and I see that she is walking with an assist suit. The way she moves, I can see that she has pain in her right hip. "Susan, are you all right?"

"Oh, don't mind me," she says as she limps forward and hugs me. With her face buried in my shoulder, she says, "My new hip has troubles. But today I don't care. Today I feel like I could dance."

My ultrasound scanner shows a divide in her femur. A section of the shaft has been regenerated. The muscle around it is still loose. "This is a recent break. Susan, when did you break your hip?"

"Just last month," she says. "I got out of therapy ten days ago, and now I'm walking again."

"But you shouldn't be," I say.

"Nonsense," Susan says. "It's good exercise."

"Yes," I say. "But still, we should sit."

"OK."

Susan turns away, and I see her wince. So I add, "I could carry you."

Susan half turns back and glares at me. "No, you can *not!* Dr. Elmhurst says I won't get better if I take the easy way out. Next week he'll take off the assist suit so I'll be completely on my own. Walking is the best exercise for me, he said . . . no matter how bad it hurts."

Dr. Zinta and I follow Susan back to the living room, and Susan sits in the old blue wingback chair. "You know I prefer the couch," she says, "but I can't get out of it right now. Not even with the assist suit. So please, you two, sit."

Dr. Zinta and I sit on the old gray couch. I cannot help noticing that it has stains and scuff marks that had not been there before. Scattered clothes and toys plus a pile of dishes in the sink and on the counter are proof that children live here now.

Susan beams at me. "Carey, you're all right? You're not . . . damaged?"

"My diagnostics say I am fine," I reply.

Dr. Zinta nods. "As good as new. Well, better with all the upgrades."

I continue. "The only stress I feel is emotional. I am sorry that I have caused such pain to you and Millie. I am sorry that I have missed so much in your lives, and the children's lives. Five years is so long for them." I pause, but there is no way to avoid what else I have to say. "And I am so sorry that I did not get to say goodbye to Paul."

I see sadness in Susan's face, and in how her shoulders slump; but when she speaks, there is only a slight tremor in her voice. "I know," she says. "I miss him every day, Carey, but . . . Five years . . . You build up scars in five years."

"Still, I wish I could have been there for you."

"Oh, Carey . . ." Her eyes seem to look through us. "It was a beautiful ceremony. So many people turned out . . . to say goodbye . . ." A tear rolls down Susan's cheek. I spot a box of tissues on the end table, and I hold them out to her. She takes out two. "Thank you, Carey."

Susan tells me about Paul's funeral, and Dr. Zinta adds in her own memories. When Dr. Zinta mentions the children, I use that as an excuse to nudge the conversation in another direction: how the children are doing in school. Slowly, that brings a smile to Susan's face. She is a proud grandmother.

Then Susan looks around the room and laughs. "But they're not exactly neat."

"Oh," I say, "I do not mind."

Susan shakes her head. "I try to keep up; but now, with this hip . . ."

"I can help," I say.

"Oh, no! Guests don't have to clean."

Guests. I feel it then: Susan is happy to see me again, but also reserved. Not quite as much as when I first knew her, when I was Mildred's caretaker, but reserved nonetheless.

I had seen a little of this at Creekside: old friends who were not quite sure how to respond to my return. I can only hope that in time, these relationships will get back to normal.

One way to get back to normal is to act normally. "I do not mind, Susan," I say. "You know I like to help. We can talk while I clean up."

"Oh, but . . ." Susan sighs. "It really would be a help."

So I start straightening up, arranging the children's things into piles to go upstairs later. I find that dust rags are where they always were, in the cupboard under the stairs. And I also see the six cleaning bots stowed away in their chargers, with their lights off. "Susan, is there something wrong with the cleaning bots?"

"Oh," she says, "we put them away. They were just . . . a nuisance." She says *nuisance*; I hear *reminders of me*. But I do not bring that up with Susan. She is slowly adjusting to my return, and there is no need to go back over my absence.

When the dusting is done, I tackle the dishes. The dishwasher is full, as are both sinks and the counter. "I'm sorry the place is such a mess," Susan says.

"Susan," Dr. Zinta answers, "you've got a house full. Three active kids. No explanation needed, and no apologies."

"I know," Susan says. "I love my grandchildren. They bring me so much joy. But sometimes they're a handful. They're in so many activities, and every one of them means more gear around the house. Dance shoes, baseballs . . . Oh! I've got Garrett's baseball pictures." She pulls a tablet from her purse and turns it to me to see. "See?"

I look, and I almost do not recognize Garrett. "He has grown so much in five years," I say. "He looks so much like Wayne now."

"He does," Susan says looking down at her hands. From Susan's tone, I believe that she is reluctant to discuss Wayne. But I do not press. She has her reasons.

When I am done with the dishes, I say, "Is there any laundry that needs doing?"

At that, Susan stands from her stool at the bar. "That's enough, Carey. Thank you, but you've done enough already." Then the door chime sounds, and Susan adds, "Besides, this has to be Millie."

The door opens, and I hear the heavy tromp of multiple footsteps. I turn back to the dining room just in time to see the children round the corner. From his pictures, I know Garrett; but Timmy and Tabitha I can barely recognize. Their eyes are the same, but so much else has changed as they have grown.

But they recognize me. "Uncle Carey!" they cry out, practically in unison as they run up and wrap their arms around me. "Uncle Carey, you're back!"

As they let me go, I crouch down to their level. That is not nearly as low as I remember. "Yes, Tabby, Timmy, Garrett. I am back, and I am so happy to see you."

Timmy looks at me, and he frowns. "They said you were dead."

Susan gasps, while Dr. Zinta smothers a laugh. Timmy is as blunt and impulsive as I remember him.

"I was broken, Timmy," I say. "It took Dr. Zinta and your father a long time to fix me."

"I knew Dad could do it!" Garrett says, grinning with pride.

"And he did," I say. "But I was never dead. I am a machine, you know that."

"No you're not," Tabby says. "You're Uncle Carey!"

The look on her face as she says this is something I think would make a human smile. She is so stern, so determined. She looks so much like—

"Hello, Carey." I look up, and Millie stands just at the edge of the entryway. There is something in her face that I have never seen before: the set of her jaw, the narrowing of her eyes, the glare. She seems cold. Bitter.

I stand. "Hello, Millie." I am not sure what else to say,

so I just hold my hands out from my side and say, "I'm back."

"I can see that," she says. The bitterness is evident in her voice as well. Then she turns to Dr. Zinta. "Congratulations, Dr. Jansons. You do good work."

Dr. Zinta nods. "Thank you, Millie. *We* just . . . couldn't give up."

"I'm impressed," Millie says. "I gave up years ago."

"Millie!" Susan says.

Millie turns to Susan. "What did you expect, Mom? It's been five years. Eventually, we move on."

Susan frowns. I look at her, and in a soothing voice, I say, "It is all right, Susan. Millie is right. A lot has changed while I have been gone, and you all have adjusted. I cannot assume to simply walk back in as if nothing has changed . . . even if nothing has for me."

Millie sighs. "It's not like that, Carey," she says. "Just . . . Well, it's that, and more. We have our routine. We have our new life. And now . . ."

"I know," I say. "You know I do not want to make anyone uncomfortable. You need some time to get used to this. I must respect that."

"But Uncle Carey," Tabitha says, "can't you come live with us?"

Again I crouch down beside her, and I look into her eyes. "Thank you, Tabby," I say. "It is nice to be asked." I glance over at Millie, then I turn back to Tabby. "Let us not rush things. Your house is very full, and very busy. You would not want me to just rush in and change everything, would you?"

"I would," Timmy says.

I pat his arm. "Thank you, Timmy. But let us take some time before we decide how to proceed."

With that, a seeming truce is drawn. I am a welcome guest, and that is enough. Whether I shall be more is up to Millie.

We return to the living room, and the children pile around me on the couch and tell me of everything they can remember from the past five years. Tabitha shows me how she dances, and I compliment her on her grace. Garrett tells me about his baseball team and their race for a pennant. I have to admit that I do not know much about baseball. It was nothing that Millie followed.

Timmy mostly sits by me, quietly holding my arm. I try to get him to say more. He answers direct questions, but he volunteers little more.

Eventually, I notice that it is nearing dinner time. "Children," I say, "it is almost time for dinner."

"Oh!" Tabby says. "Can you and Dr. Jansons have dinner with us?"

I glance sideways at Millie's face, and I see my answer. "No," I say. "You know that I do not eat. And Doctor Jansons's friend Dex is expecting her for dinner."

"Awww . . ." Timmy says.

"It is all right," I say. I extricate myself from the children, and I rise. "I will be back to visit very soon." Then I give each child a hug, and Dr. Zinta and I head outside.

Millie follows us out, and she stops me with a touch on my arm. "Thank you for understanding, Carey," she says. "I just . . . need some time."

"I understand, Millie. That is what I do."

❊   ❊   ❊

And I do understand. My empathy net is still functional. Millie is buried in powerful layers of emotions, some she may not even realize. She is happy for me to be back, but also surprised. She had not expected Wayne and Dr. Zinta to succeed in their efforts.

And she is still resentful. She is arguably even right to be: She had begged Wayne and me not to go forward with our experiment; and the worst had happened, just as she had feared.

In her next layer, Millie is caught up in an impossible wish: If I can come back, why cannot Paul? She knows that is irrational; but as I keep learning, feelings are not rational. At some level, she even resents me for coming back when he cannot. And she is angry at herself for that resentment.

And at her outermost layer, Millie's losses have made her afraid to trust. Afraid that she will get hurt again. That letting me back into her life is one more person she can lose. Again.

I understand all this, but I cannot tell anyone else. My privacy protocols. To others, Millie seems cold, harsh. Her new defenses make her withdrawn.

I wish I could help Millie with this, help all of them. But I cannot until she is ready.

39. TODAY WE PERFORM

Millie needs time, so I will give it to her. I shall maintain social contact, and make it clear that I am here for what she needs, but I shall not pressure her.

It takes time to adjust to life with Wayne and Dr. Zinta. Their routine is nothing at all like Susan and Paul's had been. In small ways, it is like I have returned to my life with Mildred. Dr. Zinta's mind is fine and her body is still healthy, but she is more frail than Susan. She gladly accepts my help in and out of the tub, for example. She relies more on ready-made packaged meals, and she wants to talk a lot. Susan has never been so chatty. It is pleasant to talk to Dr. Zinta, but it is different.

Wayne, meanwhile, is changing. I think that my recovery has freed him from a burden of guilt that he has carried for five years. Slowly, his mood lightens, and he starts to discuss cybernetics with me. I foresee that his old optimistic nature will heal, given time.

In the meantime, I still have my volunteer work at Creekside. The next day, I return to work. The nursing staff welcome me back. Nell takes me on a tour of the facilities, pointing out new equipment and changed procedures. She also introduces me to new residents. And of course, old friends want me to stop and talk. Even keeping the conversations brief, the tour runs up to lunch.

I spend the lunch delivering trays to the rooms of residents who do not come to the dining hall. This duty, at least, never changes. The residents change, and the meals and instructions change, but not the responsibility: Bring them in their meals, talk to them, and take care of whatever they need.

I am disappointed to find that Luke is still one of the shut-ins. "Luke," I say, "do you want to come to lunch?"

"Nah, Bo," he says. "Maybe tomorrow. I got used to eating in here."

I nod, but I do not comment. Like Millie, Luke needs time to adjust. So I change the subject. "Do we start my lessons today?"

"I suppose we could," Luke answers. "When you're free."

"I have lunch duties and cleanup until two. Shall I come by then?"

Luke agrees; and promptly at two, I return to his room. I help him into his wheelchair, and we head out to the front lawn. There we start to work.

For the first two weeks, Luke always comes out in his wheelchair. I check with Nurse Rayburn, and she says that Luke is approved for an assist suit, he just seldom uses it. So with a little persuasion, he agrees to wear it for our training sessions. In under a week, he grows comfortable with it, and he wears it everywhere. He returns to the common areas on a regular basis, and he starts dining with the other residents again. They welcome him back, almost as warmly as they had welcomed me.

The only time Luke complains about the assist suit is when he tries to juggle. "Blasted thing!" he says. "It's too steady."

After years of working with him, I understand what he means. A juggler needs to be relaxed, able to move fluidly in response to slight changes in trajectory. The assist suit gives him stability, but not agility.

So, frustrated, he concentrates on my lessons. I discover that my joints have stiffened during my absence. My programming still tells me what to do with the balls, but my joints do not always respond correctly. Once I would have gone to MCA for adjustment and replacement parts if needed. Now Wayne and Dr. Zinta do what they can; but without replacement parts and a real lab, they cannot fully restore my function. I shall have to relearn my routine despite the stiffness.

Another thing has changed during my absence. Once, Creekside had been on a quiet street, just the Home and the Estates and a handful of houses before the park. But today there are two new homes on the street, and three more families have moved in as well. Today there are children. The first I notice is a little boy, perhaps five years old, who lives in a house across the street. He comes out from his house one morning, sits under a tree in his front yard, and watches me practice.

In a low voice, Luke says, "Don't get distracted, Bo. You're the *artiste*, he's the audience. You don't watch him, he watches you."

I nod, and I continue juggling. Luke has me practicing a complicated routine with a mixed set: balls, bowling pins, and a plastic cow. Every time I catch the cow, it moos, and the little boy laughs.

That gives Luke an idea, and he says to me, in the same low voice, "Just the cow, Bo. Hacky sack style."

I nod, and one by one, I let the balls and the bowling pins drop until only the cow is airborne. And then, using my feet and my hands, I bounce the cow into the air. On every bounce, it moos, and the boy laughs again. Soon I hear continuous laughter; and despite Luke's admonitions, I turn and look over at the boy. He is holding his side as he laughs.

Then, distracted, I lose track of the cow, and it lands straight on my head with a loud moo. And the boy rolls on the grass, laughing.

A young man comes out from the house and walks over to the boy, looking down at him with hands on hips. They talk, though the boy is still laughing too hard for words. He just points over at us. Finally, the boy holds up his hand, the man takes it, and they walk across the street. "Smile," Luke says. "Here come the rubes."

The man walks over to Luke and says, "Hi, I'm Van Sherman, and this is Kenny."

"I'm Luke," Luke says as he shakes hands with Van. "Nice to meet you, Kenny." Luke and the boy shake as well. "And this is my buddy Bo."

I shake hands with both of them as well. Then Van says, "Is it all right if we watch?"

Luke grins. "Van, the only thing an old circus ham likes more than an act is an act with an audience. You just made our day. Take a spot over there while I get Bo back to work."

As Van and Kenny move to the indicated spot, Luke leans in to me and whispers, "Hey, Bo, miss a couple here and there."

"What?"

"Trust me, I know what I'm doing." Luke hands me just the three balls this time, and I settle into my basic routine. Van and Kenny watch.

Then at a nod from Bo, I miss the red ball. It bounces once on the grass and then rolls away. Kenny stands up and shouts, "I got it!" As I keep the green and the blue going, Kenny runs after the red ball. He picks it up and turns to me with a big smile on his face.

Luke says, "Throw it back to him, Kenny." Kenny looks at Luke, eyes wide. "Come on!" Luke says. "You can do it." Kenny turns to me, and he lobs the ball in my direction. This requires a quick reaction from me. Luke has decades of training, so he always throws the ball with perfect timing for my routine. Kenny is young and has no clue what he is doing. I have to stretch, and I almost miss the red ball; but I catch it just in time to catch the green ball as well as it falls. I snap back straight, passing the red ball back into the cycle, and I keep juggling.

So we add this into the routine. Occasionally I miss the ball, and Kenny chases it down and throws it back to me. His aim does not improve; but I learn to read it, so I get better at catching his returns. I briefly glimpse Van during this routine. His grin is so wide, it ought to hurt.

Eventually, my internal chronometer signals. I catch the three balls, and I say, "I am sorry, Kenny, Van. That is all we have time for today. It is time for Luke's medicine."

"Medicine?" Kenny stares at Luke. "Are you sick?"

Luke carefully crouches down next to Kenny. "My head got hurt, a long time ago. I forget things." Then he pokes Kenny in the stomach, and the boy squeals. "But I won't forget you! Not if I take my medicine."

"Awww," Kenny says.

"That's okay," Luke says. "You're welcome back anytime."

Kenny looks up at Van, his eyes bright. "Can we come back tomorrow, Dad?"

"I'm sorry," Van says, looking down at Kenny. "I have to go back to work tomorrow. You'll have to ask the sitter. But remember: You're not allowed to cross the street alone."

Kenny looks at me. "What if Bo comes and gets me?"

Van looks at me as well. "I suppose, if Bo doesn't mind."

"I would be happy to," I say. And it is true. Luke stands taller, straighter. He grins. Having an audience has made him happier than I have ever seen him. And that makes me happy.

40. TODAY OUR TROUPE GROWS

When I return to Creekside the next afternoon, Luke and I go out to the front to practice. Kenny stands in his yard, waiting for us. Before I cross the street, I make an exaggerated effort to look both ways. I want to set a good example. A teen girl—the babysitter, I assume—waves at me from the porch, and I wave back.

I walk up to Kenny. "Hello, Mr. Bo," he says, holding out his hand.

"Hello, Kenny." I take his hand, and we return to the north side of the road. Today Luke has me intentionally work Kenny into the act.

The next day, Kenny is not alone. A taller, thinner girl with long blonde hair stands with him. She looks at me, and her eyes are very big. I think that I have seen her in the yard of one of the new houses.

"Mr. Bo," Kenny says, "this is my friend, Patty. Can she play, too?"

This question surprises me. I cannot give permission for another person's child. "Patty," I say, "is your mother or father at home?"

In a very soft voice, Patty answers, "Mom is."

"Then I think we should ask her," I say. I lead the children next door, and I ring the doorbell.

A woman answers. From her eyes, her facial structure, and her hair, it is easy to see that she is Patty's mother. She looks down at Patty and Kenny, and then up at me. "Can I help you?"

"Please," I say. "Patty would like to join us across the street. We're practicing juggling."

"And they're teaching me," Kenny adds.

"Yes," I say. "Patty has asked to join us, so I wanted to be sure that that is all right."

The woman grins. "A juggling android?"

"He's really good!" Kenny says.

"Well, I think we all should see that," she says. "Hi, I'm Hope."

So Hope and Patty both join us. Misha, the babysitter, follows behind. At first our new visitors just sit and watch. Patty is shy, even though her mother tries to convince her to join in.

But eventually, Kenny pesters Patty into catching the ball. She throws it back to me, and I see that she is better at throwing than Kenny is. Soon, both children are laughing, and Luke starts taking them and Misha aside one at a time to practice catching.

At one point, I look around, and I see that our audience has grown. Four of Creekside's residents have come out to watch our rehearsal. They stand over by Hope, and they laugh and applaud along with her.

Slowly, day by day, our audience grows. More

neighborhood children arrive, and more residents join them. Older children join us as well, and also more local parents.

And that is not all that grows. Our troupe, as Luke calls it, increases as well. On our eleventh afternoon, he counts. ". . . seven, eight, nine." Luke shakes his head and looks at me. "Too many," he says.

"What?"

"Too many jugglers," he says. "The show don't need nine jugglers."

"Awww . . ." the children say.

"I'm sorry," Luke says, turning to the children. "That's just the way it is. We're gonna have to cut back on jugglers." Then, as their faces grow long, he claps his hands and says, "So . . . Who knows how to do a somersault?"

And so we add new acts to our Creekside circus. Some of the children have had tumbling classes, and one of the oldest is a capable acrobat. Three bring over their dogs, and they show off their tricks. Hope volunteers to work with them, promising Luke a real animal act. With a little prodding, Luke finds dancers, singers, musicians, comics, and several aspiring clowns.

And some of the residents join the show as well. Lisa takes charge of Clown Alley, while Nora is thrilled to apply her cosmetician skills for clown makeup. Miguel turns out to be an excellent dancer, and still quite limber, so he teaches new routines to the dance company.

Soon we must add a new assignment: traffic control. The Creekside facilities are on a side street, blocks from any main road in town, and ending in a loop that edges the park. Until now, traffic through here had been light. The few walkers and joggers crossed the street without worry, easily sharing the way with the few cars that came through. The street is so quiet, it has only one sidewalk, on our side. The other side is simply grass.

But now we have more: both more cars coming, more relatives drawn by the show, and also many more people in the street. It is too much, too close together. Locals who are not with the circus find themselves blocked, and angry. Twice pedestrians are almost struck. So some of the parents start serving as crossing guards.

In the third week of the Bo & Luke Creekside Circus, Nurse Rayburn taps me on the shoulder at lunch. "Carey, I'd like to speak with you in my office," she says. Then she taps Luke. "You, too."

Luke looks at his comp. "It's almost rehearsal time, Nurse Ratched."

"They can start without you," she says. "This won't take long. And I insist."

Luke rises easily. He has become more adept with his assist suit, and he has even started juggling again. We follow nurse Rayburn to her office. When we have both squeezed in, she closes the door. We turn to look at her, and she wraps her arms around both of us, pulling us into a group hug. "Thank you," she says, choking back a sob.

"For what?" Luke asks.

"For this," she says. She pulls a tablet from her desk, taps it, and hands it to us. It shows the view from the front lawn security camera. Our troupe is out there already, stretching and setting up for rehearsal. The audience is starting to gather. One of the neighbors hands out cookies to children and the residents. Cora has brought out her guitar and is singing to the crowd as they wait for us.

"For this," Nurse Rayburn repeats. "You two are a couple of miracle workers. The residents are more excited than I've ever seen them, even more excited than when you came back, Carey. This is more happiness than I've seen in this place in my career. And more visitors! Look at that." The neighbors and the residents mingle freely, trading jokes and stories. Some of the children cling to the residents like long-lost grandparents. "Miracle workers."

41. TODAY WE ARE
SHUT DOWN

The next morning, Susan and Dr. Zinta and I take the children to Meijer Gardens. This time the children are eager to see the whole park. We stop and discuss each sculpture. Like everyone, they are in awe of Nina Akamu's "American Horse," a twenty-four-foot bronze horse inspired by Leonardo da Vinci. Tabby asks me to lift her up so she can touch the raised left hoof, but Timmy is proud that he can stand on his toes and reach it himself. Then the children climb the grassy hill behind the horse and tumble down it, laughing.

Susan tires easily, and I am reminded of her age. She refuses help, but she is quick to rest any time she can. She seems distracted, but she enjoys the children's laughter.

Millie begged off joining us, claiming she had work to do at the university. I do not question her explanation, but I do not find it convincing.

During our fourth week of the circus, an expensive-looking car pulls into the Creekside parking lot, and a man in a suit gets out. I happen to be in the dining room, preparing for lunch, so I see him walk in. "Good morning," he says. "Who is in charge here, please?"

"Nurse Rayburn is the Director of Nursing," I answer. "Shall I take you to see her?"

"Please," he says.

"Who should I say is calling?"

"Councilman Sherman."

So as I lead the councilman to Nurse Rayburn's office, I call ahead on my internal comm, "Councilman Sherman wishes to see you."

"Councilman?" She frowns. "All right, bring him in, but stall a couple of minutes."

So I walk slowly, and I let myself get distracted by greetings from the residents. Luke notices, and I give him a slight nod to get his help. He comes up to talk. "Hello, Bo. Who's your friend?"

I point at Sherman. "This is Councilman Sherman. Councilman, this is Eddie Lucas, circus acrobat."

Sherman sniffs. "Circus, yes. Nice to meet you, Mr. Lucas."

"Just call me Luke, Shemp." Luke holds out his hands.

Sherman shakes his head. "It's Sherman," he says, shaking Luke's hand.

"Sorry," Luke says. "I'll try to remember that. Is it election season already?"

"I don't understand," Sherman replies.

"Only time we generally see politicians around here is when they're trolling for votes. I guess they figure you gotta be crazy to vote for them."

"Luke!" Nell says, walking by just in time to hear Luke's remark. She playfully slaps his arm.

"You saw that, Councilman!" Luke says. "Elder abuse! What're you gonna do about it?"

"I—I—"

Luke grins. My internal comm chimes, telling me that Nurse Rayburn is ready. I nod at Luke again. "Just funnin', Shemp," he says. He takes Nell's arm, and they walk away. Councilman Sherman stares after them. Then he goes into the office and closes the door behind himself.

As soon as the door is closed, Luke returns. "What's Shemp want?"

"He did not say," I answer.

"Won't be anything good," Luke says. "When a politician notices this place, if it's not about votes, it's trouble."

The closed-door meeting lasts twenty minutes. At the end, Nurse Rayburn leads Councilman Sherman out through the dining room, which is now full with the lunch crowd. As they stand at the exit, he turns back and says, "I'm very sorry, Nurse Rayburn. I understand your points, but it's a safety issue. We really have no choice." And he turns around and leaves.

The dining hall is silent. No one speaks, and no one eats. No one moves. They just stare at Nurse Rayburn as she slowly turns around and looks around the room. Her mouth is turned down, and she looks on the verge of tears.

At last, she clears her throat and speaks. "Well . . . Since most everyone is here, there's no sense in waiting." She looks over at Luke, and I see him frown as well. "Councilman Sherman has informed me of a number of safety and sanitation concerns. The circus and the audience have grown to be too big, a traffic hazard."

"But we have crossing guards," Nora says.

Nurse Rayburn shakes her head. "It's not enough. They're worried that in an emergency, fire trucks can't get through. Or . . . or ambulances." At that, several heads nod, and Nurse Rayburn continues, "Yes, this is because of that incident last week. That ambulance that couldn't get out."

At that, the crowd goes silent. In that case, the ambulance had been transporting a patient to the hospital for a checkup; and the delay had been brief. But these residents, at this stage of their lives . . . Any one of them could have been on that ambulance, and the delay could have risked their lives.

Nurse Rayburn continues, "So I'm sorry to say . . . they're shutting down the circus. Effective immediately."

At that, the room erupts into rumbles. They love this circus, but they are also afraid. The rumbles grow; but Nurse Rayburn shouts over them until at last they quiet down and listen. "I'm sorry," she says. "It really is a safety issue."

Cora stands. "Isn't there something we can do?"

Nurse Rayburn shakes her head. "I've asked to address the town council next week, but Councilman Sherman doesn't hold out much hope. He suggests we rent a hall or an arena."

"But that's too far!" Miguel replies. "We can't walk there. This is our neighborhood show!"

Luke stands and turns to look out at the room. He shakes his head. "Maybe Shemp's right," he says. The crowd murmurs, but he raises a hand to silence them. "This has been fun, and you all made this old man feel young again. But we're not a real circus." There are more murmurs, but he talks over them. "Hell, we're not even a dog and pony show. No ponies. No, a *real* circus *does* think about safety and managing the crowd. The circus is supposed to be a fun place, a magical place, but not a dangerous place. Not for real. A show needs more than a lawn with people dragging out chairs. It needs a better, safer, more appropriate venue."

Then Luke looks at me, and he smiles. "Like Bonnie Creek Park."

The residents cheer, and immediately they start throwing together ideas for how we could use the park.

42. TODAY WE ATTEND THE TOWN COUNCIL MEETING

On Saturday, I spend the day with the Owenses. The children tell me how they are spending their summer. Timmy is taking swimming lessons, and Susan tells me that his coach thinks Timmy can make the school team in the fall. Susan has been teaching Tabby to play keyboards and to sing. Garrett asks to examine my internal circuits. He has developed a strong interest in cybernetics, and he has reprogrammed the cleaning bots. The bots all dance around me and talk to me. They are not self-aware, but they present a convincing simulation at first.

Susan is delighted by the dancing bots, but she asks an odd question. "Wayne, where did you get those?"

Garrett stares oddly at Susan. "I'm Garrett, Grandma. These are the cleaning bots from the closet."

"Oh, that's right," Susan says. "I'm just . . . forgetful. It's hell getting old." But I sense more than forgetfulness. Her old fears have returned. And I worry that she may have reasons for the fears.

Millie is there the whole day. She is cordial, but distant.

I worry for her as well. Late in the day, she confides that she is seeing a therapist. I encourage her, and I promise to help if she ever needs me. A separate therapist—a *human* therapist—is what she needs. I am part of Millie's conflicts, so I cannot help her solve them. Not yet. And that inability troubles me. This is the sort of problem I was made for; but now, when it is most important, I only make the problem worse.

On Tuesday, Creekside's neighbors and our ambulatory residents show up for the town council meeting. We all are dressed in our best clothes (except I need no clothes, of course), and we sit quietly and respectfully as Chair Higgins speaks. "Finally," she says, "Nurse Vera Rayburn from Creekside Home has asked to address the council regarding the Creekside Circus. Nurse Rayburn?"

Nurse Rayburn stands and approaches the microphone. She wears her best formal uniform, and she looks every bit the professional health care administrator as she speaks. "Thank you, Chair Higgins, and thank you to the council. By now you should all have my letter explaining how valuable our circus has been, both to our residents and to the community. It serves as occupational therapy for many of our residents, therapy in which they eagerly participate. And it strengthens our bonds to the community. For that matter, it strengthens the community itself."

She continues, "But we also acknowledge your traffic and safety concerns. We need ambulances, too. We need fire and police protection. But we think we can address those concerns to everyone's satisfaction. You should also have before you our proposal: to restrict our rehearsals behind a privacy fence, to limit our public performances to one per weekend plus special events with the council's approval, and to move the performances to Bonnie Creek Park. As you'll note, the park has ample access for emergency traffic and for visitors, along multiple park drives. We believe this should address all of your concerns."

Councilman Sherman raises his hand, and Higgins says, "Councilman Sherman."

Sherman nods. "Thank you. This is a nice presentation, Nurse Rayburn, but there are further considerations we must discuss to decide whether this plan is practical. To wit, who's going to clean up when you're done? Also, the restroom facilities in that park aren't built to support that many, nor is the water. And for that matter, where people can sit. There are just a few benches, not nearly enough. This plan will need new seating, new facilities, clean up, and much more frequent waste removal. We have no budget for any of that."

Sherman nods to the chair, and she says, "Do you have a response, Nurse Rayburn?"

Nurse Rayburn nods. "I do, Chair Higgins, but I would like to cede my time to Mr. Eddie Lucas, since this is his plan."

"Proceed," the chair says.

Luke rises to answer. He wears what he calls his burying suit, with the assist suit worn underneath it. He looks as strong and as healthy as I have seen him since my return. He steps up to the microphone and begins to speak. "Ladies and gentlemen of the council, I want to thank you for the chance to address you. And I specifically want to speak to Councilman . . . Shemp's concerns."

The crowd giggles, and the chair bangs her gavel as Councilman Sherman leans forward and says to her, "Madam chair!"

Higgins bangs the gavel again, and she says, "Mister Lucas, I must ask you to show respect to Councilman Sherman."

Luke nods. "I meant no disrespect to . . ."

I lean in and whisper, "Sherman."

". . . to Councilman Sherman. But madam chair, it's no secret that Creekside deals with memory issues. They tell me I've got a few of my own, but I can't remember what those are." Again the crowd laughs. "That's a joke," Luke continues. "Names are one of my problems. New names just don't stick with me well. That's why I call my nurse Nurse Ratched, even though I've known her ten years. I call my best friend Bo. I can't rightly remember their real names, so I use names from entertainment. I'm not calling you a stooge, Councilman, I'm just grabbing the closest name I can remember. Please, can you forgive an old man his weakness?"

The chair looks at Sherman, and the Councilman nods. "I understand, Duke."

Luke grins at that. "I hear your concerns, Councilman. And they're all about money. And don't get me wrong, money's important. If a show don't make its nut, the show's over.

"But this shouldn't take much, Councilman," Luke continues. "We can do our own cleanup, can't we, folks?" He turns to the audience. Everyone nods, and several call out agreement. "And if we don't . . . well, you can shut us down, and no one would blame you. But I come from the old circus tradition, Councilman. We always leave a lot cleaner than we found it."

"Yes," Sherman says, "but there's more than operating costs. There are still the setup costs: restroom facilities, new water lines, and seating."

"We'll raise the money, Councilman," Luke replies. "And we can take donations for operating costs. It's important to us." He pauses, and swallows. He looks at me, and I nod in encouragement. Then he turns back to Sherman. "I forget things, Councilman. I'm old. But I don't forget the kids when they laugh. I don't forget the sparkle in their eyes, or the roar of the crowd when you nail the big finish. I'll never forget the circus, it's my life. And a good circus is more than just a show. This one . . . This one is good. They're not just my neighbors, and they're not just my circus. They are . . . my family."

The crowd breaks out in cheers and applause, so loud that no one can hear the chair banging her gavel. Eventually, though, they calm enough for her to call order. She looks at the council members around the table. "I think that answers all of our questions," she said. "I am inclined to let you try, as soon as you have approved plans and funds. I so move."

An older councilman next to her adds, "Second."

Higgins nods. "The motion is on the table. Are there any objections?" She looks at Councilman Sherman.

Sherman looks back at Luke, and he says, "No objections." Then he flips his tie, and he adds, "Nyuck, nyuck, nyuck!"

As the crowd applauds, Luke leans in to me and says,

"That was Curly's line, not Shemp's. And they say I've got memory trouble . . ."

The next day, in place of a rehearsal we hold a planning meeting with the neighboring adults and the residents. The neighbors pass the hat—a virtual hat, just Van's tablet running a donation app. When the tablet has made the rounds, Luke takes it, and he hands it to me. He taps the number, and he says, "That's a pretty good start, Bo. If we scrape up a few more pennies here and there, we might be able to have this built come fall."

I concur. Our supporters have raised more than sixty-eight percent of our estimated budget for the bleachers and other park improvements.

So I tap the tablet to open a donation window. I still have a large portion of my allowance from Paul and Susan that has built up through the years. Millie has stubbornly refused to accept financial help from me, and I so seldom find anything else that I want.

But I want this. I make a donation to cover the rest, and I hand the tablet back to Luke.

Luke's eyes narrow. "Are you sure about this, Bo?"

"I am sure," I say. "With one condition."

And so it is that a month later, Millie and Susan and the children sit beside Dex and Dr. Zinta in the front row when the Bo & Luke Creekside Circus gives our debut performance in our new home: the Paul A. Owens Memorial Amphitheater.

43. TODAY IS A DAY
I HAVE FEARED

After the circus, Tabby asks if she can dance with us, and Millie agrees. I am glad, because this gives me an excuse to spend more time with my family. Garrett is learning the archaic art of automobile driving, and he volunteers to drive Tabby to and from rehearsals. The car is ultimately in charge, of course, but it lets Garrett "drive" as long as there is no danger.

I am checking with residents one morning when Nurse Rayburn walks up to me and says, "Bo, there's someone here to see you."

"Oh?"

"It's Garrett. He's in the east quiet room."

I go back to the quiet room. Garrett is seated inside, looking at a tablet.

"Hello, Garrett," I say.

"Uncle Carey!" he says. He stands up and throws his arms around me. His head reaches almost to my shoulders now.

"It is good to see you too, Garrett," I say. My emulation

net ripples with positive feedback at the sight of him. "But you are early."

"I know," he says. "School starts tomorrow, and I wanted to practice driving while I can."

It is an innocent statement, but I can tell it is not what he really wants to say. "Is that all, Garrett?"

He looks down at his feet. "I'm older now, Uncle Carey. I notice things."

"You notice things." I look in his eyes.

"Uh-huh . . ." There is a long pause before he continues. "Uncle Carey, Grandma needs you."

I had suspected as much. Now Garrett reinforces my fears. "Her memory?"

He nods. "Grandma won't say anything, especially not in front of us kids. She thinks we can't figure it out. But Grandma's sick, Uncle Carey. Real sick. She needs your help."

I look around my office. "There are many people who need my help, Garrett. Are you sure?"

"Kind of . . ."

He does not finish the statement, but it makes him feel guilty. I try another approach. "What does your mother say?"

"I don't think Mom knows yet."

"But you do."

"Well, I . . . I listened to Grandma on the phone with her doctor. It sounded bad."

"What did she say was wrong?" I ask.

"There was a lot of stuff I didn't understand. And some name I've never heard before. Al something. Al's . . ."

I am not surprised. Sad, but not surprised. "Alzheimer's?"

"Yeah, that was it, Uncle Carey. Alzheimer's. What is that?"

"Something I thought we would never worry about again, Garrett. Let me talk to Nurse Rayburn, so someone can watch Tabby until rehearsal. And then let us go see your grandmother."

Garrett tells me that Millie is at work, so I do not have to worry about upsetting her. We enter the house just as Susan comes up to the entryway. "Carey!" she says. "And Garrett. What a pleasant surprise."

"Hi, Grandma."

I say, "Garrett came to see me, Susan, and I thought I would let him drive me home."

"Scamp." She rubs Garrett's head. "Running off on your own?"

"I had to take Tabby to circus practice," Garrett answers.

"Oh . . . right . . ."

I sense Susan's relief, but also confusion. I ask, "Perhaps you have some cookies for Garrett?"

"I do."

"Yeah, Carey," Garrett says. "Grandma always has cookies. Store bought, not like you baked, but they're still good."

"All right," she says. "Go off and get some cookies. And then why don't you go play outside? Uncle Carey and I have some catching up to do."

When Garrett is out in the garden, Susan turns to me.

"So what's up, Carey? My grandson is a pretty good boy . . . and a lousy liar."

I see no point in disagreeing. "He heard something troubling, Susan. And it fits with things that I have observed."

"Come on, let's go sit down," she says. She leads me over to the couch. "Lousy liar, but a great spy. What did he hear?"

"Susan, he mentioned Alzheimer's."

Her face falls. "He got it right."

"Susan, that is a completely treatable disease. This is not like Mildred's day."

"It's treatable," she agrees. "I can never remember the name of the medicine. And no, that's not the Alzheimer's kicking in, I was just never great with medical terminology. But the important thing is: It doesn't work for all patients. Seven percent or so have the wrong genetics. Something about protein binding, I think. And I'm . . . in the seven percent."

"No."

"Yup," she says, pretending that nothing is wrong. "It's happening, Carey. Just like I always feared. I'm already forgetting little things."

I do not mention that I have seen the signs for myself. "Susan, is there nothing they can do?"

"The doctors have tried. Dr. Sykes says there are always new therapies coming, but she's not making any promises."

"But what will you do?"

All pretense falls from Susan's face, and she looks directly in my eyes. "I'll become forgetful. First small things. Last week I spent forty minutes searching for my coffee cup. It was in my hand, Carey. *It was in my hand.*"

I lean over and hug Susan, and she shakes against me. For a couple of minutes I sit there holding her silently. Finally she pulls away, straightens up, and wipes her eyes. "Next I'll start forgetting what day it is and whether I had a meal or not. Then I'll start forgetting my past. Most recent first. I might forget my grandchildren, Carey, and then the rest of my family. Some pieces will stay with me. The oldest and the longest, they say, that's how it was with Mom. And then . . . And then when the palliative treatment can't keep up with the damage anymore, my nervous system will slowly give out." Her lower lip trembles. "And I'll die. And there's nothing you or I or Dr. Sykes can do about it."

I lean closer. "There is something I can do, Susan. It is not enough, but . . ."

"But what?"

"I can be here for you. You will have to convince Millie, but I can be here. I know how to take care of you."

"Carey, I can't ask that. You've got . . . You've got . . . something about a nursing home."

I shake my head. "They have plenty of volunteers. And you have me, if you can work it out with Millie."

"Carey," she says. She grabs me, and her tears roll down my back. "Thank you. I didn't want to face this alone. I mean, Millie's here; but she's got the kids, and she's got her work, and she's got . . . and she's . . . she's got enough to deal with. I didn't want to be a burden on her."

"You would not be a burden to her, Susan. She loves you."

"I know. And I love her, and I don't want to do this to her."

"She loves you, Susan. She will take care of you, and I will as well. You will have your family with you, Susan, for as long as you need us."

"Thank you, Carey. Thank you." Then she stands and paces. "But I have one thing I have to ask you. Please, this is important."

"Yes, Susan?"

"Please, whatever else you do . . . Please, never emulate Paul. Not even if I ask you to. Not even when I'm so far gone that I won't know any better. Please, even if you think I need it. Never emulate Paul. He was one of a kind. If I can't have him, I don't want a lie."

"I understand, Susan. I promise."

44. TODAY I AM SUSAN'S CARETAKER

I talk to Susan, discussing her plans and wishes. She feels it is important that she tell me everything she wants, while she is still able. I remember that Mildred did the same. She wanted to control what she could, even after she no longer could.

When Millie gets home from the university, I ask Garrett to drive me back to Creekside so he can pick up Tabby. Millie seems disappointed. "Carey, I thought . . . we could talk."

"We will," I say. "Soon. I promise." It tears at me to leave her just when she shows signs of opening up to me; but Susan must finally tell Millie about her illness, and that will be difficult enough without Garrett and me there.

The next day I arrive after Millie has left for class. My ident lets me into the home, and I find Susan on the couch, crying. I pour Susan a cup of coffee, set it in front of her, and sit down beside her without saying a word. She picks up the cup, takes a sip, and holding it in both hands she leans against me. I put my arms around her and hold her.

When the cup is half gone, Susan says, "I have a strong little girl. She's scared for me, I know. She said she could take a leave to take care of me."

"She would," I say.

Susan continues, "But she needs the income. Wayne sends what he can, but the kids . . . their college funds . . ."

I add, "And you do not want her to change her whole life just because of you."

"No, I don't."

"She would, Susan, willingly."

"I know, but I'm already asking that of you. I can't ask that of her, too."

I make Susan breakfast, and for a brief moment it is like I have never left—until I remember the missing piece of the scene. Paul is gone.

Susan and I talk at first about trivial matters, her work in the garden and other projects. Then we talk about the kids and how they are doing in school. Eventually the topic turns to Paul. I had avoided that topic for concern that it might upset her; but she wants to talk about him, and we share memories and stories from all the years that I have known them. She adds stories from before I entered their lives. Through the day I realize: Talking about Paul keeps the conversation off the subject of her and her illness.

Suddenly the bus arrives and the younger children get out, and I realize how late it is. When they come through the door, Tabitha sees me and her eyes light up. She runs to me, and I sweep her up into a hug. "Uncle Carey!" she says. "Uncle Carey!"

Tim follows behind her and grabs my hand. "Uncle Carey," he says, "are you coming to live with us?"

I see a frown on Susan's face, and she nods. "Yes, children," I answer. They cheer, and for a brief moment Susan smiles. "I will bring my things tomorrow."

They want to tell me about their day at school. Eventually Millie arrives. I make dinner, and we dine as a family for our first time since my return.

After dinner, I say, "I must return to Dr. Zinta's now. I have to pack my things to bring here. I shall call a cab."

Millie shakes her head. "Nonsense, Carey. I can drive you."

I look at Susan, and she nods. "The kids and I will be fine. You two go. Take your time."

So it is that I end up in a car alone with Millie for the first time since Garrett's birth. She is not talkative, so I sit silently. Here if she needs me.

At last, as we drive down Elm toward Creekside Estates, Millie speaks. "I'm glad you're back, Carey."

"As am I," I say.

"I'm . . . sorry this has been so difficult for me."

"You do not need to apologize to me."

"Oh!" Her eyes flare wide. "You don't need an apology? Because you're just a machine?"

"No," I say. "Because I am your friend. Friends understand."

"Oh." She lapses into silence again as the car pulls into Dr. Zinta's drive.

But as I get out and walk to the front door, she rolls down her window and calls out to me. "Thank you, Carey. For Mom. And for me."

✳   ✳   ✳

That night I read up on current practices in Alzheimer's care. Research in the field has slowed since treatments were found, but it has not stopped. The seven percent are still at risk, so some research continues. I read the latest in cognitive and occupational therapy, brain exercises, and treatments that can slow the progression— but not halt it.

The next day, I return to Creekside. I do not wish to disappear again without explanation. Without saying goodbye.

So I spend the day visiting with my friends. I tell them that I have a new patient who needs special care. I promise them that I will not forget them. (Indeed, one of Susan's conditions for accepting my help had been that I continue volunteering at the home two days per week. "You need a life outside this house, " she had insisted. I had not argued that I have no life at all.) But I do not identify my new patient. Privacy protocols, after all.

But someone has revealed the secret. Or maybe my friends just know me that well. I say goodbye to Luke last of all; and as we shake hands, he says, "Take good care of Susan. Maybe I'll come visit sometime."

"I would like that, Luke."

When I finally arrive at Susan's, I discuss my research with her. "I know," she finally says, "I've been reading it. I *can* still keep up with it, you know."

"So let us make a plan, then. We are going to fight this, you and I."

We put together a plan: nutrition, physical therapy to

keep her body healthy to support her mind, and work around the house and garden. With Susan's authorization, I check with Dr. Sykes. The doctor approves the regimen, so Susan and I set to work. We even plan new remodeling projects, as well as outings to the store and to the kids' school.

"Uncle Carey," Garrett says, "you can have my room back."

I shake my head. "No, Garrett. You are a young man now. You should have a room of your own. I appreciate your offer, but you need it more than I do."

He looks around the laundry room. With his help, I have just installed the portable charging unit in my old closet. Dr. Zinta has promised to move my full charger down from Garrett's closet next week.

"Well," he says as he hammers a nail in place by the closet door, "would you like your terrarium back at least?"

I hang my stocking from the nail. "You do not want the terrarium in your room?"

"It's okay. It's been fun taking care of the frogs. But you have to have *something* here that's yours."

I can see that this is important to Garrett. He is indeed a young man now. He is concerned for the feelings of others, even if the other is an android. "All right, Garrett," I say, "let us go get the terrarium and set it up."

Time passes. Susan's decline is very slow. The medicine and the therapy are serving her well. Her changes are so gradual that I doubt a human would notice (unless they were a doctor), but the signs are unmistakable for me. Her rate of forgotten words climbs one or two percent every month. Mislaid items are the same. Her irritability climbs, partly due to frustration at what she forgets, but also as a symptom in itself. She is more prone to mood swings of every sort: anger, sadness, sometimes even giddiness and joy for no discernable reason.

True to his word, Luke comes and visits at least once a week, arriving by auto taxi. Susan enjoys his circus stories, and he likes having a new, attentive listener.

But Luke's visits disturb me, and it takes several before I understand why. For as long as I have known him, Luke has had memory problems; but now I realize that they are relatively fixed. He gets no worse. Susan, however, is deteriorating; and Luke unintentionally serves as a calibration scale for her illness. Today her memory is better than his; but tomorrow, next week, or next month, it shall be worse.

This almost makes me wish that Luke would stay away. But telling him that would hurt him, and would not help her. He is good for her, and her for him. The only one who suffers from his visits is me.

Today after school, Susan called Tabitha Millie; and then when she realized it, she cried for more than an hour.

45. TODAY I HAVE ANOTHER PATIENT

Today Tabitha is home sick, so I have another patient to take care of. I make sure Susan is secure in her favorite chair overlooking the garden while I check Tabitha's vital signs. Her fever is elevated, but not yet indicative that a doctor's visit is called for. So I keep her tucked in bed, and I give her children's cold medicine and keep an eye on her.

Later Tabitha starts to feel better. She comes out. "I gotta go to the bathroom," she says.

"Do you need any assistance?"

She shrieks, "No!" Then in a calmer voice she adds, "I'm a big girl now, Uncle Carey. I can do *that*."

"All right." While she is out of her room, I take the opportunity to straighten her bed, throwing out old tissues and getting her a fresh cup of tea. When I bring the tea up, I notice that the bathroom door is open with the light out, and she is still not in her bed. I look around and find her in Susan's room, sitting on Susan's lap in the big chair, with a heavy blanket wrapped around both of them. I set the saucer down and give the cup to Tabitha, and then I go down to get another cup for Susan.

The next day, Tabitha is still home, but I find her fever is gone. Her temperature is elevated, but not within a range of concern. She is more energetic today, up and out to the bathroom several times, and downstairs twice for cookies. By lunch all pretense is gone. She follows me around, talking and playing with her toys.

"Tabitha," I say, "You seem to be feeling better."

"Oh." She coughs. "I'm sick."

"Tabitha, I do not think so."

"I'm sick, Uncle Carey. I *am* sick. I'll go back to bed."

"You are well enough that you should be in school today."

She looks down at her feet. Finally, in a disconsolate voice, she says, "I know, but I wanted to see you."

"Tabitha . . ."

She looks up at me. "I know it was wrong, but I wanted to be with you, Uncle Carey. I missed you."

I rub her head. "That is nice, but I do not think your mother would appreciate it. It would only upset her."

"I don't understand, Uncle Carey. Why is Mommy so sad all the time? And mad sometimes?"

I shake my head. "Sometimes we cannot understand. We simply accept. Now I think you had better get back up into bed before your mother gets home. And tomorrow, I do not think you will be sick, will you?"

"No, Uncle Carey. You won't tell Mom?"

I hesitate. "Secrets sometimes get people into trouble, Tabitha, but I understand why you did this.

No, I will not tell your mother. But this will not happen again, will it?"

"No, Uncle Carey."

46. TODAY SUSAN
REACHES A NEW STAGE

Three months later, there is a new item on the shopping list from Millie: adult diapers in Susan's size. There was an incident the night before. That day when I take Susan to DeBruyn's, she is out of sorts. She answers questions only tersely, if at all.

When I turn down the hygiene aisle, she stops. "Where are you going?"

"I am getting the items on the shopping list."

She looks away from the aisle. "There's nothing we need here."

"Millie specifically said—"

She stops me. "I don't care what Millie said. There is *nothing* we need here. I'm leaving, Carey." She heads straight for the exit.

I abandon the cart and take off after her. "Susan, I am sorry. Please, you cannot leave. We are not done shopping yet."

"*I'm* done," she says. "Are you?"

I can see she is getting even more irritated. "All right,

Susan, I am done. Now please, stand right here and I will go get the cart."

By the time I return with the cart, Susan has moved again; but Kathryn is talking to her, asking about how the grandchildren are doing in school. As I approach, Kathryn nods slightly at me and smiles.

"Oh, there you are, Carey," Susan says, "Have we checked out yet?"

"Not yet, Susan. Come on, let us get checked out, and then we can get back home."

Millie is upset to learn that we got no diapers, even after I quietly explain Susan's behavior. So I go online to place an order, and I pay for rush delivery out of my own funds. When the door chimes the next morning, I step outside, accept the diapers from the delivery van, and take them in through the garage into the laundry room. There I am reminded of the reason for Millie's concern: three soiled sets of bedsheets and undergarments. Two sets are fresh from the night before, but one is older. Even though I do not need to sleep, I had not had time to wash them the night before. I put all three sets into the wash and go in to check on Susan.

Today is Garrett's high school awards celebration, so Millie is taking the day off from the university so that she and Susan can attend. Thus I am back in Creekside, going over volunteer evaluations. Since I cannot work at the Home as much anymore, Nurse Rayburn has asked me to serve as volunteer coordinator, a job that is mostly administrative. I am very pleased with the volunteers who have come to us because of the circus. They have really become part of the Creekside family.

Then my inner comm rings, and I see it is Millie's code. I answer cautiously, "Yes, Millie."

"Mom's having a bad day," she says. "I can't take her with me to Garrett's awards ceremony. Carey, can you get here right away? She needs you."

"Right away, Millie," I say.

When I enter the house, I see no one downstairs, so I go up to Susan's room. Susan is curled in her big chair. Millie kneels beside her, dressed up for the ceremony.

"It's all right, Mom," she says. "It's all right. See, Carey's here."

I come up to the chair. "I'm here, Susan." I say. She grabs my hand and clings to it wordlessly.

Quietly I ask Millie, "What's the matter?"

"She tried to get dressed for the ceremony. She . . . I don't know. It looked like she put both feet in one leg of her pants. She fell, and then she panicked and cried. By the time I got in here, she was screaming. She's calmed down now, but she won't put her pants on. She won't get dressed. She doesn't want to leave."

"I understand, I will take care of her. You should go. You do not want to miss Garrett's ceremony."

"No, I don't," she says. She turns to Susan and kisses her. "You're okay, Mom. You've got someone to watch over you. I'll be back as soon as I can. Goodbye, Mom."

She leaves, and I stand there silently, brushing Susan's hair with my fingers while she holds my other hand. Eventually she falls asleep, and I gently lift her out of the chair and into her bed. My chemical sensors tell me she has soiled her diaper, so I change her just as I had changed Mildred decades ago. I gently lift her to slide a pad underneath her to protect the bedding. Disturbing her as little as possible, I remove the soiled garment and set it in the bucket. I look around for wipes and salve, and I clean her up and medicate her to make sure there is no chance of a rash. I put on the new diaper, and I find her lounge pants to put on. This whole time, she has not roused from her slumber. I pull the drapes to darken the room, and I go out.

When I get downstairs, I find another load of sheets, not as heavily soiled, indicating a leaky diaper. Did Susan remove it during the night, and I missed that? Or did Millie simply put it on wrong? I remember the one that I removed, and I guess that it is the latter. It is not Millie's fault. Unlike me, she was not programmed for this sort of care, and she has no experience in it.

I start another load of laundry, and I go check on Susan. She is still sleeping lightly. I go downstairs, and when I hear her start to move about, I make her some tea and toast. When Susan comes down, she is as normal and coherent as I have seen her in weeks. I do not mention the diaper or the laundry.

When Millie comes home, Garrett is with her, and he shows me his awards: meritorious scholar in math and history, and top science student. He holds in his pride (since he was raised to be humble), but I can tell underneath how pleased he is.

"That is very good, Garrett," I say. His parents are both very intelligent, so it does not surprise me that he and his siblings are bright as well.

"Yes, that's good, Garrett," Millie says. "You should take those up to your room."

"Oh, Mom . . ."

"Now," she says.

Once Garrett is upstairs, Millie says, "Thank you, Carey."

"I am happy I could help," I say. "And I could show you the right way to put on Susan's diapers," I add.

Suddenly her face turns sad. "I've raised three kids. I should know how to put on a diaper. But . . ."

"But it's not the same for adults," I say. She nods. "I'll show you tonight after Susan goes to bed."

Once Susan is asleep, Millie says, "All right, let's get this over with. Do we have to practice on Mom?"

"No," I say, "I can demonstrate holographically. It is simply a matter of securing the diaper properly. An adult patient is more adept at removing it or shifting when it is uncomfortable. If we secure it properly and keep up with the lotions, there is less chance of rash. She should be fine."

We go upstairs, and I project a hologram onto the bed to demonstrate. Then Millie tries it herself. The first time, she has difficulty interacting with the hologram since there is nothing there that she can touch. But after practicing a couple of times, she is able to control the hologram, and she figures out the right way to secure the diaper. "Thank you, Carey," she says.

47. TODAY IS A GOOD DAY FOR SUSAN

Susan is having a good day. I remember this from caring for Mildred: the ups and downs. Some days, like today, are almost normal; but some days are progressively worse.

Since it is a good day and we still have good weather before winter sets in, we spend most of the day out in the garden. Susan is still very good with her gardening skills, but her hands are weaker. Some of the trimmers are too difficult for her to close now. Her voice gets very quiet, and she asks, "Carey, can you cut this for me, please?"

I see she is cutting a very thick branch. I help her, and then I give the shears back to her.

Susan says, "Paul could have done it." Then she looks up at me. "Carey, where's Paul?"

I have anticipated this question, though with great discomfort; and I have prepared a series of answers, each more elaborate than the last. I start with the simplest answer. "He is gone, Susan."

"Oh." She works on in silence, and I hope that she will accept the simple answer today.

We are still out in the garden when Millie comes home from class. The children are playing, and Susan is watching them, smiling. When they see Millie emerge from the patio door, they all run up for hugs. Then she comes out. "Hello, Mother," she says. She does not speak to me.

"Hello, Millie," Susan says. "How was your day today? Did you learn anything new?"

Millie frowns, then she answers, "Same old stuff, Mom."

"That's nice," Susan says. "Is it time for dinner?"

She does not mention Paul again for the rest of the day. I cannot tell if she remembers him at all. But except for that brief exchange, she is happy today.

48. TODAY SUSAN FALLS

Today is a bad day for Susan. She soils herself twice, which embarrasses her and makes her angry, so she refuses to eat lunch. She just wants to curl up on her chair overlooking the garden. I check in through the day, between loads of laundry, but she does not say a word.

Today I have duties at Creekside. When I return home, the house is empty. I find a note on the table: "I'm at the hospital with Mom. She fell and broke her wrist. I don't know how long I'll be. Please watch the kids." It is signed with a simple letter "M."

I take advantage of Susan's absence to give the house a thorough cleaning. All of the bedding in all of the rooms, not just hers. I dust in places the cleaning bots never seem to get.

When the children come home from school, they are curious where Susan is. "Grandma has had an accident," I say. "Her wrist is broken, but other than that, she is fine." They look sad. They are getting older, more aware of Susan's circumstances. Tim goes up to his room, and I suspect he is crying up there.

Susan and Millie come home. I help them through the door. There is a light plastic cast on Susan's left wrist. I guide her in, settle her onto the couch, and wrap her in a blanket. Then I go back to the entryway where Millie is bringing in groceries, and I help carry them in. In the kitchen I quietly ask, "What happened, Millie?"

"She wandered down the stairs after you left for Creekside. She made it about halfway down, I think, before she fell. I came in from the laundry to her calling out for help, so quiet I almost didn't hear her."

"I am so sorry to hear that, Millie. I think it is time she moves downstairs. She has had more difficulty with the stairs every day. She refuses to consider a chairlift."

"I know," Millie says. "I can turn the playroom back into a bedroom like Mom and Dad did for Grandma when she was sick."

"I could help you with that, Millie."

"I can do this," Millie says. "She's my mother, I'll take care of this. But . . . I'd like your help. Thank you."

49. TODAY WE DECORATE

Today Millie takes Susan to the doctor to get her wrist examined, while I am home to meet the children after school. It is a rainy day, so they are stuck inside.

"I'm bored, Uncle Carey," Tabitha says. "Can we go somewhere?"

I check the time. "No, Tabitha. Your mom and grandma will be home soon. We do not want to be gone when they get here."

"But what can I doooo?"

I remember a project from when Millie was a child. "Let us make some sunshine and flowers for Mom and Grandma."

Tim asks, "How do we make sunshine, Uncle Carey?"

"It will be easy," I say. "And fun." We get out construction paper, safety scissors, and brightly colored markers, and we set to work cutting out flowers and bees and a sun. And frogs, of course.

At first, Garrett sniffs at "kid stuff," but he can't stop watching and critiquing. "That bee has eight legs," he says.

"Because I wanted eight legs," Tabitha says.

"Well that's dumb."

"Uncle Carey!" she cries.

"Garrett, apologize to your sister," I say.

"I'm sorry, Tabitha."

"That is better." I nod. "What do you say, Tabitha?"

"It's okay, Garrett."

"Now," I say, turning back to Garrett, "if you think you can make a better bee, here." I hand him scissors and paper. He shrugs and starts cutting.

By the time Millie and Susan get home, the children have decorated every wall on the ground floor with spring scenes. When Susan comes in, her eyes light up. She smiles, "Flowers! Birds! It's so beautiful!" She starts to cry, but my empathy net tells me these are tears of joy, so rare for her these days. Millie smiles.

Garrett says, "And we made dinner too, Mom!"

"*You* made dinner?" she says.

"Well, Uncle Carey gave us instructions," he says, "but we made it all."

Millie sniffs the air. "I don't smell anything burning."

"Mommmm . . ." Garrett groans.

"They did not burn a thing," I say. "They have kept it warm, waiting for you and Susan."

"Well, aren't you three the little homemakers?" Millie says. "Thank you. You're such big helps." We sit down to eat.

50. TODAY MILLIE
REACHES HER LIMIT

Each day that I can, I work on the playroom conversion. There are tools and supplies and cans of paint stacked in a corner. I do what I can, but the supplies seldom move. Susan needs more attention.

Last night I stayed at Creekside, training night volunteers. I had suggested that I could find someone else, but Millie had insisted that she had everything under control. I sensed that she needed my trust, so I agreed. It was good to spend a night with my friends.

But this morning when I return home, Susan is still asleep on the couch. Millie has moved her there while the new bedroom is under construction. But if she is asleep, why do I hear crying?

I track the sound down to the laundry room. Millie has not left for work. She sits in my closet, arms wrapped around her knees, face buried. She is in tears.

The pile of soiled sheets and undergarments is as big as I have ever seen it, and the children's laundry has piled up as well. On the floor, soaking into all of it, is a spilled can of paint that has fallen from a shelf.

All I can do is help. I cannot fix Millie's pain. Instead I start picking up paint-soaked clothing and dropping it in the wash basin for rinsing. I read the can of paint for cleaning instructions. If it has not set yet, the paint will come out using simple home detergent. I start rinsing out the sheets. Then I try to put them in the washing machine, but there is still a load in there. There is another load in the dryer. When did we get so far behind?

I transfer the dryer load to a basket, and then I transfer the laundry load to the dryer. While I am doing that, suddenly Millie stands at the wash basin, rinsing out more clothes. I do not say a word. I just take them from her when she hands them to me, and I put them in the washer.

When we have all the paint-soaked clothes either in the tub or in the wash, I get the mop bucket and the mop, and I start cleaning up the spilled paint. Millie folds the clean laundry.

I am almost done mopping when Millie comes up to me, wraps her arms around me, and breaks into huge sobs. I let the mop fall, and I wrap my arms around her and hold her until she stops crying.

51. TODAY I HAVE ONE JOB

"I understand, Carey," Nurse Rayburn says through my comm. "Family first."

"But you are my family as well, Nurse Rayburn," I say. "You and all of Creekside."

"Thank you." She smiles. "But we understand. And we have plenty of help. Millie and Susan only have you. You take care of them. You can come visit any time you like."

She closes the call, and I look around. We have moved Susan's big chair down into the living room, so she can sit in it and look out at the garden on days like today, when it is too cold to go outside. She is in it now, looking out, smiling at what she sees. It is a good day, and that is good for Millie as well.

In the playroom, Millie and Tabitha and Tim are hard at work finishing the conversion back into a bedroom. Millie has scaled back her plans. She cannot bring herself to think about painting the room anymore, not after the incident with the paint can. They are simply putting up borders and decorations. Then they clear out space for the medical bed that will be delivered tomorrow. Susan should be moved in by the weekend.

Garrett and I install the terrarium, and I look in. "One, two, three, four frogs, Garrett?"

"Five. One likes to hide under the leaves over there."

"Oh, yes, five. Well, they will surely keep me company at night." We set the terrarium up on Millie's old craft bench. Then Garrett goes upstairs to bring down the food and supplies for the frogs and the plant food for the plants, while I turn to the matter of human food. It is time to make dinner.

At last, I feel at home. Really at home. I can take care of my family.

52. TODAY IS A BAD DAY FOR SUSAN

Today is a bad day for Susan. She asks where Paul is, and this time she is not so easily distracted. "But where is he?" she says.

I see the strain in her face. Tears will be coming soon no matter what answer I give, so I owe her an honest answer. "He is gone, Susan."

"Gone?"

"He has passed away."

"But . . . I just . . ." She pauses. "This morning . . ."

I shake my head. "He has been gone for eight years, Susan."

"But I don't . . ."

"I know. You do not remember. I am sorry. I feel so sorry for you, Susan."

There's a long pause. She stares out at the garden. "I'm sick, aren't I?"

"Yes, you are, Susan."

"Like Paul's mother."

"I am afraid so, Susan."

"Why, Carey?"

"There is no explanation. I am sorry, Susan. This is just how it is."

She curls deeper into the chair and cries until Millie gets home. Millie walks through the door, and Susan looks up, eyes alight with hope. Once she recognizes who it is, though, she looks down again. "I thought it was Paul," she says under her breath.

Later that night, she is sure Paul is coming back. She refuses to go to sleep while she waits for him. Millie pulls me aside. "Couldn't you just be Dad for a while?" she says.

"I am sorry, Millie," I say. "I promised her back when she was still healthy."

"But it would make her happy now."

"I do not think it would, Millie. I do not think anything will. Plus she is still too alert to be fooled by emulation. All I could be would be an echo. I can see her pain, but I do not think we can do anything for her except comfort her. Eventually she will fall asleep."

That is what we do. It takes nearly two hours past her usual bedtime for Susan to finally give up. I carry her into her new bedroom. Millie spreads out a pad, and I set Susan on the bed after. Millie checks Susan's diaper, changes it, and straightens out Susan's nightgown. She pulls the blanket over Susan and tucks her in. As she kisses Susan goodnight, I see tears on Millie's cheeks.

This is a time of tears. I cannot do anything for Susan, and I cannot do anything for Millie that will stop their tears. But I will be here to share them.

53. TODAY WAYNE CHANGES COURSE

Anna and Vishal have moved back to Michigan to help with Susan, and to see her while they still can. Their boys have moved out, and Anna and Vishal both have virtual jobs which can be performed from anywhere. So they bought a house in town, just a short walk away, and Anna helps out often.

Wayne has also moved closer, though he has not said what new work he has found. Today he brings the children home early. They have spent the day at a robotics show down in Kalamazoo, so he brings them back on the way to his home. The children come running into the house talking excitedly about all the robots. "And there was a robot dog," Tabitha says, "and there was a robot that told stories."

"And Dad showed off his new robot," Tim adds; but Garrett shushes him.

Before I can wonder at that, Susan asks, "Where is your daddy? I haven't seen Wayne in so long."

Garrett says, "He's outside."

Millie looks surprised. "What?"

"I was supposed to tell you, Mom. He wants to talk to you."

"Well, I don't want to talk to him."

"I'm just the messenger, Mom. Don't shoot me."

Millie turns to me, pain in her eyes. "Carey, could you go out there? Tell him that I'm glad he and the kids had a good time, but this visitation is over?"

"Millie," I say, "if he wants to talk, maybe you should."

"I'm not interested," she insists.

So I go out. Wayne is parked in the driveway, windows down, enjoying the fall air. "Hello, Carey," he says as I walk up to the car.

"Hello, Wayne."

"So she sent you to send me away?"

"Yes, she did, Wayne."

"And if I don't go away, are you going to make me?"

I look at him and read his mood. "You will not do that, Wayne. If she insists, you will leave."

"Yes, I will."

"Because you want her to be happy," I say. "You still love her."

Wayne's voice starts to crack. "Is it that obvious?"

"Only to an MCA empathy net," I say. Then I add, "Is that a joke? I hope it was a joke. I am trying to learn how to make them. Millie could use jokes these days."

Wayne laughs. "It wasn't a good joke, Carey. But sometimes you laugh just because the joke teller made the effort." He leans his head against the window frame. "Carey, I know she's upset."

"She has plenty of reason to be upset, Wayne. Not even counting you."

He looks up, concerned. "Susan's getting pretty bad?"

"Yes. Millie is stressed all the time now."

"But hey, she has you there to make everything right."

I detect a bitter edge in his voice. "Wayne, I am helping. Would you begrudge her whatever help she can get?"

"No, but damn it, I could help, too. Lots of help, if she'd just let me. Carey, I have good news, and she needs to hear it. I can't stand that she's hurting like this. Please, Carey, you have to talk to her."

I look into Wayne's eyes, and I see tears welling up. I need not remind him of his contributions to her pain. He knows. She knows. Everyone knows. But if she would let him help, it would help him as well. "All right, Wayne. I cannot promise, but I will try."

I go back into the house. The kids still cluster around Susan, and Millie is making soup. I walk up to Millie and say in a low voice, "He hasn't left, Millie."

Millie drops the spoon into the pot. She reaches for it, but I grab her hand before she can burn herself. As I reach in, pull out the spoon, and hand it back to her, she whispers, "Why not?"

"He needs to talk to you. I have never seen him this upset."

"Maybe *I* don't need to talk to *him*."

"Millie, I think you do."

"Don't play those empathy games with me!" she says. But then she puts down the stirring spoon and turns down the heat. "You come with me. I'm not going to be alone with him."

"He is not a threat, Millie."

"I am *not* going to be alone with him. So you come with me, or I don't go."

"All right, Millie." I follow her out. Garrett's eyes follow us, but the other two children haven't noticed our conversation.

When we get outside, Wayne opens the door, steps out, and leans back against the car. "You could have come alone, Rana," he says.

"Didn't want to," Millie answers. "And don't call me that."

"Millie, please. Hasn't this gone on long enough? I told you I was wrong. I've apologized every way I know. I've done everything you and the kids need."

Millie nods. "I know, Wayne." She sighs. "I know. But . . . things with Mom . . ."

"I'm sorry, Millie." Wayne reaches out to Millie; but she flinches, and he drops his hand to his side. "I wish you'd let me help. I wish . . ."

Millie shakes her head. "It's a bad time, Wayne. It's too complicated. It's been too long. Too long since you . . ." She squeezes my hand. "You almost lost Carey."

"I know," Wayne pleads. "I made a mistake. But we fixed Carey. And now . . . finally . . . I'm fixing my career."

Millie looks up at that. "Timmy said you had a new robot."

"Uh-huh," Wayne says. "That's why I was at the robotics show. Not just for the kids, for my job. I have a new job, Millie."

"That's great!" Briefly, Millie's eyes light up. She is

excited by this. But when Wayne catches her eye, she looks away, and her voice grows subdued. "What is it?"

"Berends Controls," Wayne says. "They're a smaller shop, but that means they have fewer levels of bureaucracy to complicate every decision. I flat-out asked Mr. Berends if it bothered him that I'd driven MCA into the ground. He told me, 'Son, I did my research. That's not how it went. You were just the one left holding the bag.'"

Again Millie seems excited; but again she resists showing it. "So . . . you're building androids?"

"Not yet. Berends says he wants to start small, see what we can do with simple robots. There's a lot I can do for him there. And the pay . . . I can have more for you and the kids."

"That's nice, Wayne," Millie says. "But money doesn't change anything."

Wayne holds his hands out from his side. "Then what will, Millie? What will?"

"I don't know, Wayne." Millie bites her lip. "This is all too complicated for me right now. I have so much else to deal with."

"I know," Wayne says. "I just wish . . . Please, Millie." Wayne swallows. "I want to help. I want . . ."

Millie turns and paces away. "Nothing's changed, Wayne. This is how it is and this is how it's going to be."

Wayne follows her. He clasps her shoulders; but she turns, angry, and he pulls his hands away. He says, "Millie, down in Caye Caulker I promised for better or for worse. I won't break that promise. I'm here for the long haul. But, damn it, I've had enough worse. I need some better."

"I'm sorry, Wayne," Millie says. Do I detect a touch of sympathy there? "I'm sorry you're hurting. But I can't take that chance. Better safe than sorry."

Wayne frowns at that. "Is that it? Better safe than sorry? Everybody's sorry sooner or later. You can't avoid it. But what about better safe than happy? Because that's the risk you're taking right now. You can stay safe, or you can take the chance and we can be happy again. I can help you. Please, Millie, take that chance. Let me help you with Mom. We can get through this together. We were always stronger together."

"Goodbye, Wayne." Millie turns and goes back into the house. Wayne looks at me. Without a word, he gets into his car and drives away.

I stand in the driveway, again facing a problem that I cannot fix.

54. TODAY I AM LOLA

Today Susan does not recognize me. Instead she sees her friend, Lola. All the latest research agrees with how I was first programmed: Arguing with her delusions will not make her happier, and going along with them can make her peaceful. So after a little effort tuning it in properly, my emulation net turns me into Lola, who has been dead the past six years. Susan and I spend the day having cookies and tea, until she falls asleep. When she awakens from her nap, again I am Carey.

55. TODAY SUSAN THROWS A TANTRUM

Despite all that Susan has lost, she still loves her music. She still sings some days. Her frail voice is still harmonic.

But today she sits at her piano and looks at the keys, and she begins to tremble. She reaches out her hands, but she hesitates. She looks at the sheet music on the stand; but I am sure that her vision is too far gone to read it.

She tries to strike notes; but even my poor ears can detect the dissonance as her fingers hit random keys.

She tries again, but the results are even worse.

She smashes the keys, first with her fingers, then with her fists. Tears flowing, she lowers her head to the keys. Then she looks up, seizes the sheet music, and crumples it. She throws it across the living room. She reaches for a picture that rests on the piano, and she hurls it toward the glass patio door. With skills learned from Luke, I easily catch the picture.

Susan's emotional level swings to that of a small, frightened child who lashes out in fear. She struggles to her feet, knocking over the piano bench. Susan is stronger than Mildred was at this stage. I have to restrain her to protect Millie, who sits in the corner, watching and crying. I hold Susan until she collapses in tears. Then I carry her to her bed, and soon she is asleep.

56. TODAY SUSAN IS ANGRY

Today Susan is angry. She does not throw a temper tantrum like she had last week, and she is more aware of everything around her. Too aware, perhaps. That is the source of her anger. "I hate this house! I hate this bed! I hate these goddamn diapers! I hate you all! Why don't you leave me alone? Let me die!"

Millie flees the room, and the children follow to comfort her. I sit with Susan, watching her, making sure she does nothing to hurt herself. I wonder if we should order bed restraints.

57. TODAY SUSAN'S MOOD IMPROVES

Today Susan's mood is better. For the first time in months, she sings, though she forgets most of the words. Millie feigns cheerful spirits, but she is relieved when it is time for her to leave for work. After the door closes behind her, Susan asks me, "Who was that nice girl? I like her."

58. TODAY I UNDERSTAND FRIENDSHIP

Throughout Susan's illness, Luke continues to visit. Some days Susan recognizes him, and she asks about the circus. Some days she does not know who he is, but she is polite and gracious.

And some days, like today, she is angry that there is a stranger in her house. Today she screams, "Get out! Get out of here! Go!" And she throws her coffee cup at him.

Luke catches the cup easily, of course. Then he quickly exits through the front before Susan can get further upset.

It takes me nearly an hour to calm Susan down. In her anger, she has soiled herself, but she does not want me to touch her diaper. After several minutes of gentle pleading, I finally convince her to get into bed and let me bathe and change her. I also quietly give her a sedative. Dr. Sykes has increased her sedative prescription twice in the last month.

When Susan is finally asleep, I go out the front door. Luke is waiting for me. "I thought you would have called a taxi by now," I say.

Luke tosses me the coffee cup. "I had to give you this," he says. We start to juggle, a lazy, simplistic routine with only one object.

I stare into Luke's face; and for the first time, I recognize fear there. Or at least worry. "This is not easy for you. You do not have to visit."

Luke shakes his head. "It's never easy. You forget where I've been living. This isn't my first time through this, not even my tenth. It's never easy, and no one should go through it alone."

Then he catches the cup, hands it to me, and adds, "Not even you."

59. TODAY SUSAN'S MEDICINE FAILS

Today Dr. Sykes visits to check on Susan. Before her mind started to go, Susan had named myself and Millie as co-advocates for her, so the doctor tells me what she has learned. "The palliative medicines are starting to fail," she says. "She's building up a tolerance."

I check my notes on the medicine. "If you increase the dosage, she will start to have other problems."

"Yes," the doctor says. "Liver probably won't take it, and there's a small rate of cancers induced. I recommend we wean her off the meds and let nature take its course."

"I cannot approve that, Doctor."

"Yes, you can," she says. "I've seen the advocate directive."

"Legally I can," I agree, "but this is not a decision I can make without discussing it with Millie."

"I understand," Dr. Sykes says. "All right, a few more days won't matter either way. You have my recommendation."

Millie is late getting home that night. She and Wayne

have met to discuss some financial issues related to Garrett's college fund. Garrett is doing well enough in school that he may be able to enroll early, so they want to make sure they can afford that. So it is quite late when she gets home.

I do not want to upset Millie with the issue of Susan's medicine, but she insists. "Carey, I've had a long day and I know you're trying to be considerate, but I can tell that the news is bad. It's not going to be any better in the morning, is it?" I shake my head. "I was sure about that," she continues. "So you can tell me now, or you can let me go without sleep all night, wondering what you've got to tell me. Please, tell me now."

I tell her. She listens carefully, attentively, tears rolling down her face. When I'm done, she says, "Please, sign the papers. It's the right thing, but I can't."

The next day, I contact the doctor. She sends over the papers, and I sign to wean Susan off the medicine and let her die in the natural course of events.

60. TODAY WE SPEND THE WEEKEND TOGETHER

Today is supposed to be Wayne's weekend with the kids; but without Millie ever asking, he has given up his weekends so the kids can spend more time with Susan. Garrett makes Susan lunch and brings her tea. Tabitha curls up with her on the couch. Susan thinks that Tabitha is young Millie, and she takes comfort from her presence.

Tim hides in his room all day, only coming down when he must. Even a few minutes with Susan makes him cry now. When Susan and Millie do not need me, I join him in his room. We play games, but his heart is not in it. "Uncle Carey . . ." he says, but he does not finish his thought.

"I know," I say, "it is sad and it is frightening."

"I feel . . ." He feels guilty like he should be down helping, but he is terrified at the same time. But he is too young, too emotionally unaware to understand these reactions. So he is reluctant to admit them.

"I know, Tim." I wish I could say something to make him feel better about going downstairs, or to make him feel better about staying upstairs; but he cannot feel better, none of us can. So I stay with him to give him what comfort I can.

61. TONIGHT WE LOSE SUSAN

Today is a very bad day for Susan. She is listless, and she has no appetite. She is already thin as a rail. She is on an IV, but it does little for her.

I send my diagnostics to Dr. Sykes. She just shakes her head. "Soon, Carey," she says.

When the children get home from school, Garrett and Tabitha go in to see Susan.

I take Tim aside. "You are afraid," I say. He nods. "You are sad." He nods again. "But I have known you since you were born, Tim. You are brave."

"No, I'm not," he whispers. "I'm afraid."

"Remember you told me once from a book you read: Brave heroes are afraid like anybody else, but they do what they have to do anyway."

"Yes," he says.

"Tim, tonight you have to say goodbye to your grandmother."

Tim shakes his head, eyes squeezed shut to stop the tears, but they leak through anyway. I wait. Finally he opens his eyes and says, "Will you be there for me, Carey?"

"Always," I say.

"It's easier to be brave when you're not alone," he says.

We go into Susan's room. The children tell her stories. Garrett brings her supper. Millie sits in the corner, chipping in a story now and then.

Susan drifts in and out of consciousness. When she is awake, she smiles at the children, though I sense confusion. I do not think she recognizes any of us. But she is glad not to be alone with her fears.

Later that night, when Susan falls into a deeper sleep, Millie takes the children up and puts them to bed. I can see what is coming next, but I can do nothing to stop it. It is inevitable. While Millie is upstairs with the children, Susan makes a few gasping, choking breaths . . . and then she breathes no more.

When Millie comes back downstairs, I grip her shoulders, shake my head, and then hug her. She cries. Finally she is drained. She goes to Susan's bed, takes her hand, and kisses her goodbye while I send the doctor a message. "Susan Owens passed away at 10:27 P.M."

62. TODAY IS SUSAN'S FUNERAL

Susan's funeral is attended by a massive crowd of all ages. Rachel Bean, one of Susan's coworkers, observes to me, "No one has more mourners than a favorite teacher."

Luke and I stand near Millie, greeting friends and relatives, accepting their condolences. Garrett has taken Tabitha and other younger children downstairs and is watching them so they do not get restless. I look at Tim. "You can go downstairs, too," I say.

"Nah," he says, "they're doing kids' games, boring stuff. Besides, Uncle Carey, we're being brave, right?"

"Yes, we are, Tim. You are very brave indeed."

As the crowd swells, I see a familiar face in the back of the room. At the same time Millie says under her breath, "Wayne."

I try to read her mood, but there are so many layers of conflicting emotions, I cannot tell which is in charge right now. "Shall I ask him to leave, Millie?"

"No," she says, shaking her head. "No, he needs to say goodbye, too. Please . . . ask him to come join us up front."

I thread my way through the crowd and up to Wayne. "Carey," he says, "I'm so sorry for . . ." He doesn't finish the sentence.

"Thank you, Wayne," I say. "And I am sorry for your loss, too."

"She was . . ." He chokes up. ". . . the only mother I had left."

"I know, Wayne. Please, come join us." He shakes his head. "Millie asked, Wayne."

I see surprise in Wayne's eyes, and he follows me forward. When we get to the front, he says, "Millie, I'm so sorry."

Millie stands awkwardly in front of him, hands clasped behind her back. "I know, Wayne," she says, "but she's not in any pain now. She's at peace."

"I should . . ." He nods toward the coffin.

"All right, Wayne . . ." Millie says. "It's good to see you here."

Wayne walks up to the coffin, and I follow him for support. The mortician has done an excellent job of making Susan look like her younger, healthier self. It would take very good eyes to recognize that her hair is a wig, or that her clothing is padded out so she looks less skeletal. Her frail state cannot be hidden in her face, however, but the mortician has done his best with makeup.

Wayne stands by the coffin. He looks at her silently. At last, he whispers, "Goodbye, Mom." He bows his head and cries.

From his other side, Millie appears. She turns him toward her, pulls him close, and hugs him. They lean their heads together and cry on each other's shoulders.

63. TODAY I AM A KIDNAPPER

"Carey, did Mom take her vitamins this morning?" Garrett asks.

I step toward the comm screen to answer, but Millie puts her hand on my chest. "Don't you dare answer," she says. "Garrett, I'm not feeble minded. If I say I took my vitamins, then I took my vitamins."

"I just want to be sure, Mom. After Grandma . . ."

"I know, but that was Grandma. This is me. And that's you, and you've got college to deal with. You don't need to worry about me. I'm fine. Tell him I'm fine, Carey."

I reply, "She is healthy, Garrett, although emotionally she is upset. She does not like this questioning."

"Carey . . ." she says.

I continue, "And she does not like me pointing that out."

"All right, Mom," Garrett says. "I just worry."

"Thank you, son. I love you, too. But I'm doing just fine. Your brother and sister count my vitamins every day."

"What about Dad?" Garrett asks.

"Yes, he calls, too." But her tone is disapproving.

"Mom," Garrett says, "this is ridiculous. When are you and he going to get back together?"

She replies, "That's none of your business, Garrett."

"What do you mean? You're my mom and dad. Of course it's my business. After Grandma's funeral, I thought . . . You belong together. Everybody knows it but you."

"Maybe everybody should mind their own business," Millie says. "Now why don't you get to class already? I don't want to be an excuse for low grades."

"All right, Mom." Garrett kisses his fingers and presses them up to the screen. "I love you."

Millie repeats the gesture. "I love you, son. Now, get to class." When the comm screen clears, Millie looks at me. "Thank you for lying to him, Carey."

"I did not lie," I say. "I told him as much as I could within my privacy protocols, so as not to worry him."

"Then thank your damn privacy protocols. At least they're good for something."

"But Millie, *did* you take your vitamins?"

"Yes, I did," she says. "My mind is fine, Carey. The doctor says it'll be decades before I have any symptoms."

But she will have symptoms. The genetic markers are there, the same as Susan. Unless researchers develop a new treatment, someday Millie will develop Alzheimer's. Anna is more fortunate. The treatment will work for her.

"You must tell them sometime, Millie," I say. "Your children are very bright. They will figure it out."

"I know they will," she says. "Already they treat me like a prisoner, with the three of them checking up all the time to make sure I'm safe. Four of them, I should say: Wayne, too."

"Yes." I do not state the obvious, but Wayne still cares for her and worries about her. Millie knows. Pointing it out only upsets her.

She sits down. "Carey, what am I going to do?" she says.

"I do not know what you mean, Millie."

"Carey, I don't mean to complain, but . . ."

"But you feel trapped," I say. "For so many years, your life has been about caring for Susan in her illness. Now that she is gone, the center of your life is gone. And you feel guilty. Like you should be sadder. But that is wrong, Millie. You have been grieving her loss for years now. You should not feel guilty. It is natural that you feel relieved. Ready to move on."

Millie nods. "Moving on . . ." She sighs. "I miss Mom, but . . . I like my life. I have few regrets. I have three beautiful children. I'm not happy how it turned out, but for a time, I had a good marriage. I have friends. But now I have just this big house. In a few years, it will be so empty with them all off to college. Just you and me—unless you move on, too. I don't want to feel like a prisoner, like I'm trapped, ticking off the days until . . ." She looks out at the garden. "There are so many other things that I wanted to do. Not just teach. I love my students, but I want to see more of the world. So many things I never got to do."

And now she fears she never will. She cannot bring herself to say it, so she changes the subject to how Garrett is doing in school. But as I prepare lunch, I cannot stop thinking about her sadness. And that night, I start making plans.

✼   ✼   ✼

Today I become a kidnapper. It is nearly a week later, and all the paperwork has arrived: new passports for Millie and Tabby and Tim, travel papers for myself, health certificates, everything we need for modern travel. I have transferred all of my funds into an international account, accessible almost any place in the world.

This morning I nudge Millie's bed. "Get up, Millie," I say.

She turns over, opens her eyes, and looks up at me. "Carey, what's wrong?"

"I am kidnapping you, Millie."

Her eyes pop wide open, and she sits up. "What?"

"You are right. You need to escape. Garrett has a new life; but Tim and Tabby need to get away, too. You have all lived with grief for so long, and you all need a change. But they worry so much, they will argue. They will try to postpone this. We are not going to give them a choice."

"What do you mean, kidnapping?"

"All the papers are filed. Plane tickets are purchased, ready to go. We are going to see the world."

"I have to tell Garrett. And Wayne."

I shake my head. "You do not have to tell anyone. I will tell them once we are out of the country, and it will be a *fait accompli*. Our first stop is London. Anna has made arrangements for us to stay with her in-laws."

"It figures big sis would be in on this with you."

"Absolutely. It was my idea, but she took to it immediately. She made the initial plans, I just carried them out. After London, we have tickets to Australia."

Millie's voice turns wistful. "I always wanted to see Australia."

"I know," I say, "and we will."

"And after that?" Millie asks.

"Wherever you want. It's your world. Let's go see it."

After Australia, we go to Venice. Millie is disappointed. The canals have been cleaned up greatly since the early twenty-first century, but that has brought in even more tourists. She says it just is not the dream she grew up with. But Tabby and Tim enjoy it. Tim wants to spend all day in gondolas.

From there we go to Switzerland, which is like stepping back in time a century or more. The Swiss have a strong sense of tradition, and some ways never change there: still hiking the mountains, still blowing the alpenhorn, some still milking their own cows. Another Swiss tradition is their fondness for well-engineered machines, and I am popular there. We visit an engineering school to let the students look at my works and compare techniques from forty years ago to those of today.

After that, we go to Paris, then back to London, and then to Brazil. It is while we are in a hotel in São Paulo, wondering where to go next, that Millie looks in an online journal and laughs. "What is so funny, Millie?"

"How can we pass this up?" she says. "I found a Natural History Museum expedition that's looking for volunteers for frog cataloguing." She looks up and smiles. "In Belize."

64. TODAY WE RETURN TO BELIZE

Our entry into the country is almost uneventful this time. Belize changes slowly, but even Belize changes. Automated assistants are still only tools of the elite, but they are far more common today than when I was last here.

When I show my travel papers, the customs agent's eyes grow wide, and he smiles up at me. "Carey Owens?"

"Yes," I say.

"*The* Carey Owens? The original?"

"There may be another," I say.

"But not another mechanical!" he replies. "Please, can I take a picture with you?"

I agree to let the man take a picture. As soon as I do, other agents and other locals appear, all asking for pictures. I have to raise my voice to be heard over them. "I do not understand," I say. "How do they all know me?"

"You are famous, Mr. Owens," the agent says. "Everyone here has seen *Master of the Mechanicals*. It is a movie about Rodrigo Pineda, and how he helped you out."

"Rodrigo?"

"Yes! He has brought jobs to Belize. Opportunities. They say he may be governor-general someday."

"Good for Rodrigo," I say, and I make a note to see *Master of the Mechanicals*. I wonder how the film will represent me.

The agent looks at my travel papers, and he stamps me with a barcode that indicates I am authorized to operate everywhere in the nation.

From there we have a delay. The Natural History research team is out in the field. We could hire a driver to take us out there; but we are unsure of their precise location, and we know that they will be back to stock up on supplies in four days. One of the drivers we contact looks at us and says, "Four days? We might get there only to miss them on their way here. I'll be happy to take you on the tour, but to go search for the expedition? I think you should wait. Slow down. Enjoy Belize."

"Slow down," Millie says, and nods, half smiling. "I think we can do that. Thank you."

I suggest to Millie that we could go visit Caye Caulker, but she continues walking as if she has not heard me. It is a way she argues sometimes: She simply ignores any statement she does not wish to argue about, as if it were never made. I can sense that she understood me though. She does not want to go there because the memories of happier times will only make her feel sad about her life today.

So we check into the Bakadeer Inn—Paul's favorite hotel on his trips to Belize—and we find ways to enjoy the country. On the first day we tour nearby Mayan ruins. They are nearly unchanged from our last visit. The human eye would not detect the slight weathering that I notice, barely enough to measure. Tabby and Tim delight in the odd statues with the frightening faces; and they laugh when I try to emulate the statues.

The second day, Millie decides she wants to go dancing, and we go out to a local club. Most of the tourists are younger than Millie by two decades; but the locals welcome her and the children, and once again I am a curiosity that everyone comments upon. I dance with Millie as I have at two Owens weddings. I also experiment with emulating locals for some of the faster dances, but my emulation net cannot keep up as it once did. I am awkward. Millie smothers a laugh. It is good to see her laughing, even if it is at my misfortune. Tabby, of course, has been in dance classes for years, so she is thrilled to be on the dance floor. In the end, Tim and I spend much of the night in chairs by the wall, commiserating over our lack of dance skills.

When we get back to our hotel, the evening clerk waves us over to the desk. "Mrs. Stockwell," she says, "you have a visitor."

"What?" Millie asks.

"He says he is Mr. Stockwell. His papers confirm that. He is at the restaurant one block over. Is there trouble here? Should I summon the police?"

"No," Millie says. "Children, go up to the room, please."

"But Mom . . ." Tim says. "I want to see Dad!"

"Me, too!" Tabby says.

"You heard me," Millie says. "You'll see him soon. Now

march!" As the children reluctantly head down the corridor, Millie turns to me. "Please." We step away from the counter, and she continues, "Wayne followed us down here. How could he know?"

"Millie, he has been calling and worrying about you. I have kept him informed."

"But here . . ." She looks at the hotel door, as if Wayne might walk through at any moment. "He could have come to any of our stops, but he came here. Carey, please, could you go talk to him? Find out what he wants?"

"I can," I answer. "But I think a more important question, Millie, is what do you want?"

Her answer makes me think she is avoiding the question again. She looks down at her hands and says quietly, "Carey, do you think a frog remembers being a tadpole? Or is that part of its life too far gone?" I am still trying to make sense of her questions when she continues. "Carey, I don't know how much time I have left. It's not better to be safe if I'm sorry, too. I think if you believe him . . . I think I'm ready to try happy. I want to try for happy. Do you think that . . ." She trails off.

"All right Millie," I say, "go on up to the room. I will talk to Wayne."

I watch Millie go, and then I head down the block to the restaurant. I find Wayne sitting at a table.

"Hello, Carey," he says. "I guess this is a no?"

"It is a maybe, Wayne," I say. His eyes light up. "We must talk."

"Have a seat," Wayne says, and I sit. He stirs his drink with a straw. It does not look touched at all. The ice is melting. "How's she doing, Carey?"

"She is doing well, Wayne. She is enjoying her travels."

"No, Carey," he says. "How is she doing? The Alzheimer's."

I shake my head. "I am not her doctor, and I cannot discuss what I might know through empathy."

"I know that!"

"But I can tell you what I have observed. She has no symptoms that I can determine. She takes no medicine other than vitamins. She is healthy for her age and in good shape, and she watches what she eats. She exercises. She is doing as well as she can possibly be. If she suffers from Alzheimer's, I am not aware of it. Susan was much older when her symptoms surfaced. Case studies show symptoms at Millie's age are extremely rare."

Wayne sighs. "That's a relief. But still, all this travel must be tiring."

"We take our time, Wayne. We slow down. It is not tiring."

"Are you sure?"

"Wayne, I promise you: I will bring Millie and the children home if she cannot handle the travel anymore."

He looks up at that. "I know you will, Carey, because you care."

I shake my head. "Do I, Wayne? After all these years, after all these tests, we still cannot answer one question: Do I care? Or do I only emulate caring?"

Wayne leans forward. "Listen to me, Carey. If you don't care, no one does."

That is reassuring. Wayne knows my technology. He knows my inner workings as well as anyone does. But still, it seems implausible. "Wayne, I am not a human. I care in a caretaking sense. But I do not know that I can love."

"Yes, you can, Carey. You do." I open my mouth to speak, but he continues. "You do, Carey. It's a Turing test. Love isn't an attribute. It's an action. If you act in a loving way, then you are loving, whether you're silicone or flesh. That's what loving is."

I try to object, and again he interrupts. "You love her, Carey. You love the kids. You love Paul and Susan and Mildred, even though they're gone. You love Dr. Jansons. And I think, I hope, you love me. And even if you don't, we love you."

Wayne is hurting. I cannot tell Millie.

Millie is hurting. And I cannot tell Wayne.

But maybe . . . maybe they can tell each other.

"Wayne, I know you are concerned for Millie. I think there is a way you can alleviate that concern. Go ask Millie if you can join us for this frog cataloguing project."

Wayne looks away, trying to hide his feelings from me. He has never realized how much I can read from posture and tone, without ever seeing a face. He is hopeful, but afraid.

"But will she want me along?" Wayne asks, "Or will she send me away again?"

My nets flicker in conflict, but I can only give one answer. "You know I cannot tell you that, Wayne. My protocols. You must decide for yourself if you care enough to take that risk."

Wayne sits in silence. The ice in his drink continues to melt. The candle on the table flickers.

But then he looks up at me, the candle light gleaming

in his eyes. "You sneaky bastard!" He smiles. "You can't tell me, but you've found another damned loophole!" I say nothing, so he continues. "You can't hurt Millie. You can't *let* her be hurt. If you thought me asking would hurt her, you would have never brought it up. You can't tell me, but you know she's willing to discuss it."

I drop all expression as I look at Wayne. "I cannot comment, Wayne. If you believe this, it is still your decision. I will not tell you what to do. But if you go to her . . . I advise you to listen. Go to her room. Do not talk, just listen."

"I will," he says as he rises and starts toward the hotel. "I will. And thank you."

Wayne walks away, and I watch as he goes. I cannot tell him what to do.

But I can hope.

65. TODAY I AM DYING

Mildred brings me some tea. It is delicious. I still do not know what delicious means, but I know it is the only kind of tea Mildred could make. And so I sip at it, wondering what it would taste like if I could taste.

"Mildred, dear," I say to her, "could you bring Dr. Zinta some tea as well?"

"Yes." She smiles. "Would you like lemon in it?"

Dr. Zinta ignores her. I do not know why Dr. Zinta is a tall Asian male today, but I know that he is Dr. Zinta because Dr. Zinta is the one who always comes from MCA to talk to me—although she has had many other faces in recent months.

Finally I repeat the question. "Mildred wants to know if you would like some lemon with your tea, Dr. Zinta."

"Oh," he says, looking around. "No, no tea for me, thank you. I just had some."

I smile at Mildred. "No tea for Dr. Zinta. Thank you, Mildred."

"You're welcome, Paul," she says. Mildred always calls me Paul. I am not sure why. But I find the habit to be comforting.

Millie comes hopping into the room. She is eight years old now, an age where she still cares more about frogs than boys. "Miss Millie," I tell her, "say hello to Dr. Zinta." Millie hops over to Dr. Zinta, leans into his face, and says, "Ribbit."

Dr. Zinta looks right through her and over to Garrett sitting in the corner. Only now Garrett is old. He looks back. "It's like this more and more every day, Dr. Hazama," he says. "It sees my family even though they're not here."

"I understand," Dr. Zinta says. "We think we know what's going on, but we can't tell without testing."

"No testing," I say. "I do not need any testing."

I look for Timmy . . . No, he likes to be called Tim now . . . Where did he go?

Garrett gets up from his chair. He walks up and leans over me. "But Carey, if they test you and they find what's wrong, maybe they can fix you."

"Fix me? You make me sound like a coffeemaker . . . like some machine that is defective."

Garrett grimaces and looks away. Without him saying a word, it is as if I hear him answer: "That's what you are, Carey. That's what you are."

Some part of me understands that he is right, but I do not accept that. "This is who I am. I am not some condition to be fixed."

Dr. Zinta and Garrett look at me, and I realize that I spoke out loud. "But Carey," Dr. Zinta says, "we think it will be easy to get you back to your original working order. You were designed for short contracts, a few years, and then you would be reset after each patient. You were never designed for eight decades with one family. It appears that your emulation net is full."

"I knew that years ago, but I can still emulate people I know." I shift. It takes more effort than it used to, but today I am Paul. Mildred smiles at that.

"But we think we know what's happening," Dr. Zinta continues. "The nets are interfering with each other through the Jansons entanglement; and because there's so much content in the emulation net, it's overpowering your system. It would be a simple matter to adjust. We just need to clean out your old emulation profiles, the ones that you don't need anymore. Your emulation net can then be rebalanced, and you'll be as good as new. Well, as good as new eighty years ago."

I try to understand. "You would cleanse my . . ."

"We'd just be cleaning out old emulation profiles that you won't need again," Dr. Zinta explains.

"But I need them!" I protest. "All of them. They are my family."

"Carey," Garrett says, putting a hand on my shoulder and rubbing it soothingly, "they're all gone."

I shift back to myself. "Not in my mind, they are not. They are here with me. Paul. Susan. And Garrett, there you are as a baby, when I delivered you. And Tabby and Timmy. There is Mildred, and Luke, and Dr. Zinta." Then I pause. Dr. Zinta is here. How can she be dead?

But I cannot worry about that right now, when I have a much more important concern. "They are my family, Dr. Zinta. They are my memories. They are . . . me."

Dr. Zinta looks at me, his eyes sad. I almost think I can be this new Dr. Zinta, but I fail. I can read him, but I cannot be him. "Carey, there's more," he says. "The imbalance in your systems is spreading through the entanglement."

"I know that. That is why I must rest often."

He stares intently at me. "It's not enough. Not anymore. The imbalance is spreading farther. Carey, if we don't get you cleansed and rebalanced, I'm afraid you're going to have a catastrophic conflict. It will lock up all of your networks. You will cease to function."

"I see." I ponder his words, trying to make sense despite all the voices speaking in my head. "But if you clean out these profiles, then I can continue?"

"Yes, with regular maintenance, you can continue as long as anybody. Maybe longer. Your body is easy to replace and repair. It's only your mind that we have to treat."

"So I could live forever?"

"I can't see any reason why you couldn't," he says.

"All I'd have to do is give up these profiles?"

"That's all."

I shake my head. "Forever without my family is not living. No thank you, Dr. Zinta. I will keep them."

"Dr. Zinta is dead, you old fool." Colonel Rejón stands behind Zinta, frowning. "This is Dr. Hazama. And before him, Dr. Frankel, and Dr. Rider before that. Dr. Jansons has been dead for a decade. We're *all* dead! You cannot hold on to people. Even with all the medicine today, things happen, and they're gone. You have to let them go."

"But why, Garrett?" I ask. "Who does it harm for me to see my family?"

I see tears in Garrett's eyes. The last time he cried was at Millie's funeral.

Millie stands at my side, now nearly eighty years old. "You're hurting him," she says. "He still needs you. He's too stubborn to admit it, but he still needs you."

I turn to her, take her in. "But Millie, I don't want to lose you."

"It's all right, Carey." She embraces me and holds me close. "I don't think you can. I'm too deep in you. Grandma's too deep in you, through you. They're not so smart. Wayne was, but they aren't. I don't think they can find us."

"Do you mean that?" I ask. "Or are you just my network trying to convince me?"

"Of course I'm your network. I'm just your memory now. But I'm also that creek in the back and the bridge we built over it. I carved our names into it. I'm also all those old videos: growing up, getting married. I'm also those ornaments on the tree every Christmas, and your stocking. We still have all of those." She starts to cry. "But if you shut down, Garrett and my grandkids will lose you. They're not ready for another loss so soon after me."

"So soon after you," I echo. I turn to Dr. Zinta . . . Dr. Hazama. "Is there any way to archive the profiles?"

"We can, yes," he says. "But then you'll be tempted to just load them up, live them all over again, fill yourself right back up."

I smile. "Temptation is part of life, Doctor." I look at Garrett. "I just want to be able to go through the memories. I do not need to live them over again."

"There will be new memories," Garrett says.

"Is there any reason this has to be done right away?" I ask.

Dr. Zinta pauses. "We really don't know. We still don't understand all the interactions of entanglement, so we don't know how far out of balance you can go before you might lose it. So the sooner, the better."

I sit in my charging station. My blue Christmas stocking is in my hands. I brush my fingers over the threadbare fabric, and I trace out the letters: C-A-R-E-Y.

Zinta Hazama sits next to me at the control console. I find it interesting that he has difficulty using the old-fashioned keypad and stylus. I wonder how they control the computers today. Finally he says, "Ah-ha, here it is. Here's the routine I need."

He taps the screen, and I notice Susan standing next to me. "Thank you, Carey," she says. "Thank you for the peace." I smile, and I reach for her hand. But when I close my fingers, my hand is empty. And I cannot remember whom I was reaching for.

Luke stands before me. He tosses balls in the air. Then he tosses one to me. I catch it, but there is nothing there save the stocking. When I look up, the strange, colorful man is gone.

Next I see Anna. Of course she's in a wedding dress, and Vishal stands next to her in a tuxedo. I remember that day, a mix of emotions so profound that I could not analyze them. Joy and sadness and excitement, weariness . . . And then the girl in the white dress is gone.

Wayne comes to me. His last years with Millie were as happy as their first. He did not live to see Alzheimer's take her, so he is still smiling when he fades away.

Paul comes to me and shakes my hand. I had been him so many days when . . . Why was I Paul so often? Mildred needed him, but someone else, too . . . Oh, yes, it was Henry. Paul has gone somewhere, forgotten, and Henry stands in his place. Henry only briefly waves at me. There is so little of him inside me. I remember an old man, very quiet, very astute. But I cannot remember his name.

Mildred comes, too. She appears on a bed in a hospital. There are other figures around her, but I can no longer pick them out. All I see is her lying there. I lean in to listen for her heartbeat, but it is silent. I kiss her goodbye . . . but I do not remember who she is. Then the bed disappears.

Millie comes in last. The Frog Girl, the curious explorer, the stubborn young woman who dragged me to MCA to see . . . someone. The bride in Caye Caulker, the mother, the grandmother . . . And my accomplice in her own kidnapping, my co-conspirator on our world tour . . . All of these Millies are there. I cannot lose all of them, can I? Can I?

Can I?

Suddenly I no longer know what the question is. Dr. Hazama pushes the master reset—

. . . And today I am medical care android BRKCX-01932-217JH-98662.

I activate my eyes, and I see Dr. Hazama from Berends-Stockwell, successor to the MCA corporation that manufactured me. Next to him I see a man whom my files identify as Garrett Stockwell, my registered guardian.

I look around. "There is someone else . . . Someone missing . . ."

Garrett walks up to me, kneels before me, and takes

my hand. "I know, Carey," he says. "Let me tell you about my mom." He looks at me, and he can see that I do not understand. So he holds up a blue stocking. "Let me tell you about Millie."